Environment and Utopia
A Synthesis

THE PLENUM SOCIAL ECOLOGY SERIES

Series Editor: Rudolf Moos
Stanford University, Stanford, California and
Veterans Administration Hospital, Palo Alto, California

Environment and Utopia • Rudolf Moos and Robert Brownstein

A Continuation Order Plan is available for this series. A continuation order will bring delivery of each new volume immediately upon publication. Volumes are billed only upon actual shipment. For further information please contact the publisher.

Environment and Utopia
A Synthesis

Rudolf Moos
and
Robert Brownstein

Stanford University
Stanford, California
and
Veterans Administration Hospital
Palo Alto, California

PLENUM PRESS · NEW YORK AND LONDON

Library of Congress Cataloging in Publication Data

Moos, Rudolf H   1934-
  Environment and utopia.

  (The Plenum social ecology series)
  Includes index.
  1. Human ecology. 2. Utopias. I. Brownstein, Robert, joint author. II. Title.
HM206.M65 1977   301.31   77-23272
ISBN 0-306-30985-8

© 1977 Plenum Press, New York
A Division of Plenum Publishing Corporation
227 West 17th Street, New York, N.Y. 10011

Printed in the United States of America

Contents

PART III: A SYNTHESIS OF ENVIRONMENTAL AND
UTOPIAN PERSPECTIVES

PART I: CONCEPTUAL AND PHILOSOPHICAL BACKGROUND

CHAPTER 1

Environmental and Ecological Thought

Conventional wisdom increasingly describes modern man as disoriented and disturbed by the unfolding of his own future. Indeed, there is a sense in which the concept of the future has become reified; it is seen as something to be awaited fearfully by a helpless humanity. The inhabitants of industrial societies foresee their destiny as a great beast threatening to restructure the earth in some horrendous fashion.

We seek to challenge this passive and pessimistic attitude. Despair can be a self-fulfilling prophecy, a perspective which ensures the absence of that preparation and planning which might yet yield significant improvement in the human condition. Whatever the future holds, it must arise out of the material and social dynamics of the present. In fact, active planning must begin at once if vitally necessary social transformations are to be effected. We can create our own future, and we cannot abdicate responsibility for the quality of that creation.

However, it is naive to imply that the future stretches before us as soft clay to be shaped into any conceivable mold. Karl Marx's insightful observation made over a century ago remains applicable today: "Men make their own history, but they do not make it just as they please; they do not make it under circumstances chosen by themselves, but under circumstances directly encountered, given and transmitted from the past." [1] The future results from an interaction of human creative impulse with material and social reality—circumstances not of our own choosing.

Mankind's attempts to design its future must be based on an understanding and appreciation of this interaction. We must merge our capacity to imagine and innovate with our ability to comprehend and manipulate natural and social forces. We must produce constructive contact between our visions of hope and our scientific knowledge of the physical and social environment. This work is an effort to further that contact.

We seek to focus upon the future relationship between man and his environment. Specifically, we attempt to synthesize two distinct approaches to this issue: environmental theory and utopian speculation. These two perspectives have rarely, if ever, been deliberately focused upon one another. We believe that each suggests new questions and hopefully new answers that would not normally be revealed through the separate insights of the other discipline.

Both perspectives have existed in one form or another for centuries. Yet today, there is an increased urgency for their mutual development and interaction. This century, to its loss, has tended to abandon utopian speculation. We witness "a retreat from constructive thinking about the future in order to dig oneself into the trenches of the present. It is a ruthless elimination of future-centered idealism by today-centered realism. We have lost the ability to see any further than the end of our collective nose." [2]

At the same time, contemporary research on the environment suggests an urgent need for change in basic patterns of human behavior, for the formation of new institutions and social structure. As regards the physical environment, ecological studies have emphasized the relationship between man and the ecosystem in which he lives, and the implications of environmental factors for the future of humanity. At the root of these analyses is the recognition that ecosystems exist in balance. All parts of the system are linked to each other through interflows of matter and energy. No single part can act in isolation. Every ecological act produces—sometime, somewhere—an ecological reaction. In addition, ecosystems are homeostatic. If one part of the system behaves so as to upset the system's balance, other parts will respond so as to restore equilibrium.

Ecologists have applied this notion of balance on a global scale to man and the ecosystem that sustains him, the planet earth. Their findings indicate that man has for generations been upsetting the ecological balance of his habitat. Among the most disturbing trends are an increase in human population (especially in relation to food supplies), the depletion of mineral and energy resources, and the pollution of air and water. For example, a comparison of projected world population levels with the earth's food production capability quickly leads one to the conclusion that the rate of population growth cannot be sustained. Even with the full benefits of the best agricultural technology, food production probably cannot keep ahead of population growth for more than two more decades.

The possibility that the technologically developed nations may run out of critical minerals and metals was raised at least a decade ago by a study of the relationship between demands and known supplies of petroleum, bauxite, uranium, and various other materials vitally necessary in the manufacturing processes of advanced economies.[3] The geographic dispersal of deposits of many of these substances made the supply problem seem more critical. Cobalt, for example, is found in the Congo; diamonds and gold are largely concentrated in South Africa. Should these nations, for economic or political reasons, decide to withhold the substances from the world market, an untenable situation would quickly develop. Recent comprehensive studies of the resource picture of the United States have reached similar conclusions.[4] By the year 2050, we may have run out of several economically important substances for which no substitute is known: helium, natural gas, lead, copper, zinc, and petroleum.[5]

The implication of resource depletion, pollution, and population growth is that it is necessary to move toward a stable society to avert worldwide ecological catastrophe.[6] Most important of all is the realization that the above trends cannot continue indefinitely. At some point—the precise timetable being a matter of dispute—natural balance will be restored. And the processes of homeostasis may be catastrophic, at least from the human point of view. Excess population may lead to famine; resource shortage may cause war and the collapse of industry; pollutants may poison whole populations. In the logic of ecology, the creature that makes its habitat unlivable destroys itself. Thus, the Club of Rome, in its manifesto published as *The Limits of Growth,* presented a prediction technical in style but apocalyptic in scope:

> If the present growth trends in world population, industrialization, pollution, food production and resource depletion continue unchanged, the limits to growth on this planet will be reached sometime within the next one hundred years. The most probable result will be a rather sudden and uncontrollable decline in both population and industrial capacity.[7]

To survive, men must restructure their political, economic, and social activities, and their values, so as to terminate their disequilibriating effects on the environment.[8]

There is also a second environmental crisis—an environmental crisis in human dignity:

> A great deal more is involved than the blight of the ghetto, the noise of the city, the monotonous ugliness of the landscape or the appalling inadequacy of some public high-rising projects. The crisis lies not just in the over-use, the mis-use, and the decay of both the immediate and broader physical environment, but rather in how we conceive of the individual in relation to any exist-

ing setting, including the newest ones and those still on the drawing board. This is true regardless of whether the setting is an apartment, family home, school room, business office, playground, subway car, college dorm, bathroom, government building, neighborhood setting, and so on.[9]

Physical and social settings combine to threaten human values. The blight of urban ghettos threatens the dignity of the ghetto dweller. Certain environments threaten the aged, the mental patient, the blind or handicapped person, and the like. Crowded, noisy urban milieus devalue individuals. Most settings are designed without regard for the "human" properties of people. Many workers feel dissatisfied and unproductive; many students feel a sense of anonymity and isolation. Participation in modern bureaucracies often leads to overwhelming feelings of alienation and anomie.

These two environmental crises suggest the need for broad social change. But what kind of society should we construct? We need guidelines for social change and models for alternative types of optimal societies. We must plan for a variety of possible futures. We seek to demonstrate that the environmental scientist and the utopian, working together, can significantly assist in this search.

We adopt the following procedure to carry out our comparative analysis. Part I focuses on the conceptual background for our inquiry. In this chapter, we examine major perspectives of environmental and ecological thought, noting the internal tensions and limitations within these perspectives. In Chapter 2, we present a brief historical review of utopias and utopian thought and introduce a conceptual framework through which we can focus on the structural complexity of individual utopias. This framework provides a perspective on how utopists deal with issues salient to environmental theory and suggests guidelines for a detailed analysis of human environments.

We employ this conceptual framework in four case studies. Three experimental utopian communities—the Oneida Community, the Israeli kibbutzim, and the new town of Columbia, Maryland—are analyzed in Chapters 3, 4, and 5, and one literary utopia (B. F. Skinner's *Walden II*) is analyzed in Chapter 6.

In Chapters 7, 8, and 9, we use the foregoing material in a critical discussion of environmental and utopian thought. We seek to synthesize the two perspectives, thereby indicating potential directions for future thought and experimentation. We find that the underlying goals of environmental and utopian thought are congruent. We suggest how environmental thought can contribute to the further development of utopias and how utopian thought can provide a human perspective within which environmental and ecological thought can be creatively applied in the future development of society.

ENVIRONMENTAL THOUGHT

Environmental theory is earthbound and oriented to reality. Its objective is the discovery of laws and relationships that typify the dynamics of nature and the interaction between man and his environment. The particular methods adopted have changed throughout history. Ancient hypotheses employed astrological and mystical elements. Modern work emphasizes scientific procedure: empirical classification, formation of hypothesis, examination and testing of data, and generalized conclusions. Recent environmental thought demonstrates high degrees of scientific rigor, including applications of statistics, systems theory, and computer analysis. Still, the direction of study has remained steady. Environmental theory seeks to comprehend an environment, not to create one. It seeks to identify the processes of nature, not to evaluate them. A successful analysis indicates how things are, not how they ought to be.

Substantive conclusions of environmental theorists have varied with time and with changes of method. Despite this diversity, a common thesis can be discerned in almost all environmental theories, although it is presented with varying degrees of insight and emphasis. Essentially, environmental thought emphasizes the ability of nature to limit the ambitions and achievements of mankind.

Determinism

Environmental determinism is the purest case of a theory that defines man as helpless before the forces of nature. Determinism is more than a belief in the environment's ability to limit human endeavor. It speculates that nature retains *causal* power over the actions of men. Culture and social institutions are responses to environmental conditions; free will is an illusion (indeed, an illusion presumably produced by environmental forces).

A determinist perspective was advanced by the classical scholars of both the Greek and the Roman world, as well as by Arab scholars during the Middle Ages.[10] Environmental determinism remained a dominant theoretical approach through the beginning of the 20th century. However, determinist analyses did reveal greater rigor in method and comprehensiveness in scope. Rather than specifying direct causal relationships between environmental factors and human responses, determinists began to view environmental inputs as interacting with a complex network of social and economic institutions.[11] One highly influential school of thought exemplary of this new determinism was developed by the French mining engineer turned social theorist, Frédéric Le Play.[12]

Le Play selected the family as the basic unit of society and sought to examine its behavior through quantitative analyses of family budgets. He recognized that the basic functions of the family could be understood only by an analysis of the forces external to it. In particular, every family faced the problem of providing the means of subsistence for its members: the problem of work. Occupations, in turn, are affected by the location in which the family lives: by place. This set of deductions produced the famous Le Play formula for the study of society: place, work, family. It also produced a mode of social analysis clearly linking the environment and human activity. An excellent illustration of the full determinist application of this method is provided by one of Le Play's students, Edmond Demolins.

Demolins sought to account for the diversity of the peoples on the earth's surface. He eventually concluded that the environmental features of regions people pass through when they migrate, as well as the conditions in the places from which they start and in which they finally settle, are the determinants of their character and social institutions.[13]

As an example, Demolins discussed the original inhabitants of the steppes, large tracts of level grasslands in southeast Europe and Asia. Because the principal vegetation on the steppes is grass, it is an ideal region for the pastoral life-style of nomadic shepherds. Pastoralism requires a dependence on animals, especially the horse, which allows the herdsman sufficient mobility to follow his flocks as they seek new pasture. Demolins observed that horses flourish on the steppes. Thus, an environmental law was revealed: the steppes are essentially adapted to the horse, and it is the horse that adapts the steppes to man.

Pastoralism as a mode of work determines other aspects of the steppe dweller's culture. His food and the material for his crafts are limited to the by-products of his herds. Since the nomad is always on the move, his dwellings and tools must be rugged and easily transportable. There is no room for large, complex machinery or long-lasting buildings or luxury goods. The limited scale of production does not require any economic organization more complicated than handcraftsmanship. The steppe people thus have little or no division of labor or unemployment, and few wage rates; work is communal, centered in the family workshop.

Geographic factors also affect property relationships. Grass grows spontaneously and demands no cultivation. Once the grass cover has been consumed, the land loses all value to the herdsman and he moves on. Thus, no motivation exists for the institution of private property in land.

Furthermore, since land and work are communal and the family is the only basis of social organization, patriarchal structures that feature common property and common subordination to a single father–leader appear. This mode of family life can be credited with affecting the personal characteristics of its members. Patriarchy suppresses individual initiative and promotes traditionalism and conservative attitudes. [14]

As the 19th century progressed, attempts to apply new developments in the natural sciences to the study of man proliferated. Darwin revolutionized the social and several of the natural sciences with his theory of natural selection. Karl Marx launched frontal assaults against prevailing economic and philosophical traditions, arguing for dialectical materialism as the science of history. Comte and Durkheim were advancing sociology as an independent discipline employing empirical theory. The study of man's relationship to the geographic environment could hardly remain unaffected.

One of the most well-known and most controversial of the post-Darwinian 19th-century geographers was Frederich Ratzel. Ratzel developed several hypotheses concerning climatic influences on civilizations. He held that the most invigorating temperate climate was one in which isothermal lines group together, thus producing a region of varying and contrasting climates. He even considered winds significant, either as factors in trade during the era of sailing vessels or as causes of destruction, thus intensifying the struggle for existence and stimulating progress. He also emphasized geographic location as a factor in national development. [15]

Ratzel's thought reached the United States through the work of his disciple Ellen Semple, whose *Influences of the Geographic Environment* was published in 1911. She and Ellsworth Huntington, a professor of history at Yale, promulgated environmental determinism in the United States throughout the first half of the 20th century. [16] During this time, the determinist position became the target of substantial criticism. Critics charged that the evidence offered by determinists was vague, that it was often contradicted by data available in other sources, [17] that simple correlations were not proof of causation, and the like. [18]

Even if it was granted that the environment had some influence on human activity, critics objected to the argument that it was the major influence. Numerous cases were advanced of situations in which other, non-environmental factors had predominant causal impact. Thus, some critics questioned the relationship between environment and patterns of food consumption by noting that the difference in consumption between social classes within a given geographical area is often greater than the difference between residents of differing areas. In addition, the environment rarely changes to a significant degree over the time span relevant to recorded history. Critics of determinism wished to know how major changes in social and political organization could take place in a context of environmental stability if the latter phenomena determined the structure of the former.

Critics also objected to conceptualizing the environment as an autonomous variable without considering the nature of the organism whose environment was in question. For example, an evaluation of the earth's environment from the perspective of fishes is the precise opposite of an evaluation from the perspective of humanity—at least in terms of the percentage of the earth's surface that is habitable. Further, in evaluating the claim that soil and climate affect a society's accumulation of wealth, Sorokin indicated that the wealth-producing capacities of a geographic area are a function not simply of its physical attributes but also of the culture that inhabits it. Fertile soil is of limited value to a people who have not yet discovered agriculture; likewise, coal and oil represent wealth only when a certain level of technological capability has been attained.

Possibilism

As a reaction against determinism, there appeared a new theory, possibilism, which emphasized the role of man in the unfolding of history. Lucien Febvre provided the single sentence that best encapsulates its central thesis: "There are no necessities, but everywhere possibilities; and man as master of the possibilities is the judge of their use." [19]

According to this view, man is not a passive creature helpless before environmental pressures. Rather man is "in the first place." The environment of each locality offers a set of opportunities (possibilities), but it is man who evaluates the options and selects those that he will pursue. Opportunities define what can be done, not what will be done.

However, possibilism never claimed that man could do whatever he pleased with regard to nature. On the contrary, the options of human action are always limited. This point is perhaps best illustrated in the writings of Jean Brunhes the French geographer. Brunhes believed that human beings enjoy enormous latitude in the kinds of activities they can initiate. Nevertheless, he stressed that there are limits which have to be taken seriously. All human beings have unavoidable needs for food, clothing, and shelter. Man's relationship to nature must meet these needs.

Nor did Brunhes assume that man's increased technological capacities liberated him from natural limitations. To Brunhes, the attempt to press beyond natural limits involved grave risks, and "The penalty exacted for acting contrary to physical facts is all the more cruel as man's victory over them is great and glorious." There was ample evidence to prove his point:

> When man succeeds in building dikes to hold back the waters of a Po or a Hoang-ho, or manages to drive the North Sea back and win the Dutch polders, the risks he runs are proportional to the fruitfulness of his efforts. An invasion of the sea or an abnormal flooding of these rivers is destructive to the very extent that the natural forces were victoriously tamed.[20]

In addition, the possibilists were aware of economic and social limits on the environmental possibilities that could be realized. Human time and resources are finite; everything feasible cannot be accomplished, and there is a consequent opportunity cost on those projects which do take place. As Bowman quipped, men can move mountains, but not without first floating a bond issue.

As an example of the possibilist approach to substantive problems, one can consider the question of the effect of environmental factors on the stagnation or decline of civilizations. A determinist might argue that such phenomena can be understood as an inexorable effect of a limited supply of natural resources. Yet, the possibilist geographer Isaiah Bowman insisted that human institutions are the primary causal factors: "It may be shown that there has never been a civilization that declined because it exhausted the possibilities of the land. No nation has ever fully developed its frontier! The earth has never gone back on man, but man has found himself entangled in the unpredictable effects of his own system."[21]

Bowman agreed that the environment presents some limitations to human cultures, but he maintained that declining civilizations fail to take advantage of possibilities that still exist. Thus, he argued that in China during the 1920s:

> The prevailing type of her culture makes it impossible for her people to occupy semi-arid regions that are suited to extensive machine cultivation, like the western fringe of settlement in the United States. It has been estimated that if China were to employ such lands they would add more than 500 million acres to the present total. . . . But the required change in type of farm practice would be as revolutionary to the Chinese as migration to a new land. Moreover, it would demand a beginning with capital for machine equipment, and

this cannot be got from either private sources or government at this time. So
the population stays bound to the crop and land cultivation system created
through the ages.[22]

No doubt Bowman would consider the new environmental possibilities
opened up by the revolutionary political and social forces of modern China
as contemporary proof of his point.

Probabilism and Pragmatism

For several decades, possibilism and determinism defined the parameters within which geographers debated the relationship between man and
environment. The bases of the dispute became extremely confused. One
problem concerned the difficulty of deciding whether factual evidence
should be interpreted as proof of determinism or possibilism. Consider a
hypothetical case in which man makes a technological response to his environment, such as the introduction of air conditioning in the tropics. Does
this demonstrate that the environment has determined the direction of
man's technological development? Or does it indicate that man has mas-
tered the environment by managing to escape its unpleasant characteristics?
The evidence can be used either way. A simple correlation between human
action and an environmental condition is insufficient to indicate whether an
act represents determinism or the free selection of an advantageous possibility. W. E. Wallis provided an intriguing argument on this point:

> The correlation between man's economic life and his geographical environment
> is not evidence of the influence of physical environments. The correlation
> shows the extent to which he has compelled it to minister to his needs, to
> serve his purposes, to respond to his will . . . . if "being influenced" by the en-
> vironment means making the most of it, then it is the best part of wisdom to
> be influenced.[23]

A second problem in the determinist–possibilist debate involved the
degree of difference between the two positions. If natural regions encompass definite systems of possibilities, and if these possibilities can be
ranked in their ability to satisfy human needs, then how much of a difference is there between designating the most likely possibility and modified determinism? What distinguishes the argument that the desert
requires a nomadic life-style from the position that other social patterns
could exist in the desert, but nomadism is by far the most common, practical, and probable alternative? In such a context, the possibilists could
only insist that their point of view included a belief in free will. Yet, that

response simply removed the issue from the domain of empirical theory and transferred it to philosophy.[24]

Dissatisfaction with these ambiguities led post-World War II geographers to reexamine the usefulness of the determinism–possibilism dichotomy. One alternative was to eliminate the debate by developing a new perspective that bridged the gap between environmental causality and free will. O. H. K. Spate suggested such a theory, which he titled *probabilism*. Spate never developed his notion with any rigor. All he meant by the term was a literal recognition that some possibilities were more likely than others and that one could learn something about the probability that a given project would be carried out by examining environmental factors.[25]

Probabilistic theories of decision making may involve complex statistical and mathematical models designed to predict the likely results of alternative environmental policies. One study of this type is Peter Gould's application of game theory to the problems of farmers in the barren middle zone of Ghana. Essentially, game theory attempts to show how, under conditions of uncertainty, rational decisions can be made to outwit an opponent or at least maintain a superior position with regard to an opponent. In order to employ such a perspective in an analysis of man–environment relationships, Gould must assume the following. First, it is possible for men to make rational decisions. Second, different choices as to interaction with the environment (whether or not to expand cultivation) will have different utilities (size of harvest) depending on how environmental processes operate (whether there is enough rain). Third, from the human point of view, the environment is unpredictable; no one knows whether next year will provide sufficient rain. Fourth, the environment is a game player. This is not a pantheist notion; we are all well aware that nature does not consciously decide whether it will rain or not. For the purposes of this model, however, man and nature are opposing players in a competitive game, and man remains uncertain as to what the environment's next move will be.

In Gould's analysis, Ghanaian farmers are playing a two-person, five-strategy, zero-sum game against nature. In other words, there are two players (the farmers and nature), five strategies (the five crops that the farmers may plant in any year: yams, maize, cassava, millet, and hill rice), and the contest is zero-sum (what one side wins, the other side loses; the loss of a crop is considered a win for nature). For purposes of simplicity, nature gets only two moves: dry years and wet years (inadequate rainfall and adequate rainfall). A round in this game would look something like the following: farmer plays a crop of half maize and half millet, nature plays a dry year, and the harvest is the payoff. The objective of Gould's analysis is to devise the best moves for the farmers. If we know how much of a given crop a farmer can produce in dry and wet years, we can create a payoff matrix that indicates the returns for each of the five possible crop strategies.

Gould's game predicts how to produce a maximum yield under conditions of uncertainty. If one knows how to predict future rainfall or can reduce uncertainty by estimating probabilities of future rainfall, then different strategies are called for. However, it is important to note that a winning strategy may offer no more than the best of a bad situation. The environment limits the maximum yield whatever the crop mixture, and if the terrain is bleak, even the maximum return may not provide more than bare subsistence.[26]

Few environmental theorists are formal adherents of probabilism. The approach of most of those seeking to move beyond the determinism–possibilism controversy can best be referred to as *pragmatism*. Pragmatists do not know whether the universe is organized according to determinism or free will. They do not know how to find out. And they are unwilling to delay substantive research until they are capable of resolving what they perceive to be philosophical questions. They accept as a working hypothesis a qualified determinism, the assumption that natural and human processes of sufficient regularity do exist. This pragmatic attitude is clearly in the mainstream of contemporary practice in the social sciences.[27]

Neodeterminism

In the preceding discussion, we explained the probabilist argument that human beings are more likely to select one geographic possibility than others. In some situations, however, the probable alternative is not merely more likely to occur but virtually certain. Where probabilities reach such levels, one can reasonably argue that in essence the environment is determining human action.

Betty Meggers, an anthropologist, has developed a neodeterminist theory of the environment. Meggers observed that efforts to empirically demonstrate specific relationships between environment and culture have generally yielded negative results. Meggers believes that the source of the problem is not the absence of a relationship but rather the failure to discern the fundamental factors involved in the relationship. In particular, efforts to correlate culture and environment have classified the environment according to categories employed by geographers. What results would follow if a different classificatory standard were used?

Since the primary contact between culture and environment is through subsistence activity, Meggers proceeded to define four types of environment in terms of agricultural potential: no potential, limited potential, improvable potential, and unlimited potential. Her field studies, particularly in South American rain forests, provided evidence of the following patterns. Tropical rain forests (limited potential) precluded certain levels of cultural complexity (large concentration of population, stable settlements, and so on). In addition, advanced cultural traits did not diffuse into these regions from adjacent areas. Finally, when advanced cultures migrated into the limited-potential area, they were unable to preserve their former level of development, and they thus declined.

Studies of other areas that exhibited similar patterns led Meggers to offer the following thesis: "The level to which a culture can develop is dependent upon the agricultural potentiality of the environment it occupies. As this potentiality is improved, culture will advance. If it cannot be improved the culture will become stabilized at a level compatible with the food resources." [28] Thus, Meggers argued that the environment limits what man can do; it does not ordain what he will do within those limits. Many societies do not develop to as high a level as their agricultural potential permits. Megger's law does not imply that higher civilizations can never transfer their cultures to low-potential regions. She maintained only that such civilizations could not appear indigenously in those areas, nor could they survive if restricted to the resources available there. As long as other areas of high agricultural potential provide sufficient products and services to "underwrite" the low-potential region, a civilization can encompass both.

HUMAN ECOLOGY

Throughout the late 19th and early 20th century, as geographers struggled to comprehend the interaction between man and his environment, a kindred discipline, which would focus on similar questions, was emerging. *Ecology,* a term derived from the Greek *oikos* ("a house" or "place to live in"), first appeared in German biologist Ernst Haeckel's studies of plant life in 1868. Since that time, the field has broadened to include both animals and human beings.[29]

From its inception, ecology was overtly Darwinian; it focused upon the "web of life," those interactions through which organisms adapt to each other and to the world around them in a struggle for existence. Living organisms exist in the "web of life," in which they "struggle for existence" in relation to the environment. This process fits and adapts the individual to the particular character of its environment. Thus, the environment has a limiting or constraining impact on the organism.

Human ecologists developed a holistic approach to these phenomena and processes.[30] This perspective permits a broader definition of the environment than that employed in much of the previous literature. Ecology encompasses the whole spectrum of organic life (plants, animals, microbes), as well as all of the physical resources relevant to the existence of living organisms. There is no need to limit inquiry to surface features or climate. Ecology emphasizes the totality of relationships among organisms and between them and their physical environment. It includes the complete analysis of food chains, energy flows, and other complex and dynamic cycles.[31]

Ecology has been defined as the study of the relation of organisms or groups of organisms to their environment:

> every organism, plant and animal—including man—is in constant process of adjustment to an environment external to itself. The life of an organism, in other words, is inescapably bound up with the conditions of the environment which comprise not only topography, climate, drainage, etc. but other organisms and their activities as well . . . . all organisms are engaged in activities which have as their logical conclusion adjustment to environment.[32]

Some authors see human ecology as a general perspective useful to the scientific study of social life. Human ecology is distinguished from plant and animal ecology by the unique characteristics of man and the human community. Unlike plants and animals, human beings can construct their own environment. They are not necessarily attached to the immediate environment in which they are placed by nature. Men also have an elaborate technology and culture. They are regulated by conscious controls, by rules, norms, laws, and formal organizations.

Human ecology was thus slowly reconceptualized as a social and cultural science. According to Hawley, the unique aspect of human ecology is the study of communal adaptation. Human beings cannot adapt to their environment alone. They are highly dependent on their fellow human beings. Adaptation to the conditions of the physical environment is facilitated by adaptation to (and cooperation with) other living beings. Human beings confront the environment as a "human aggregate" and make cooperative efforts at adaptation. The distinctive hypothesis of human ecology is that the human community is an essential adaptive mechanism in man's relation to the environment.[33]

ECOSYSTEM PERSPECTIVES

In recent years, ecologists have developed a fundamental concept for their discipline—that of the ecosystem—which permits expanded inquiry into the relationships between organisms and their environment. As defined by Fossberg, *ecosystem* refers to:

> a functioning interacting system composed of one or more living organisms and their effective environment, both physical and biological . . . the description of an ecosystem may include its spatial relationships, inventories of its physical features, its habitats and ecological niches, its organisms and its basic reserves of matter and energy; the nature of its income (or input) of matter and energy; and the behavior or trend of its entropy level.[34]

This framework has valuable properties for analyses of the environment. First, it includes, within a common rubric, man, the physical environment, animals, and plants. Previous approaches often employed an arbitrary dualism, a dichotomy between man and nature. Also, they tended to exaggerate a single relationship, the environment's impact on human activity. The ecosystem concept directs attention to the unity of its member elements in interlocking and ongoing processes; for example, it calls attention to man's impact on the environment. Second, the relationship between the parts of an ecosystem exhibit a more-or-less orderly structure that can be identified and studied. Third, ecosystems function. There is a continuous flow of matter and energy between component elements, and, at least in simple ecosystems, this entire process can be examined quantitatively. Fourth, as a form of general system, ecosystems can be examined from the vantage point of general systems theory (formally, the ecosystem is an open system tending toward a steady state and obeying the laws of open-system thermodynamics). Depending upon the complexity of the specific problem and the relevant level of analysis, a variety of forms of model construction become possible: "Systems may be built at the framework level (e.g., settlement hierarchies or transport nets) or as simple cybernetic systems (e.g., the mechanism of supply and demand and of Malthus' doctrine), or at the more complex level of social systems and living organisms."[35]

At first reading, the current ecological perspective may appear highly deterministic. Nature (via ecosystems) requires that man obey its rules. If he fails to do so, he must pay an incalculable price for his futile efforts at autonomy. Closer examination, however, reveals that the ecologists leave substantial room for man to shape his own destiny. Unlike pure determinism, ecological theory does not stipulate that an environmental impetus accounts for human responses. On the contrary, its major assertion is that human action (whose sources are left unexplained) inevitably leads to environmental consequences. The environment limits man's activities because these consequences cannot be continually postponed or avoided. However, the possibility of attempting new modes of action with different consequences still remains. Indeed, it is the existence of such options that accounts for the ecologist's determined efforts to effect change in modern social institutions.

What are the new practices that will permit a restoration of ecological balance? No single blueprint has been suggested. However, several major changes in human social organization are commonly discussed as necessary elements for an environmentally stable planet. The first and foremost of these is control of human population. While early theorists hoped to rely on voluntary population planning by individual families, there has increasingly developed an awareness that control must be considered in its literal sense. Voluntary birth control is unlikely to produce the desired results, since many couples want more than the two or three children necessary to sustain populations at their current levels. Government-controlled and -enforced birth control programs may thus be the only way to avert natural catastrophe.[36]

Second, environmental balance requires a steady-state economy, as opposed to contemporary growth-oriented systems. *Steady-state economy* refers to a mode of organization typified by a relatively constant population and stock of physical wealth with a minimal rate of throughput, that is, depletion of resources through use. A steady-state society would probably demonstrate a low birth rate, a low death rate, a low level of production, a low level of consumption, and a high life expectancy. Also, since the argument that economic inequality is a spur to productivity would be negated by the society's very premises, it would be difficult to see how anything less than egalitarian distribution of goods and resources could either be legitimated or prove politically tolerable.[37]

Third, man's ecosystem is planet-sized, as indicated by the "spaceship earth" analogy. And to carry that analogy one step further, spaceships cannot afford to have their passengers fighting over the controls. Ecological balance requires the organization of human and material resources on a world scale, an actuality hardly likely to result from consultations between sovereign and potentially hostile nation-states. Hence, world order is considered a prerequisite for environmental stability.[38]

Finally, a society that seeks to maintain ecological balance will require a new set of values. To a large extent, Western man's ethos defines progress in quantitative terms. National goals are ever higher levels of industrialization and consumerism. Nature remains the helpless object of man's insatiable passion to produce. This outlook is incompatible with a steady state. Ecologically responsible people must conceive of themselves as the partners rather than the masters of nature. New goals must replace those that are irrevocably linked to growth. The substance of such a new ethics, however, is probably that aspect of an environmentally stable social order that ecologists are least competent and least likely to predict.[39]

The British historian Arnold Toynbee has suggested that the histories of individuals, of communities, and of entire civilizations fall into successive stages. In each stage, some groups of people are confronted by a specific challenge that imposes an ordeal. Different individuals react in different ways to these common ordeals. The majority succumb. Some just barely manage to survive. Some, however, discover a response to the challenge that not only allows them to cope with the ordeal of the moment but puts them in a favorable position for undergoing the next ordeal. Other people follow these leaders into the next stage of civilization. Toynbee proposed the basic idea of *challenge and response* as a mechanism stimulating the evolutionary process. The role of the "external factor" (the environment) is to supply the "inner creative factor" with an adequately challenging stimulus sufficient to evoke a creative response.

In Toynbee's view, the environment presents a challenge to which man must respond. If the challenge is too weak (i.e., the environment is too easy), human potential will remain unfulfilled. If the challenge is excessive, human attempts to cope with it will result in failure and decline. When the challenge is optimal, human beings will be stimulated to new creative heights. The challenge of the environment is a necessary condition for man to grow and to develop higher civilizations. It is the stimulus of the battle that allows people to prove their potential.[40]

There are times in the development of human history when basic structural changes in society are needed. Totally different social models must be constructed. According to Toynbee, a major social change or movement is much more likely to occur when there is a major crisis—such as our current ecological crisis. This radical and holistic change needs effort and struggle, but a new stage in the development of man may result if a creative and successful response to the crisis can be found. We believe that utopian thinking may provide the overall perspective within which ecologically necessary social changes can be planned.

REFERENCES AND NOTES

1. Marx, K., and Engels, F. *Selected works.* New York: International Publishers, 1968, p. 97.
2. Polak, F. *The image of the future.* San Francisco: Jossey-Bass, 1973, p. 195.
3. Landsberg, H., Fischman, L., and Fisher, J. *Resources in America's future: Patterns of requirements and availabilities, 1960–2000.* Baltimore: Johns Hopkins University Press, 1963.
4. Study of critical environmental problems (SCEP). *Man's impact on the global environment.* Cambridge, Mass.: MIT Press, 1970.
5. Cloud, P. Mineral resources in fact and fancy; and Hubbert, M. Energy resources. In W. Murdoch (Ed.), *Environment: Resources, pollution and society.* Stamford, Conn.: Sinauer Associates, Inc., 1971, pp. 71–116.
6. Goldsmith, E., Allen, R., Allaby, M., Davoll, J., and Lawrence, S. *Blueprint for survival.* Boston: Houghton Mifflin, 1972.
7. Meadows, D. H., Meadows, D. L., Randers, J., and Behrens, W., III. *The limits to growth.* New York: New American Library, 1972.
8. Disch, R. (Ed.). *The ecological conscience.* Englewood Cliffs, N.J.: Prentice-Hall, 1970.
9. Proshansky, H. The environmental crisis in human dignity. *Journal of Social Issues, 29:*1–20, 1973.
10. Thomas, F. *The environmental basis of society.* New York: The Century Company, 1925. Kristof, L. K. D., The origins and evolution of geopolitics. *Journal of Conflict Resolution, 4:*15–51, 1960.
11. Tatham, G. Geography in the 19th century. In G. Taylor (Ed.), *Geography in the 20th century.* New York: Philosophical Library, 1957.
12. Sorokin, P. A. *Contemporary sociological theories.* New York: Harper & Bros., 1928, pp. 83–86.
13. Tatham, G. Environmentalism and possibilism. In G. Taylor (Ed.), *Geography in the 20th century.* New York: Philosophical Library, 1957 (quote on p. 86).
14. Sorokin, op. cit., pp. 73–79.
15. Thomas, op. cit., pp. 78–79.
16. Semple, E. *Influences of the geographic environment.* New York: Henry Holt, 1911. Huntington, E., *Mainstreams of civilization.* New York: Wiley, 1945.
17. Clarkson, J. Ecology and spatial analysis. *Annals of the Association of American Geographers, 60:*700–716, 1970 (quote from pp. 703–704).
18. Sorokin, op. cit., pp. 163–164.
19. Febvre, L. *A geographical introduction to history.* New York: Alfred A. Knopf, 1925 (quote from p. 236).
20. Brunhes, J. *Human geography.* Chicago: Rand McNally, 1920 (quote from p. 227).
21. Bowman, I. *The pioneer fringe.* Worcester, Mass.: The American Geographical Society, 1931 (quote from p. 42).

22. Ibid., pp. 42–44.
23. Wallis, W. Geographical environment and culture. *Social Forces, 4*:702–708, 1926 (quote from pp. 707–708).
24. For discussions of possibilism, determinism, and free will see: Febvre, op. cit., 181–182, 238–240; Brunhes, op. cit., pp. 225–226; Sprout, H., and Sprout, M., *The ecological perspective on human affairs.* Princeton: Princeton University Press, 1965, pp. 94–97.
25. Spate, O. H. K. Toynbee and Huntington: A study in determinism. *Geographical Journal, 118*:406–428, 1952.
26. Gould, P. R. Man against his environment: A game theoretic framework. In T. W. English and R. Mayfield (Eds.), *Man, space and environment.* New York: Oxford University Press, 1972, pp. 147–151.
27. See the distinction between tactical determinism and strategic determinism in: Lewthwaite, G. Environmentalism and determinism: A search for clarification. *Annals of the Association of American Geographers, 56*:1–23, 1966.
28. Meggers, B. Environmental limitations on the development of culture. *Anthropologist, 56*:801–824, 1954 (quote from p. 815).
29. Hawley, A. H. *Human ecology.* New York: Ronald Press, 1950, pp. 3–10.
30. Stoddard, D. R. Darwin's impact on geography. In W. Davies (Ed.), *The conceptual revolution in geography.* London: University of London Press, 1970, pp. 57–61.
31. For basic texts on modern ecology see: Odum, E. *Fundamentals of ecology.* Philadelphia: W. Saunders Co., 1971. Boughey, A. S. *Fundamental ecology.* Scranton, Pa.: Intext Educational Publishers, 1971.
32. Hawley, op. cit., p. 3.
33. Hawley, op. cit., p. 52.
34. Stoddard, D. R. Geography and the ecological approach. In English and Mayfield, op. cit., p. 157.
35. Ibid., pp. 157–161 (quote from p. 161).
36. Keyfitz, N. The numbers and distribution of mankind. In W. Murdoch, op. cit., pp. 31–52. See also: Davis, K. Population policy: Will current programs succeed? (p. 105); Hardin, G. Tragedy of the Commons (pp. 107–121). Both in C. Johnson (Ed.), *Eco crisis.* New York: Wiley, 1970.
37. Daly, H. Toward a stationary state economy. In J. Harte and R. Socolow (Eds.), *Patient earth.* New York: Holt, Rinehart and Winston, 1971, pp. 226–244.
38. Salk, R. Adapting world order to the global ecosystem. In Harte and Socolow, op. cit., pp. 245–257.
39. See: Caldwell, L. *Environment: A challenge for modern society.* Garden City, N.Y.: Natural History Press, 1970.
40. Toynbee, A. *The study of history,* Vols. 1 and 2, *The genesis of civilization.* New York: Oxford University Press, 1962.

CHAPTER 2

Utopias and Utopian Thought

Unlike environmental theory, utopian thought is concerned with a future world, a world that does not yet exist but that perhaps could come to be. Utopists examine the future rather than the present. Despite this future orientation, utopists make no claim to describe definitively what will be. Their vision is one of the potential of mankind and a call to realize that potential.

Utopian speculation employs methods of analysis foreign to the deliberate procedures of environmental theory. The ecologist seeks empirical data according to the tenets of scientific observation. His logic is inductive; he attempts to arrive at patterns and generalizations that depict aspects of environmental systems. The utopist begins with values. He starts with a set of normative principles around which he believes human life can best be organized. His procedure is deductive. He attempts to determine what structures are compatible with his primary tenets. But the utopist is not merely a logician. His final objective is to translate his principles into viable social forms. He must conceive of forms of social organization that are compatible with his values. For this process, his primary method of investigation is the imagination. He employs a visionary perspective, restrained only by the limits of human hopes and human dreams.

Utopian design and environmental science share a common object in that the utopian model is always linked to a physical environment. Every utopia is a society of people somewhere on earth, and, consequently, every utopia represents the interaction of human institutions and organization with common environmental and ecological characteristics. Thus, the utopist and the environmental theorist have a basis for a meeting of the minds.

There is one other way in which utopian and environmental methods are related. The ultimate test of the final product of both modes and thought lies in human action. In the last analysis, environmental theory is proved when men initiate activity based upon its predictions and are successful in their endeavor. For utopias, the measure of value is more problematic. Theoretically, a successful utopian model is one that is perceived as the best of all possible worlds, even after its realization. No society has ever passed such a test. A more modest objective is to demand that those who construct a utopia agree that they have established a society superior to the one they abandoned when beginning the utopian project. So defined, utopias have played a progressive role in human affairs.

In lay terminology, a utopia represents a fanciful projection of a perfect society. Several fundamental characteristics identify the utopian genre of social thought and action. However, the utopian mode has varied in both form and content through history, and as we argue later, it may be useful to carry that variation further still. Several features of utopias reveal the basic crux of the utopian effort.

To begin, utopias describe a society that does not exist in the present and that has never existed in the past. When one enters utopia, one leaves the empirical world, the world of "is," and enters the realm of possibility, of "can and ought to be." Formal written utopias are works of literature, not works of history or of social science. Attempts to bring utopia into reality are also excursions into the social unknown, or, if you will, experiments in human development. An effort to duplicate an ongoing mode of social organization in a new environment may be innovative and challenging, but it is not utopian.

Secondly, utopias are holistic. They seek to create, in image or in practice, a complete society with all its necessary components. The blueprint for specific utopias does not include every aspect of the physical and social environment. A utopia seeks to reveal the crucial factors in a society—those that are most significant in realizing its values. Holism is not a substitute for the setting of priorities. On the contrary, the utopists' model stresses specific features and thus demonstrates the core structural elements of a society.

The fact that utopias are holistic does not imply that they must necessarily be totally planned or be communitarian. Holism refers to the breadth of a social project; it is a formal characteristic that does not define the actual institutions or organizations that may be contained within an overall framework. True, from a historical perspective, most utopias have been communitarian, and as we argue later, there are sound reasons why a modern utopia should be planned. However, a visionary scheme based on an individualist ethic may be perfectly compatible with the definitions of utopia and holism, provided that it specifies the range of institutions required to realize that ethic in practice.

Utopias are functional models. They do not simply express certain ideas and values; they embody these principles in actual institutions, organizations, and behavior patterns. The utopist cannot sit securely behind the barriers of abstraction. He must demonstrate what it is like to live according to his proposal. At the least, this requires a model, the elements of which are compatible in motion. The utopist must devise procedures for assuring a balance between educational practices and the skills required of adults. He cannot ignore the interconnectedness of social life.

A fourth characteristic of utopias is that they are idealist. Utopists believe that social perfection is conceivable. Human potential, untapped by the existing order, awaits its release through new modes of organization. Once perfection is accepted as a possibility, it becomes a goal. To utopists, man has the power to shape his own destiny; such capacity must be used to the fullest. Thus, utopists do not merely seek a better society; their objective is nothing less than the ultimate resultant of human design and achievement.

Fifth, a utopia transcends the structure of the existing social order. The realization of a utopia requires the transformation of the political–economic–social organizations that compose the status quo. This quality of transcendence illuminates the gulf that a utopia sets between things as they are and things as the utopian believes they ought to be. A utopia goes beyond a claim to perfect existing institutions to achieve optimal performance. It is not a program of reform or adjustment; it is a model of a new social system. However, utopian speculation does not take place in a historical vacuum. Rather, utopian writers are acutely aware of the flaws in existing social structures. Thus, it is common for a utopia to be designed to resolve the major crises with which the status quo seems incapable of coping.

The transcendant quality of a utopia leads logically to its next characteristic; a utopia is critical of the existing social system. Even where criticism is not the deliberate objective of the utopian project, an attempt to create a system fundamentally distinct from the status quo, and qualitatively superior to present institutions, constitutes an implied critique. This disclaimer notwithstanding, the utopian's critical stance is usually quite deliberate. It is the disenchanted and the rebellious who don the utopian mantle to demonstrate that the present system is neither pure nor permanent, that the future remains to be created, and that its form may include new vistas for human development. Indeed, in the mind of the utopian writer, the function of criticism sometimes supersedes the function of social design. Often a specific institution or practice is included in a utopia primarily because it satirically reveals a shortcoming of the status quo.[1]

If utopias have some broad similarities of form, they nevertheless present a wide choice of contents. Indeed, through the rich history of utopian speculation, flawless societies have been designed to offer an enormous gamut of institutions, structures, and life styles. Such diversity is to be expected, considering the different historical challenges that utopian writers and practitioners have sought to confront. Also, changes in human social and cultural development have rendered elements of one century's utopia the next century's reality (especially in matters of technology). Still, as the following brief survey reveals, some elements in even the first utopias occur in subsequent works, including the most modern.

CLASSICAL UTOPIAN MODELS

While several of the lectures of the biblical Hebrew prophets contain utopian features—at least a belief in the final messianic triumph of righteousness—the first full examples of literary utopias must be credited to the ancient Greeks. Of these, Plato's *Republic* is of greatest import. Written during a period of decline in Athens, the *Republic* envisioned a new, perfected form for the Athenian model of social organization, the city-state. Like the contemporary city-states, the Republic would be small, the population level being limited to that number compatible with political unity. Economic activity would consist of agriculture and some small-craft production and would never move beyond this stage. For both ethical and pragmatic reasons, Plato preferred the virtue of restraining excessive desires to an attempt to satisfy them through economic growth.

In his political and social conceptions, Plato was more imaginative. Society would be divided into three castes—philosophers, warriors, and workers—each composed of those who demonstrated a specific value: wisdom, courage, and temperance, respectively. If each caste diligently carried out the duties for which it was best suited, justice, the harmony of the entire social order, would necessarily result. In accordance with Plato's idealist philosophy, the philosophers, those most capable of comprehending the "good" through contemplation, would rule.

If the philosophers and warriors were to carry out their functions fully, they would have to yield all selfish desires and devote themselves to the welfare of the state. To Plato, such an attitude could flourish only under conditions of communal living. As Ernest Barker observes, Plato considered the home, so precious to modern man, as anathema. "Pull down the walls," the Greek theorist argued, "they shelter at best a restricted family feeling; they harbour at the worst avarice and ignorance. Pull down the walls, and let the free air of a common life blow over the place where they have been." [2] Indeed, all aspects of the lives of these castes would be communized; they would share their property, their children, and their women.

The working class in the Republic would play no role in its government. The philosophers would be empowered to assign each individual to his work and to regulate the economy. Similarly, the philosophers would manage all education and could employ deception and censorship to ensure that the workers would harbor beliefs appropriate to social stability. [3]

During the medieval period, the utopian project, strictly defined, declined as a mode of speculation. Within Christendom, man's deepest hopes and desires were projected beyond this world to a heavenly future; utopia became supplanted by eschatology. Among literary works, even St. Augustine's *City of God,* the work of the era closest to the projection of a formal utopia, reflected a dualistic notion of life and of the future. Since Augustine considered men's eternal lives to be more significant than their mundane existences, his work emphasizes man's ideal relation with God rather than the perfected structure of social institutions. In social and political life, some Christian millennial movements did advocate the creation of the Kingdom of Justice on Earth, however their ideologies were often expedient, vague, and fragmentary, and they lacked the rigor or clarity of a serious social model. [4]

POSTMEDIEVAL UTOPIAS

Utopian thought achieved a spectacular resurrection with the decline of feudalism and the beginning of the Renaissance. An ethical civilization was still the ultimate objective, but the new writers devoted greater attention to the economic requirements for the "good" life, recognizing the significance of a sound agricultural base for a utopian city. Thus, manual labor, particularly farm labor, was often deemed a civic duty, rather than a burden relegated to a lower caste.

Another commonality consisted of a general anti-individualist tendency, probably a reaction against the social and economic chaos that accompanied the rise of the bourgeoisie. Consequently, community of property was extended to all social strata. Postmedieval utopias may have returned to the task of designing earthly instead of heavenly paradises, but they still faced the problem of coping with a significant religious tradition. Indeed, religion played a major role in most Renaissance utopias, perhaps as an effort to soften the implied heresy of perfection on earth rather than in heaven.

A notable effort to redesign man's conception of a superior social order was *City of the Sun,* written by Tomasso Campanella, a philosopher, friar, poet, astrologer, and political rebel who, although brutally tortured by the Inquisition, still managed to produce a utopian vision. Architecturally, Campanella's city on a hill reveals an intriguing mixture of mysticism, imagination, and functionality. It is divided into seven defensible rings named for seven planets; the connections between the rings are by four streets through four gates that face toward the main points of the compass; and, on the seven walls, the totality of the society's scientific knowledge is portrayed in paintings. Politically, the city is governed by a popelike leader of great philosophic insight, Metaphysic, assisted by a trinity of princes— Power, Wisdom, and Love—whose duties correspond to their titles. Communization of property, women, and all other objects of desire directs the loyalty of the citizens away from selfish pursuits and toward the state. In fact, in all areas, the society is managed for the good of the commonwealth rather than of private individuals. Children are bred "for the preservation of the species and not for individual pleasure." [5] However, here the state reveals the ruthlessness with which it demands compliance with its purposes. Should any woman wear makeup or high heels, thereby injecting artificiality into the selection of mates, she may be put to death.[6]

charming

Thomas More's Utopia

One of the leading intellectuals of late medieval Christendom, Thomas More (1478–1535), combined in a single career the successful practice of law, diplomacy, politics, and scholarship. He did so at a time of religious dispute and social dissension. An older feudal order faced supersession by the forces of economic and cultural individualism. The rise of capitalism thrust much of the English population into poverty; and political conflict reached to the ranks of the Church and its leadership. In such a context, traditional conceptions of social structure and values stood open to critical evaluation. More's essay, *Utopia,* completed in 1516, depicted a perfect human society, the institutions of which contrasted markedly with contemporary English practice. It thus served to focus attention on the shortcomings of currently prevailing institutions.[7]

In More's Utopia, stable urban planning is assured through the regulation of population density at every level of social organization. No family can have less than 10 or more than 16 members, and no city more than 6000 families. Presumably, economic welfare is the primary objective, with overpopulation straining resources and underpopulation restricting labor and intensive production. Productive economic activity itself is completely socialized. The means of production are under community control, and everyone (officials, priests, and full-time students excepted) is required to work.

The family is the basic social unit in Utopia. It is both the smallest functional political entity and the economic focal point for production and distribution. Authority resides with the patriarch. Other family members must respect the general rule of deference that wives serve husbands, children their parents, and youth their elders. More believed that people must be integrated into the larger community through membership in a small, tightly organized subgroup rather than as isolated individuals, accounting for the extensiveness of the family's role in Utopia.

In Thomas More's thought, Utopian political organization preserves the liberty of the people against enslavement or tyranny. It does so, however, through a hierarchy of subelites who resist one-man rule, rather than through genuine popular control. The fundamental electoral unit is the family, not the individual, and, as mentioned above, the Utopian family is highly autocratic. Also, Utopia prohibits political discourse outside formal assemblies, a measure that precludes the minimal level of interpersonal debate necessary to mobilize organized opposition to established power. The government consists of several levels, the lowest ranking of which are elected from a constituency of 30 families. Political decisions are generally made by a council elected from these public officials, which meets every few days in consultation with a prince. Particularly important issues are referred to the entire body of elected officials or to the populace in assembly.

Although Utopia is an extremely supportive cohesive society, it is also quite regimented and autocratic. Everyone in the city has the same work schedule, housing and clothing are uniform, and travel between cities requires a passport. One can choose a new job, but only with public agreement that one's new skill will be socially valuable. People are free to enjoy leisure, but there is strong social pressure for leisure time to be used constructively for reading, lectures, or voluntary labor. The pursuit of pleasure is also profoundly tempered by rational and religious qualifications, so as to be compatible with orderly social relationships. The Utopians employ socialization, sanctions, and the pragmatic structuring of situations, so that ethical behavior is satisfying and misbehavior detestable and violations result in severe penalties. It is this authoritarian and coercive aspect that has led strident critics to argue that utopias are in fact antiutopian because of their lack of freedom and human spontaneity (see below).

SEVENTEENTH- AND EIGHTEENTH-CENTURY UTOPIAS

In Francis Bacon's *New Atlantis,* one discovers a marked change in the utopian attitude. But the innovative features of his perspective are based on an accommodation of traditional values. Shipwrecked sailors discover the island of Bensalem, a self-sufficient, agricultural monarchy, highly moralistic and devoutly Christian. On Bensalem, however, is located a unique foundation, the House of Salomon. The objective of this foundation, states its governor, "is the knowledge of causes, and secret motions of things; and the enlarging of the bounds of human empire, to the effecting of all things possible." [8] Indeed, the house possesses incredible laboratories and equipment to enable it to fulfill such a goal. Here, Bacon has broken with the past. Popular welfare rivals the achievement of virtue as a social goal. The mean through which that welfare is to be achieved is experimental science. Also, one notes in *New Atlantis* the beginning of the scientific arrogance common to modern man. Unlike previous utopian writers, Bacon suggested a domination of nature by man rather than a stable balance with nature.

Even as he endorsed science, Bacon qualified the recommendation. If science held the key to human development, it still did not follow that all scientific achievements would have beneficial social consequences. In a prophetic statement, which has been universally ignored in modern practice, Bacon's scientists affirm their willingness to deny the fruits of their intellects to state authority. To quote their governor, "we have consultations, which of the innovations and experiences which we have discovered shall be published, and which not: and take all an oath of secrecy for the concealing of those which we think fit to keep secret: though some of those we do reveal sometime to the state, and some not." [9]

Utopias of the 18th century reflect the intellectual objective of the enlightenment: to expose the flaws of custom and tradition before the standard of human reason. Particularly in France, where political repression stifled dissent, utopias became a vehicle for social criticism disguised in the garb of fantasy. Thus, these works are less noticeable for the new social structures they designed than for their attacks on prevailing ideology, two of the favorite targets being restrictive sexual mores and Catholicism, deemed a theological bastion of the monarchy.[10]

One of the favorite techniques of this period was the glorification of primitive peoples, noble savages uncorrupted by the vices of the prevailing culture. A prime example of this approach was provided by Denis Diderot in his *Supplement to Bougainville's Voyage*. Diderot depicted an imaginary life-style of the natives of Tahiti, an island that had actually been visited by the explorer Louis Bougainville in the 1760s. In Diderot's *Supplement*, Tahiti's people enjoy a free and natural existence, unencumbered by private property, monogamy, restrictive religion, material luxury, or government. The contrast with allegedly advanced French institutions is explicit. To the question "must we civilize man or abandon him to his instincts?" Diderot replies:

> If you propose to be his tyrant, then civilize him, persecute him all you are able with a morality contrary to nature; fetter him in all ways; impede his actions with a thousand obstacles . . . and let the natural men be always shackled at the feet of the moral man. But do you want him to be happy and free? Then don't meddle with his affairs. . . . And always remain convinced, that it is not for your sake but for theirs that these cunning law-givers have moulded you and made you unnatural like you are. . . . Beware of anyone who wants to order things.[11]

It should be recognized that this position had a critical objective. Diderot was neither suggesting that primitive society was actually like his "Tahiti" nor recommending that mankind return to that state. He was, however, calling attention to the natural qualities lost in contemporary civilization. In fact, the utopian and philosophical judgment that the Enlightenment carried forward to the Revolution of 1789, perhaps best expressed in Rousseau, was that the freedom of the "noble savage" could never be regained. If mankind sought liberation from oppressive institutions, it must find its freedom within society.

NINETEENTH-CENTURY UTOPIAS

In the 19th century, utopists confronted the political and economic potential released by the French Revolution and the Industrial Revolution. Monarchy had been swept aside; now capitalist and proletarian waged war over the productive spoils spawned by technology and the open market. For the first time, equality of abundance appeared realizable, and utopian writers, "shamelessly materialistic," fervently pursued that goal. Among the early socialist visions was Étienne Cabet's *Voyage to Icaria.* Written while its author suffered exile for his antigovernment activities in France, it depicts a society in which the marriage of science and state power provides material well-being for all in an atmosphere of equality and brotherhood. The price of these economic benefits is every vestige of individual freedom. All aspects of life in Icaria—diet, clothing, architecture, education—are determined by committees of experts. Literature and art are subjected to vigorous censorship. Mumford is lenient when he dismisses Cabet's ideal with the comment, "If the good life could be perpetrated by a junta of busybodies . . . Icaria would be a model community." [12]

Edward Bellamy's *Looking Backward,* an enormously popular utopian novel, depicted a socialist order only slightly less regimented than Cabet's. Unlike earlier works that located utopia in some remote geographical region, Bellamy has his narrator fall into hypnotic sleep in 1887 to awaken in the utopian year 2000. Gradual monopolization of capitalist industry has resulted in the formation of a single, gigantic trust, a state enterprise that controls the entire American economy. In consequence, the labor force is nationalized, forming an industrial army which conscripts everybody at 17 and discharges them at 45. Bellamy's use of the army image is no accident, for it is the combination of equality in the ranks and efficient organization, common to military institutions, that he finds attractive. While production is regimented, consumption becomes a realm of freedom. State warehouses are amply stocked to provide for citizens' material needs, with technical innovation assuring the availability of sufficient goods to satisfy the soldier-workers' tastes. [13]

Despite their differences, Cabet and Bellamy adopted a relatively similar perspective within the utopian socialist tradition of the 19th century. Both writers based their vision of a better future on the prospect of continuing industrialization. In their utopias, the material wealth generated by the industrial system permits the elimination of poverty and the organization of a comfortable and satisfying life for all. The burdens of the industrial process, like the benefits, are to be shared equally. But the burdens—particularly compulsory factory-type labor—are considered unavoidable. Other utopists of this period rejected the centralization of power, the mechanization of work, and the regimentation of daily life common to the proindustrial socialist models.

An exponent of innovative cosmological, sociological, and psychological theories, Charles Fourier developed a complex model of societal organization predicated on the belief that a perfect social order requires the full release of natural human passions, albeit in a particular balance that guarantees overall harmony. Fourier called for the creation of unique, specially designed structures, named *phalanxes,* that would be populated with selected individuals with particular emotional tendencies. Although these settlements would not be completely egalitarian (members were to receive income according to their financial contribution to the endeavor), Fourier sought to prevent class conflict by combining in each individual the role of capitalist, worker, and consumer.

Designed as small communities of roughly 2000 persons, the phalanxes were expected to possess a land area sufficient to permit the practice of both agriculture and industry. While phalanxes would eventually form a federated organization with other similar units, the Fourierist scheme emphasized decentralization and local autonomy. In addition, Fourier differed from the industrial utopias in his views on the regulation of labor. According to Fourier, work should be pleasurable, with tasks fashioned to meet the abilities and interests of the worker. Forced periods of drudgery and monotonous effort would be eliminated.[14]

Another well-known proponent of the nonindustrial socialist utopia was the British poet and craftsman William Morris. In *News From Nowhere,* he transformed the atmosphere of the 19th-century utopia from factory and barracks to a romanticized conception of an English village in the Middle Ages. Morris's society presents a naturalistic and aesthetic quality markedly in contrast to the urban rigidity of industrial models. In utopian England, cities have been replaced by rural villages. Architecture is elegant and functional. Dress is decorative and pleasing. Not only did Morris recognize the undesirable concomitants of industrialization, he also questioned the worth of the machine age's alleged blessings. Criticizing the notion that constantly expanding production is to be equated with progress, he argued that much of the plenitude that industry creates is useless and unrelated to human needs.[15]

Crucial to Morris's vision was his belief that work can be a joyful experience rather than an unpleasant social requirement. In his utopia, men and women work only at activities they find agreeable. Fortunately, and inexplicably, the distribution of tasks that people wish to perform and the needs that consumers wish to have satisfied appear to be in near-perfect balance.

Politically, Morris offered a model of democratic anarchism. Government, as a central authoritative institution, no longer exists. The old

House of Parliament is a storehouse for dung. There are no courts, police, prisons, or other accouterments of executive power. Where the common interest is involved, decision making takes place at the local level according to majority rule. Not only does the minority avoid obstructing the will of the majority, it usually acquiesces willingly and helps implement majority decisions.

Although *News From Nowhere* contains an unusually captivating utopia, it nonetheless offers an implausible framework of social organization. The mechanisms of coordination between production and distribution on a national scale—certainly necessary in a society that effectively employs power-driven machinery—are never explained. Human character has conveniently improved so as to essentially eliminate the need for social control. Acute pressure of population on resources, and the technical innovation that that situation may require, is an unforeseen and unanalyzed danger. Still, the issues that Morris raised, and the values he struggled to realize, remain highly relevant to modern utopian aspirations. Current social reformists wonder whether the scale of industrial activity can be reduced, whether the products industry generates are worth the human cost in production, whether work can become more meaningful and spontaneous, and whether a simpler, quieter, more peaceful life-style is possible.

So enamored did 19th-century dreamers become of utopian prospects that many of them attempted to create experimental utopian communities. The enormous supply of open and underpopulated land in North America was seemingly waiting to give birth to a new civilization. Cabet launched several efforts to develop small-scale Icarias in Texas and Illinois, all of which ended in failure. Several dozen communities based on Fourier's prescriptions were started throughout the United States, the most famous being Brook Farm in Massachusetts; most collapsed quickly. Other communities with a religious basis were set up by Shakers, Zoar separatists, Hutterites, and Perfectionists.[16] A settlement of the latter group, the Oneida Community, is discussed in Chapter 3.

TWENTIETH-CENTURY UTOPIAS

Modern utopias are an unusual literary event. However, H. G. Wells, the British social theorist, produced several utopias among his other speculative works. One of these, *A Modern Utopia,* is an example of the crest of the wave of Western liberal optimism, which crashed abruptly against the realities of the 20th century. Wells sought to design conditions to assure popular welfare without threatening personal liberty. Of course, absolute liberty would be undesirable. "Consider how much liberty we gain," Wells suggested, "by the loss of the common liberty to kill." The state must act in careful balance, adopting only those restrictions that actually serve to maximize popular freedom.[17]

Wells's concern for individual liberty did not restrain him from advocating governmental centralization. Indeed, he insisted that utopia could take place only on a world scale. However, in very unliberal fashion, he did not fear the state apparatus he had envisioned. In matters of political power, he returned to Plato for guidance and staffed the utopian government with a class of samurai, modernized philosopher–kings, with special education and commitment to a rigorous moral code. Perhaps because he was unusually sensitive to man's prospects in the coming century, Wells's utopian visions are less extravagant than those of many of his predecessors. For example, he viewed nature as unmanageable and potentially dangerous. And he maintained that some segment of the human population would prove hopelessly criminal and would have to be exiled to prison islands.

Antiutopian Criticisms

As the 20th century has progressed, fewer and fewer utopian projects have been suggested. In part, this decline reflects a loss of confidence in the prospects of Western civilization, which began with World War I and which continues today. However, it also results from the development of a counterutopian perspective, a point of view that attacks the value of the utopian objective itself. Despite the utopian theorist's unquestioned commitment to the goal of human and social perfection, antiutopians insist that the end point of utopian logic is precisely the opposite of what is desired, the worst rather than the best of all possible worlds. For example, the Russian philosopher Nicolas Berdiaev warned "Utopias appear to be much more capable of realization than they did in the past. And we find ourselves faced by a much more distressing problem. How can we prevent their final realization?"[18] What reasons could cause men of goodwill to reject vehemently the quest for utopia?

While there is no single reason or set of reasons common to every critic, it is possible to differentiate the most frequent objections raised against utopia. To begin, there is the conservative reaction. All utopias imply criticism of the established order; none legitimate the society in which they are created. Thus, to those who are defenders of the status quo, the drive to utopia is viewed as an act of heresy, incitement to rebellion, or advocacy of cultural decline. For example, Bellamy's socialist utopia in *Looking Backward* so distressed conservatives that they responded with a decade's worth of antiutopian, and procapitalist, rejoinders.[19]

Some conservative antiutopians are less enamored of prevailing conditions than they are fearful of the unpredictable effects of large-scale social change. They see the history of the 20th century—the rise of communism in Russia, of fascism in Germany, and of technological capitalism in the United States—as a logbook of attempts to bring utopian visions to fruition. But yesteryear's dream has become today's nightmare, and to borrow Eugen Weber's analogy, those who have awakened from nightmares are reluctant to attempt further dreaming.

Second, utopias must confront a romantic critique. Although formally works of literature, utopias are less artistic than they are rational constructs, orderly efforts to form societies according to specific principles and hypotheses. Hence, they are in conflict with those who demand the triumph of the aesthetic, a world open to uninhibited spontaneity and self-expression. The imagination is, after all, without rational or moral limits. And that minimal coherency necessary to every planned society may be perceived as a restriction on the vitality of art. The locus of hope to these antiutopians lies in the strength of the instincts, of fantasy, and of the irrational—"in the peculiarly individualistic and egoistic characteristics most likely to shatter any system or order."[20]

A third basis of opposition to utopia concerns the prospects for human freedom in a perfect society. At the outset, utopias deny people the opportunity of determining their own destiny, since they prescribe a new social order. Defending the unqualified right of political choice, Berneri observed, "The builders of utopia claimed to give freedom to the people, but freedom which is given ceases to be freedom."[21]

Beyond this general coerciveness, there are specific political and social structures common to many utopias that can be considered threats to human freedom. Utopias often include a monolithic and centralized state apparatus, powerful enough to defend the perfect society and provide for the popular welfare, but also powerful enough to crush dissent. This central control may be lodged in the hands of an intellectual elite, as in the Republic or Icaria, a practice that may only improve a government's competence in managing all aspects of its citizens' lives. Or the state's authority may be buttressed by technology, as in Orwell's *1984*.

In addition, antiutopians often view science and technology as threats to freedom, regardless of their connection to some totalitarian administration. The very machines that provide abundance may require that the soci-

ety that depends upon them orient its workers' lives to their operational
requirements. Indeed, Engels, in a characteristically determinist but unusually pessimistic declaration, suggested that the following sign might be
hung above the entrance to any industrial factory, "Abandon all autonomy
ye who enter here." [22] The needs of men must be subordinated to the needs
of the engines of production.

Also, the logic of science may prove as deadly to human liberty as the
mechanisms it helps to create. Zamiatin's *We* is an antiutopian novel de-
picting a future in which all human spontaneity has been sacrificed before
the order of mathematical perfection. Indeed, the main character—himself
a number, D-503—expresses his satisfaction at mankind's development to
logical purity as follows:

> "The ancient god created the ancient man, i.e., the man capable of mistakes,
> ergo the ancient god himself made a mistake. The multiplication table is more
> wise and more absolute than the ancient god, for the multiplication table
> never (do you understand—*never*) makes mistakes! There are no more fortunate
> and happy people than those who live according to the correct, eternal laws of
> the multiplication table. No hesitation! No errors! There is but one truth and
> there is but one path to it; and that truth is: four, and that path is: two times
> two. Would it not seem preposterous for these happily multiplied twos sud-
> denly to begin thinking of some foolish kind of freedom?" [23]

Still another criticism of utopia is directed toward the notion of pure
social perfection. Once a perfect order has been established, there is no
longer any basis for improvement or innovation. Utopia must remain a
static society, ever faithful to its ideal routine. Yet, such a state denies to
its members that creative impulse that motivated the utopian writers themselves, the desire to change one's world for the better. Without such progressive movement, a society could only permit the perfection of uniformity and stagnation. Zamiatin argued that any change, even the unknown,
is preferable to such stasis when he had a character who opposes the perfect
state exclaim, " 'Tomorrow, nobody knows what . . . do you understand?
Neither I nor anyone else knows; it is unknown! Do you realize what a joy
it is? Do you realize that all that was certain has come to an end? Now
. . . things will be new, improbable, unforeseen!' " [24]

A fifth reason for viewing utopia with dismay involves the quality of
"perfected" human life. There are many elements to this argument. They
include the contention that neurosis is the fundamental source of great art
as well as the elitist view that abundance would prove an unspeakable bore.
But a deeper thesis suggests that human happiness and pleasure cannot be
divorced from pain and unhappiness. There is a dialectical relationship be-

tween the poles of experience; one state cannot be known without the possibility of encountering its opposite. An effort to eliminate the depths of despair restricts the heights of ecstasy. It is this point of view that explains the astounding speech of the Savage in Aldous Huxley's antiutopian novel *Brave New World:*

> "But I don't want comfort. I want God. I want poetry, I want real danger, I want freedom, I want goodness. I want sin . . . . I'm claiming the right to be unhappy. . . . . Not to mention the right to grow old and ugly and impotent; the right to have syphilis and cancer; the right to have too little to eat; the right to be lousy; the right to live in constant apprehension of what may happen tomorrow; the right to catch typhoid; the right to be tortured by unspeakable pains of every kind . . . I claim them all." [25]

MODERN UTOPIAS

With the advent of the postwar period, the utopian tradition confronted significant obstacles to its continued relevance as a mode of social speculation. The material and psychological devastation of world war and world economic depression made the hope of human perfection seem futile, perhaps absurd. Antiutopians argued that the quest for the "impossible dream" should be avoided as a sociological island of sirens that concealed the rocks of regimentation and tyranny. And yet, phoenixlike, utopias have continued to arise. Historically no stranger to social crisis, the utopist recognizes, in the confusion and contradictions of an existing mode of social organization, the rationale for serious consideration of a model that can replace it. Thus, as Plato confronted the decline of Athens, and Bellamy and Cabet the chaos of the Industrial Revolution, modern utopias seek a way to move beyond the political, economic, and environmental difficulties of our own era.

Writing in the dawn of the Atomic Age, B. F. Skinner brought forward one of the most controversial of postwar utopias, based on his theories of learning and psychological conditioning. While many stood in awe of the destruction that modern science had wrought, Skinner boldly insisted that it would be through an extension of scientific reasoning—to the social as well as the physical sciences—that man might construct a superior civilization. His novel, *Walden II,* is discussed in Chapter 6.

As if to provide living proof that antiutopian fears and utopian aspirations can coexist in a single human mind, Aldous Huxley, whose celebrated *Brave New World* was a formidable critique of the utopian spirit, brought forth in 1962 an unadulterated utopia, *Island.* Huxley's novel represents a half-wistful, half-defiant recognition of the obstacles facing the realization of a perfect vision in a perfect world. In this case, Utopia occurs on a "forbidden" island, hidden away somewhere near Indonesia, where the ideological descendants of a Scottish doctor and a Buddhist king reject the enticements of capitalism and communism and decide instead to combine the best of Western and Oriental culture. Whereas *Brave New World* carries technological logic to a dehumanizing and antiutopian extreme, *Island* examines a social model in which man is capable of mastering the technological impulse. Huxley's antiutopian reasoning convinced him that unregulated technological development would lead to disaster. Utopia remains a possibility if machines are permitted only a limited role restricted by the need to maintain stability and balance both with nature and within the human community. In contrast to Lenin's thesis that electricity plus socialism equals communism, the island utopians suggest that electricity minus heavy industry (plus birth control) equals democracy.[26]

Huxley yielded to utopian aspirations long enough to envision a near-perfect social microcosm, but he remembered the vulnerability of that model to its broader social environment. More and Bacon could leave their utopias in remote and uncharted seas. Huxley knew too well that in 1962 utopian islands could not keep the world at bay. Indeed, he vividly demonstrated the hopelessness of the island utopia as a plausible societal entity by burdening the antimaterialistic inhabitants with vast reserves of oil. In the novel's final pages, utopia succumbs to invasion from a neighboring military dictatorship, while sinister oil interests wait offshore to begin exploitation of their prize.

When major emphasis is placed on antiutopian objections to certain trends in utopian thinking, a form of utopianism that extends or modifies the normal structure of the genre sometimes develops. This is the case in Robert Nozick's *Anarchy, State and Utopia,* a work that includes a utopian program in an eclectic discourse on political philosophy.[27] Nozick is disturbed by the prospect of utopia, especially the concentration of state power, the regimentation of individual behavior, and the infringement of natural rights. Indeed, considering the wide diversity in human preferences, he finds the notion that there can be a single best society for everyone to be foolhardy, if not repugnant. Instead of following the usual utopian practice of imagining a perfect society, Nozick presented a more libertarian proposal:

> Imagine a possible world in which to live; this world need not contain everyone else now alive, and it may contain beings who have never actually lived. Every rational creature in this world you have imagined will have the same

rights of imagining a possible world for himself to live in (in which all other rational inhabitants have the same imagining rights, and so on) as you have. The other inhabitants of the world you have imagined may choose to stay in the world which has been created for them (they have been created for) or they may choose to leave it and inhabit a world of their own imagining. If they choose to leave your world and live in another, your world is now without them. You may choose to abandon your imagined world, now without its emigrants. This process goes on; worlds are created, people leave them, create new worlds, and so on.[28]

In developing the logical implications of this vision, Nozick concluded with a conception of utopia that is in fact a "framework" for utopias. Central to this framework is freedom of choice. Utopia represents the opportunity to join voluntarily with others to create a new society; it does not include the option to impose one's image of perfection on anyone else. Thus, unless Novick's premise of human diversity is in error, utopia will be a metautopia. It will be "the environment in which utopian experiments may be tried out; the environment in which people are free to do their own thing." [29]

Such a framework offers less than one usually finds in a utopia. Nozick has not designed a future society; he has only offered a minimal set of rules for the design of a future society. However, in light of his values, Nozick has carried utopian speculation as far as he can. To set out further details of a specific model would interfere with the freedom of imagination he wishes to assure to all other utopians. Nozick's unwillingness to describe functioning utopian institutions and organizations nonetheless limits the value of his proposal. The effort to bring a utopia into being often reveals that the actual physical and social environment can block avenues that seemed open to the imagination. The specificity of most utopias is conducive to a clear evaluation of their prospects as working models. Since Nozick's framework remains at the level of abstract principles, the gulf between its theoretical formulation and its practical realization remains wide.

There is another way in which the metautopian schema fails to live up to utopian expectations. Utopias usually attempt to provide solutions to contradictions with which the social order that they originate in is struggling. Nozick's proposal provides no insight as to concrete means of coping with political, economic, or ecological crises. His framework is procedural, and it remains for those who act within that procedure to devise mechanisms for avoiding or correcting their community's problems.

Postwar utopian aspirations have not been limited to literary endeavors. In the 1960s, the United States experienced the largest wave of communal living experiments since the great period of utopian community formation in the mid-19th century. It is not possible to determine the precise number of experiments attempted, since many of them were hidden or short-lived. Nevertheless, serious observers suggest that between 1000 and 3000 intentional communities appeared during this decade.[30]

Most of those who founded or joined communes were young, white, and of middle-class origin. Often, they lacked assets or income, productive skills, or experience in organizations. Moreover, the new communards generally had a much clearer understanding of the faults of the society they sought to abandon—materialism, spiritual bankruptcy, environmental decay, insane competitiveness, racism, and militarism—than they did of the form the alternative communities should take. These factors contributed to basic structural characteristics common to the communes: small size; transient, unstable membership; and with a few notable exceptions—such as Twin Oaks in Virginia, the Lama Foundation in New Mexico, and the Brotherhood of the Spirit in Massachusetts—lack of a formal organizational structure.[31]

Aside from noting the prevailing tendency toward little or no structure, it is impossible to generalize concerning specific institutional forms in the communes. Some collectively allocated labor; some survived through the efforts of a minority who chose to work; and some subsisted on welfare or outside contributions, preferring to avoid work altogether. Political arrangements also varied considerably, ranging from intense charismatic authoritarianism to anarchy.[32]

In their value orientations, the communes reflected the composite of attitudes and preferences common to the counterculture of the 1960s. Commune dwellers sought simplicity in their mode of living; they learned rustic crafts and minimized the use of modern technology. The selection of a rural environment usually involved a desire for harmony with nature, as shown by the proclivity for organic farming. Communards preferred spontaneity to rigid organization, although in a few communes, regimented structures were accepted. They detested competition and attempted to share resources and obligations, with varying degrees of success. Communards endorsed an extraordinary degree of sexual liberation, but sexual equality, also a goal in many communes, proved much more difficult to achieve. In addition, many commune members sought to achieve expansions of consciousness through mystical or psychological techniques or through the use of drugs.

A major communal value was the transcendence of the isolation and loneliness many members had known in urban life through a profound unity with other group members. Veysey described this vision as "a constant, spontaneous merger of individuals into a loving group. In its purest form, no one was held to be special; anyone could join, and all divisive memories would be dissolved in a total bodily and psychic fusion." [33] However, the value of communal union conflicted with another major counterculture norm: the desire for self-direction and individualism. Many individuals joined communes to escape restrictions on the free expression of their impulses.

While the values described above appeared regularly at many communes, the new communards avoided any commitment to a codified ideology or specific program. They were steadfastly antiplanning, and often antirational and anti-intellectual as well. Adopting a psychological more than a social or political view of man, they emphasized the goals of personal fulfillment and self-growth rather than organizational achievement or social mission.

Few of the communes of the 1960s demonstrated a capacity for historical longevity. The average life span of a rural commune was only about one to two years, and less than half of the 1960s communes are thought to have lasted for even five years. Only a few communes, generally of the more structured variety, have shown any promise of surviving for longer periods. Both external and internal difficulties accounted for the failure of the communal experiments. Some fell victim to legal and extralegal attacks from conservative neighbors. Others collapsed over a variety of crises: inability to resolve conflicts, unwillingness or inability to earn income, indefinite or confused goals, inadequate structure to maintain basic living conditions. [34]

From an overall perspective, the communes of the 1960s have not had a major impact on the structure or institutions of American society. In part, this resulted from the fact that many of them never sought any impact other than that which could be achieved through the force of example. The communes failed to develop alternative political institutions or programs for achieving power. In addition, the communes never presented a viable, structural alternative for the bulk of the population enmeshed in a complex, urban environment. Nor did the communes, whose members were the product of affluent communities, offer much appeal to the less privileged sectors of the American public. However, the communes did have an impact on American values and culture—particularly in their emphasis on spirituality and on individual craftsmanship and in their opposition to consumerism and technology. Specific ideas and practices with which they experimented may still achieve widespread realization as part of a more broad-based and politically effective social movement.

Another recent utopian project, albeit one much less radical in principle than the communes, is the New Town movement. Unlike the tiny counterculture communities, a single New Town can become the home of tens of thousands of persons. Necessarily, therefore, the New Towns must deal with the practical problems of life in an urban or quasi-urban environment. A planned community of this type, the New Town at Columbia, Maryland, is one of the case studies discussed in Chapter 5.

As further evidence of continuing utopian energy, a new written utopia appeared in 1975 that tackled the environmental crisis head on. *Ecotopia,* by Ernest Callenbach, envisions a future for North America in which Northern California, Oregon, and Washington have seceded from the United States and established themselves as an independent nation. The primary objective of the denizens of this society is to develop modes of social organization that maintain a balance with the natural environment.[35]

Many current institutions and practices that result in environmental deterioration have been abandoned or modified. Ecotopians have given up the automobile; transport is by electric vehicle, by bicycle, or on foot. Oil- and gas-fired power plants have been closed. Ecotopians employ fission nuclear plants, while their research aims at a full conversion to other energy sources—including fusion and solar power. New biodegradable plastics have replaced materials that cannot be recycled. Instead of receiving minor fines, those guilty of deliberate pollution receive severe prison sentences. Not only has zero population growth been achieved, but the ecotopian population is declining.

What should prove impressive to antiutopians is that this environmentally stable organization operates without mass regimentation or an authoritarian central-state apparatus. On the contrary, decentralization is the ecotopian norm. Medical and educational services and agricultural and forestry enterprises have been reorganized to serve local needs. Ecotopian business enterprises have been reorganized to serve local needs. Ecotopian business enterprises are owned by the persons who operate them. The businesses do compete with each other, but no firm can use its profits to acquire control of another. In their social relationships, ecotopians are particularly informal and spontaneous. Since they live close to nature, they favor the immediate and uninhibited release of natural emotions and passions.

Callenbach's work is clearly not the final word in the utopian response to environmental crisis. It can be criticized on many grounds. For example, the notion of a separate secessionist country coexisting with the United States, and interacting on a relatively amicable basis with the rest of the world reveals a considerable political naiveté. However, Callenbach is well aware that he does not have all the answers. In some areas, such as race relations, he has failed to offer a utopian solution. In others, like the use of energy sources, he has wisely delayed a decision until further evidence is in. Thus, even if *Ecotopia* is unlikely to induce irate Californians to close the border at Donner Pass, it does direct utopian thinking toward issues of which all who would contemplate man's future must remain aware.

A CONCEPTUAL FRAMEWORK FOR THE ANALYSIS OF UTOPIAN MODELS

We currently need a new type of utopian model. This model must deal with the twin problems of inherent environmental limitations and of human needs for stimulation and change, which preclude the development of a static social system. Utopias are to provide an ideal environment for human growth and productivity. But how can ideal human environments be described? Our framework is composed of five types of dimensions by which characteristics of human environments have been related to indices of human functioning.

Ecological Dimensions

Ecological dimensions include both geography and meteorology, on the one hand, and architecture and physical design, on the other. Since geographical and meteorological characteristics have been discussed above, they are not reviewed here. The evidence suggests that these variables are quite important in influencing human behavior. Man is increasingly creating his own geographical and meteorological environment, and trends in this area are concerned with the relationship of man-made variables, such as radiation and air pollution, to mood changes and to mental and physical symptoms.[36]

Architecture and Physical Design. People necessarily function in a specific physical context that can impose constraints on the range of possible behaviors, and that can serve to determine certain patterns of individual action. The design of buildings and cities has an effect on the behavior of the people who live and work in them. The arrangement of apartments, hallways, and exits in housing units can encourage the formation of friendships among neighbors and discourage the occurrence of crime. The pattern of streets may promote their use as playgrounds in one neighborhood and thoroughfares in another. The placement of chairs in a room may facilitate or inhibit open discussion.

For example, Harvey Osmond has offered a basic bipolar dimension along which physical environments vary. At one end of the continuum are sociofugal environments that discourage social contacts and the formation of interpersonal relationships. Railway stations, hotels, and most mental hospitals are examples of this type of design. At the other pole are sociopetal environments, such as teepees, igloos, and small seminar rooms, which encourage contacts and the development of interpersonal relationships. A circular or radial design for group living quarters would encourage interaction by placing bedrooms at the outer circumference of the structure and common recreation and meeting areas in the center, thus eliminating all hallways. People going from bedroom to bedroom, or into the lounge, would be frequently put into contact with others. These unavoidable contacts would provide people with practical opportunities to increase involvement and social cohesion.[37]

Architectural design can have a wide impact by affecting the life styles and values of people. One aspect of suburban life that has received considerable attention is the possibility that it discourages individuality. William Whyte has discussed the consequences of a neighborhood design that tends to encourage interaction and make isolation and privacy impossible. As Whyte noted, "The court, like the double bed, enforces intimacy, and self-imposed isolation becomes psychologically untenable." A leveling, homogenizing process may take place with both positive and negative consequences. One unexpected consequence of intense interaction and group cohesion in small neighborhood areas may be little participation in civic or cultural affairs. People active in the overall community that Whyte studied came from less socially active, less cohesive courts, and conversely, the courts where interaction was most intense contributed few civic leaders. The major point for our purposes is that architectural variable may exert an important impact on behavior and thus must be carefully considered in the planning of an optimum human environment.[38]

The Human Aggregate

Various aggregate characteristics of the individual inhabiting a particular environment—for example, average age, ability level, and educational attainment—are situational variables in that they partly define relevant characteristics of the environment. This idea is based on the notion that most of the social and cultural environment is transmitted through other people. It implies that the character of an environment is dependent in part on the typical characteristics of its members. For example, vocational satis-

faction, stability, and achievement depend in part on the congruence between one's personality and the environment (composed largely of other
people) in which one works. John Holland has proposed six model environments to characterize the common physical and social environments in our
culture and six personality types or personal orientations identified by the
type of vocation to which a person belongs. Since both the environmental
models and the personality types are derived from the same basic concepts
(realistic, intellectual, social, conventional, enterprising, and artistic), it is
possible to classify people and environments in the same terms and to assess
the degree of person–environment congruence and its effects.[39]

These environmental characteristics and the personal traits they foster
are important because people tend to become more like the other people in
the settings in which they function. For example, college students' career
choices tended to conform over time to the modal career choices in their
college environment, particularly in the cases of engineering, teaching,
law, and business. This effect was conceptualized as a *process* that both discouraged students who were planning relatively popular careers from aban-
doning their initial choice and encouraged those in less popular careers to
switch to more popular ones. Appropriately, this process was labeled *progressive conformity*.[40]

By analogy, the types of people in a utopian society, and their background and performance characteristics, can differentially influence the experience and behavior of new inhabitants. In fact, the more cohesive and
socially integrated a community becomes, the greater its power to influence
its members. Assume that an adolescent boy joins a communal living group
that emphasizes cultural and religious activities, fervent discussions about
intellectually stimulating topics, arguments and debates among members,
religious revival meetings, group-sponsored shows and plays, and the like.
The new member would be exposed to these and related stimuli and thus
might feel anxiety about not being intelligent or devout enough (a change
in immediate subjective experience), experience greater involvement and
cohesion in relation to fellow members, or have increased feelings of competitiveness and inferiority. Presumably, this boy would be affected dif-
ferently if he joined a different communal living group. In terms of short-
term behavioral effects, he may increase the time he devotes to intellectual
and religious activities, spend more time in enhancing his creative abilities,
and perhaps increase his intellectual aggression.

There may also be longer-lasting alterations in his self-concept and/or
relatively permanent changes in behavior that may persist beyond his time
in the particular communal living group (e.g., devoting a great deal of

energy to religious activities or continually engaging in competitive activities with others). A person's experiences, and their short- and long-term consequences, can thus be influenced by environmental stimuli that are dependent in part on the typical characteristics of the people in the social group to which that person belongs. These issues are important in the planning of a utopian society, since the characteristics of a group's new members will eventually determine the nature of that group as older members are replaced.

Dimensions of Organizational Structure and Functioning

One dominant characteristic of the 20th century is the rapid expansion and the increased scope of large organizations. Although formal organizations have existed throughout history, the 20th century might well be called the "organization age" because of the pervasiveness of large organizations. Consider the range of activities we pursue in organizational settings:

> We are born in organizations, educated by organizations, and many of us spend much of our lives working for organizations. We spend much of our leisure time paying, playing and praying in organizations. Most of us will die in an organization, and, when the time comes to burial, the largest organization of all—the state—must grant official permission. [41]

An organization is in part a formal structure "established for the pursuit of relatively specific objectives." [42] As a formal structure, it has both size (e.g., number of people) and shape (e.g., number of levels of authority). An organization is also an environment with explicit rules, roles, and responsibilities. Like most environments, an organization influences the behaviors and attitudes of the people who participate in it. This influence can often be traced to the very structure of an organization, that is, its size and shape.

For example, size is one of the most important structural factors in organizations. Most people intuitively believe that small size is more desirable than large size; in fact, throughout history there has been a consensus about the negative effects of large size. Aristotle felt that democracy could not work effectively in large-sized states where citizens did not know "one another's character." These concerns were echoed centuries later by Émile Durkheim, who felt that "small scale industry . . . displays a relative harmony between worker and employer. It is only in large scale industry that these relations are in a sickly state." [43]

Just as the structural properties of organizations can influence the behavior and attitudes of the people in them, structural changes can have a powerful impact. For example, the effects of automation and increasing technology and specialization have been the subject of a long and heated debate. The advocates of automation applaud the material benefits associated with technological progress, whereas social critics blame automation for the discontent of industrial and white-collar workers. In fact, there are both advantages and costs, depending on the level of automation and the type of industry involved.[44]

Factors related to organizational structure and change may thus have important impacts on the members of an organization. In our analysis of utopian communities, we focus on four of the major organizational structures within a society: government, economy, family, and education. Research on organizations such as government bureaucracies, educational organizations, industrial factories, and manufacturing plants indicates that these major societal structures influence their members and the basic character and quality of a society.[45]

Behavior Settings

Roger Barker and his associates have developed the concept of the behavior setting, which they consider to be the essential element in studies of the ecological environment. They believe that this unit provides the "basic building block" of ecological psychology. Behavior settings are extraindividual; that is, behavior settings refer not to the behavior of particular individuals but to groups of individuals behaving together. When you attend a lecture, go to a baseball game, shop in a grocery store, or go to the dentist, you are participating in a behavior setting.[46]

The behavior-setting unit includes temporal and physical aspects of the environment, the standing patterns of behavior in the environment, and the relationship between the two. In addition, the behavior-setting unit is intermediate in size. It is not as small as the behavior of a single individual, nor is it as large as a school or a factory. Behavior settings can serve as an important link between the behavior of a particular individual and that of large contexts, such as organizations or schools.

It is possible to survey the entire population of behavior settings in a small town, that is, in an environmental unit that is approximately the same size as some utopian communities. In fact, one study examined all 455 settings identified in one town in terms of 43 different descriptive variables. This study identified 12 behavior setting types, for example, government settings (township board meetings, city council meetings), local business settings (banks, barber shops, lumberyards, grocery stores), family-oriented settings (picnics, public dinners), religious settings (religion classes, worship services, fellowship meetings), and so on. This type of classification may provide hypotheses concerning the economic, political, and behavior-control functions of social settings in the context of an entire community.[47]

Behavior settings have important impacts on the people who function within them and are therefore of major importance in the planning of an optimal society. Descriptions of one or two behavior settings may help provide a concrete "flavor" of what life in a utopian community would actually be like.[48]

Social Climate

The social-climate perspective assumes that environments have unique "personalities," just as people do. Social environments can be portrayed with a great deal of accuracy and detail. Some people are more supportive than others; likewise, some social environments are more supportive than others. Some people feel a strong need to control others; similarly, some social environments are extremely rigid, autocratic, and controlling. Order, clarity, and structure are important to many people. Correspondingly, many social environments strongly emphasize order, clarity, and organization.

Almost everyone intuitively believes that the social environment or social climate has a significant impact on the people functioning in it. For example, many people feel that the current social climate in the United States fosters aggressive and criminal behavior. One can cogently argue that every institution in our society—and every society as a whole—attempts to set up social environments to maximize certain directions of personal growth and development. Families, social groups, business organizations, colleges and universities, military companies, and communal living groups all arrange social and environmental conditions that they hope will maximize "desirable" behaviors and minimize "undesirable" ones.

But how can the "blooming, buzzing confusion" of a natural social environment be adequately assessed? Recent research has shown that vastly different social environments can be described by common or similar sets of dimensions. These dimensions are conceptualized in three broad categories: relationship dimensions, personal-development or personal-growth dimensions, and system-maintenance and system-change dimensions. These categories of dimensions are similar across many environments, although vastly different settings may impose unique variations within the general categories.

Personal-Growth Dimensions. These assess the basic directions along which personal growth and self-enhancement tend to occur in a particular environment. The exact nature of these dimensions varies somewhat among different environments, depending upon their underlying purposes and goals. These dimensions assess the directions along which people are encouraged to develop, for example, independence (the extent to which people are encouraged to be self-sufficient and to make their own decisions); intellectual–cultural orientation (the extent to which the environment emphasizes discussions about political, social, and cultural issues); and moral–religious emphasis (the extent to which ethical and religious issues and values are discussed and emphasized). Other personal-growth goals include competition, academic achievement, self-understanding, and task orientation. We will analyze each utopian community in terms of its basic ideology, that is, the personal-growth goals or values it seeks to foster.

Relationship Dimensions. These identify the nature and intensity of personal relationships within the environment. They assess the extent to which people are involved in the environment, the extent to which they support and help each other, and the extent to which there is spontaneity and free and open expression among them. The basic dimensions are very similar in different environments. Involvement reflects how far people are concerned in and committed to their activities and how enthusiastic and constructive they are in the setting.

The degree of support present in an environment is especially important. Support reflects the extent of manifest concern for others in the group, efforts to aid one another with personal difficulties and problems, and an emphasis on open and honest communication. A separate dimension of expressiveness or spontaneity is identified in many environments and is clearly relevant to utopian societies. There are thus basically three relationship dimensions that characterize all environments: involvement, support, and expressiveness.

System-Maintenance and System-Change Dimensions. These are relatively similar across all types of environments. These dimensions assess the extent to which the environment is orderly, is clear in its expectations, maintains control, and is responsive to change. The basic dimensions are order and organization, clarity, control, and innovation. For example, clarity in a work milieu assesses to what extent workers know what to expect in their daily routines and how explicitly rules and policies are communicated. Clarity in a classroom assesses the emphasis on following a clear set of rules and on students' knowing what the consequences will be if they do not follow them. The degree of social control and of responsiveness to change is clearly relevant to—and clearly discriminates among—utopian societies. Different social environmental dimensions have pervasive impacts on people, particularly in small, relatively close-knit, and closed societies, such as many utopian living groups.[49]

Visions of ideal environments have attracted humanity ever since God summarily dismissed Adam and Eve from paradise. How have utopian environments been described? Is there any consistency in their characteristics? All utopias are necessarily free of crowding and noise and air pollution, but what types of architecture and physical design do ideal human environments have? Have certain geographic and weather conditions been suggested as most conducive to a utopian environment?

What kind of organizational structure do utopian environments have? How have the government, the economy, and the family been structured? What types of people have lived there? Can all types of people be integrated within one ideal environment? What kinds of behavior settings have been included? And finally, what type of social climate has been thought to be characteristic of an ideal human community? Are cohesiveness and spontaneity sufficient, or is some measure of order and control essential? In the next four chapters we present case-study analyses of utopian societies to provide some relevant data on these issues.

REFERENCES AND NOTES

1. For discussions of the nature of the utopian genre, see: Mumford, L. *The story of utopias.* New York: Viking, 1922, pp. 11–26; Negley G., and Patrick, J. M. *The quest for utopia.* New York: H. Schuman, 1952, pp. 2–8; Hertzler, J. O. *The history of utopian thought.* New York: MacMillan, 1923, pp. 257–269.
2. Barker, E. *The political thought of Plato and Aristotle.* New York: Russel & Russel, 1959, p. 143.
3. For discussions of *The Republic,* see: Barker, op. cit., pp. 81–163; Mumford, op. cit., pp. 29–56; Negley and Patrick, op. cit., pp. 251–261; Hertzler, op. cit., pp. 99–120; M. L. Berneri, *Journey through utopia.* Boston: Beacon Press, 1950, pp. 9–33.
4. Mumford, op. cit., pp. 59–60; Hertzler, op. cit., pp. 69–74; for a discussion of visionary social and political movements during the Middle Ages, see: Cohn, N. *The pursuit of the millennium.* New York: Harper, 1961.

5. Campanella, T. *City of the sun.* In *Ideal commonwealths.* London: G. Routledge and Sons, 1899, pp. 235–236.

6. For discussions of *City of the sun,* see: Berneri, op. cit., pp. 88–102; Mumford, op. cit., pp. 103–106; Negley and Patrick, op. cit., pp. 314–317; Hertzler, op. cit., pp. 153–165.

7. For excerpts from 16th-century and modern analyses of More's *Utopia,* see: Gallagher, L. (Ed.), *More's Utopia and its critics.* Chicago: Scott, Foresman, 1964, pp. 69–169. See also: Negley and Patrick, op. cit., pp. 262–267; Berneri, op. cit., pp. 58–61.

8. Bacon, F. *New Atlantis.* In *Ideal commonwealths,* op. cit., p. 202.

9. Ibid., pp. 211–212. For discussions of *New Atlantis,* see: Berneri, op. cit., pp. 126–137; Hertzler, op. cit., pp. 146–153; Negley and Patrick, op. cit., pp. 360–361; Mumford, op. cit., pp. 106–109.

10. Berneri, op. cit., pp. 174–184.

11. Diderot, D. *Supplement to Bougainville's voyage.* In J. Kemp (Ed.), *Diderot: Selected writings.* New York: International Publishers, 1963, p. 188.

12. Mumford, op. cit., pp. 158–159. See also: Berneri, op. cit., pp. 219–235.

13. Berneri, op. cit., pp. 243–255; Mumford, op. cit., pp. 159–169.

14. A general selection of Fourier's writings can be found in: Poster, M. (Ed.). *Harmonian man.* Garden City, N.Y.: Doubleday, 1971.

15. Morris, W. *News from nowhere.* New York: Vanguard, 1926, p. 120.

16. Kanter, R. *Commitment and community.* Cambridge, Mass.: Harvard University Press, 1972, pp. 3–8. For an eyewitness account of numerous experimental utopian communities in the 19th-century United States, see: Nordhoff, C. *The communistic societies of the United States.* New York: Hillary House, 1960.

17. Wells, H. G. *A modern utopia.* London: Thomas Nelson and Sons, Ltd., 1909, pp. 40–51 (quote from p. 42).

18. Berdiaev's statement is used as an introduction by Aldous Huxley in his anti-utopian novel *Brave new world.* New York: Harper, 1946.

19. Walsh, C. *From utopia to nightmare.* London: Goeffrey Bles, 1962, pp. 74–75.

20. Weber, E. The anti-utopia of the twentieth century. In G. Kateb (Ed.), *Utopia.* New York: Atherton Press, 1971, p. 88. For a fuller analysis of both the conservative and romantic critiques of utopia, see: Shklar, J. *After utopia.* Princeton: Princeton University Press, 1957.

21. Berneri, op. cit., p. 3.

22. *Marx and Engels: Selected works.* Moscow: Foreign Languages Publishing House, 1962, p. 637. See also E. Weber, op. cit., pp. 82–83.

23. Zamiatin, E. *We.* New York: Dutton, 1924, p. 79.

24. Ibid., p. 179.

25. Huxley, op. cit., p. 288. See: Kateb, op. cit., pp. 17–19; Kateb, G. *Utopia and its enemies.* London: Free Press of Glencoe, 1963, pp. 17–19.

26. Huxley, A. *Island.* New York: Harper & Row, 1962.

27. Nozick, R. *Anarchy, state and utopia.* New York: Basic Books, 1974.

28. Ibid., p. 299.
29. Ibid., p. 312.
30. Houriet, R. *Getting back together.* New York: Coward, McCann & Geoghegan, 1971, p. xiii; Kanter, R., op. cit., 1972, p. 116; Veysey, L., *The communal experience.* New York: Harper & Row, 1973, p. 457. See also: Melville, K. *Communes in the counter culture.* New York: William Morrow, 1972, pp. 53–82; Bouvard, M. *The intentional community movement.* Port Washington, N.Y.: Kennikat Press, 1975.
31. Veysey, op. cit., p. 458. For descriptions of these three communes, see: Houriet, op. cit., pp. 277–327, 346–371.
32. The works of Bouvard, op. cit.; Melville, op. cit.; Houriet, op. cit.; and Kanter, op. cit., all indicate the extensive diversity that existed among the communes. Veysey, op. cit., focuses on two varieties: anarchist communes and mystical communes.
33. Melville, op. cit., p. 183; Veysey, op. cit., p. 427.
34. For a report of one commune destroyed by outside pressure, see: Houriet, op. cit., pp. xxi–xxxv. See also: Melville, op. cit., p. 184; Veysey, op. cit., p. 457.
35. Callenbach, E. *Ecotopia.* Berkeley: Banyan Tree Books, 1975.
36. Moos, R. *The human context.* New York: Wiley, 1976, Chs. 2 and 3.
37. Osmond, H. Function as the basis of psychiatric ward design. *Mental Hospitals,* 8:23–29, 1957. See also: Moos, R. *The Human Context.* New York: Wiley, 1976, Ch. 4.
38. Whyte, W. *The organization man.* New York: Simon and Schuster, 1956 (quote from pp. 330–331). See also Michelson, W. *Man and his urban environment: A sociological approach.* Reading, Mass.: Addison-Wesley, 1970.
39. Holland, J. *Making vocational choices: A theory of careers.* Englewood Cliffs, N.J.: Prentice-Hall, 1973.
40. Astin, A., and Panos, R. The educational and vocational development of college students. Washington, D.C.: American Council on Education, 1969.
41. Etzioni, A. *Modern organizations.* Englewood Cliffs, N.J.: Prentice-Hall, 1964, p. 1.
42. Scott, W. Theory of organizations. In E. Faris (Ed.), *The handbook of modern sociology.* Chicago: Rand McNally, 1964, p. 488.
43. Durkheim, É. *The division of labour in society* (trans. G. Simpson). Glencoe, Ill.: Free Press of Glencoe, 1933, p. 356.
44. See, for example: Mann, F., and Hoffman, L. *Automation and the worker: A study of social change in power plants.* New York: Henry Holt, 1960.
45. For a review of the impact of organizational structure and change, see: Bromet, E., and Moos, R. The impact of organizational structure and change. In R. Moos (Ed.), *The human context.* New York: Wiley, 1976, Ch. 8.
46. Barker, R. *Ecological psychology.* Stanford, Calif.: Stanford University Press, 1968.

47. Price, R. Behavior setting theory and research. In R. Moos (Ed.), *The human context*. New York: Wiley, 1976, Ch. 7.

48. Barker, R. Ecology and Motivation. In M. R. Jones (Ed.), *Nebraska Symposium on Motivation*. Lincoln: University of Nebraska Press, 1960, p. 33. See also: Barker, R., and Schoggen, P. *Qualities of community life*. San Francisco: Jossey-Bass, 1973.

49. Moos, R. (Ed.). *The human context*. New York: Wiley, 1976, Ch. 10.

PART II: CASE STUDIES OF OPTIMAL COMMUNITIES

CHAPTER 3

The Oneida Community

INTRODUCTION

In the early decades of the 19th century, much of the intellectual curiosity, social experimentation, and moral fervor of the inhabitants of the fledgling American republic focused on questions of religion. New economic and political structures sought stable form through the test of speculative ideas and ventures. The traditional issues and methods of faith and salvation faced continual and passionate critical reexamination. As Robert Parker observed:

> Revivals swept the country like prairie fires. Strange, uncouth evangelists scattered the pollen of myths and harsh doctrines in remote villages, backwoods settlements, forest clearings. They were gifted with rudimentary dramatic power and showmanship, and they tapped an almost bottomless reservoir of credulity.[1]

Nowhere were such phenomena more prevalent than in central and western New York State, a region so exhausted by religious frenzy that it became known as the "burned-over district." [2]

It was at a "protracted meeting" (revival) in Putney, Vermont in 1831 that a young and sceptical attorney, John Humphrey Noyes, underwent a full conversion and determined to devote himself to the service of his God. Four weeks later, he had abandoned his previous career, entered Andover Theological Seminary, and begun the religious quest that resulted in the formation of a new Protestant sect and the creation of an experimental utopia, the Oneida Community.[3]

To understand the background and reality of the Oneida Community, one must understand the life experiences and character of John H. Noyes. It was Noyes who organized the community and who developed the theology that guided its practices, and it was the absence of Noyes that accounted for the community's collapse after 30 relatively successful years.

Noyes was highly intelligent and capable of the intense analysis of theoretical issues. Nevertheless, he tended to accept the intrinsic validity of his feelings. Rather than attempt to subordinate his emotions to rational control, he usually used his intellect to create rationalizations for the legitimacy of his desires. Traditional values held little power over him, and he was willing to contest the prevailing modes of religious, social, and political practice if they conflicted with his own judgment. Although described as shy and soft-spoken (he suffered a speech impediment later in life that prevented him from speaking loudly), he inspired great loyalty from his followers, many of whom believed him to be divinely inspired.[4]

As a recent convert to evangelical Christianity, Noyes found Andover to be imbued with professionalism rather than passionate commitment. After only a year in residence, he transferred to the seminary at Yale, from which he received his license to preach in 1833, at the age of 22. During his life in New Haven, Noyes became involved in a radical "free church"; here he engaged in discussions of a new doctrine known as Perfectionism, which was loosely based on Wesleyan Methodism.

Perfectionist thought challenged the established church's concern with man's sinful nature, suggesting sinless behavior as an attainable goal in one's moral life. To be sure, the achievement of perfection required great study, prayer, and faith. Most important, the achievement of such perfection in no way ensured sinless behavior. Noyes was aware of the rejected antinomianism, the conviction that faith alone, regardless of one's actions, ensured salvation. He argued that man possessed an inner and an outer self and that the purity of the former offered the possibility but not the certainty of the purity of the latter. This point is crucial, for the understanding that perfection in behavior is a challenge, rather than an automatic correlate of spiritual perfection, led Noyes to design a community that would be conducive to sinlessness in action.[5]

During its brief period of existence (1838–1847), the Putney group of Perfectionists only gradually developed into a practicing community. Beginning as a study group based primarily on Noyes's family, it eventually numbered 28 adults and 9 children, who formed a joint economy, accepted theocratic government, and eventually embraced group marriage. It was this last practice that resulted in the destruction of their effort. As word of their relationships spread, outraged moralists in neighboring communities brought charges against the communitarians. Facing the possibility of imprisonment for adultery and/or mob violence, Noyes fled to New York and the Putney community collapsed.

However, Perfectionist communitarianism was soon reestablished. Several months earlier, a small group of New York Perfectionists decided to form a "heavenly association" in the central regions of their own state. At the time of Noyes's flight from Vermont, a few families had just begun to gather at a small 40-acre property near a sawmill at Oneida Creek in Madison County. After brief discussions, it was agreed that the remnants of the Putney group would reassemble at Oneida, and a new community was born.[6]

ECOLOGICAL DIMENSIONS: GEOGRAPHIC AND ARCHITECTURAL FEATURES

Lying at the northern end of a secluded valley, the land of the Oneida community was situated almost precisely in the center of New York State. Oneida Creek flowed through the property; Oneida Lake was only nine miles to the south, and five miles northward ran the Erie Canal. In addition to its uses in agriculture, the water supply served as a source of mechanical power, first for the sawmill that had previously existed on the land and later for the community's numerous industries.[7]

Oneida's lands were fertile and suitable for farming. Despite its rigorous winter, the northern temperate climate permitted the growth of numerous crops, including corn, beans, peas, and a variety of fruits and other vegetables. Also included in the property were woodlands, providing construction material, and meadows on which to pasture livestock. Furthermore, the area, although rural and sparsely populated, maintained easy contact with urban and commercial centers; three miles north of the community was the Oneida depot, a way station on the Utica-to-Syracuse rail line.[8]

Something in this region must have made it particularly attractive to utopian and/or religious movements. As has already been noted, it provided innumerable converts as waves of revivalism passed through its towns and farms. In addition, the area hosted a Shaker colony, three Owenite communities, and seven Fourier phalanxes. It was also in rural New York that Joseph Smith claimed to have received the Mormon scriptures from the prophet Moroni and that the Millerites anticipated the end of the world in 1844. And it was here that the Oneida Perfectionists attempted to design utopia.

Analysis of the decision to settle near Oneida Creek, and of the community's later response to its physical environment, suggests that geographic factors did not play a crucial role in the formation or practices of the community. Moreover, John H. Noyes had no particular theological reason for selecting New York farmland—or for that matter, any agricultural area—for his community. Noyes simply wanted a location that would permit him to carry out his social experiment. All that was required of the geographic environment was that it be suitable for the economic survival of the community. The presence of water power, a resource Oneida exploited to the fullest, enormously enhanced the industrial potential of the community.

The Oneida model was relatively independent of the particular characteristics of its local geographic environment, as judged by the community's willingness to expand. Not only did the central settlement grow from 23 acres at its inception to 654 at the time of its collapse, but other "colonies" were established in a variety of places, including Putney, Vermont (a continuation of the first community); Brooklyn, New York; Newark, New Jersey; and Wallingford, Connecticut. Only the latter ever achieved significant size or longevity. It eventually included about 50 persons on 240 acres and served as a convenient opportunity for variety and a change in environment for Oneida members.[9]

Upon arrival at Oneida Creek, the first community members found few structures to accommodate them. There were only two small farmhouses, a few cabins, a shed, and the sawmill. Work was quickly begun on a communal building that would serve as a single home for the community's membership. The ground floor of this "Mansion House" was divided into three compartments: the front two became the kitchen and dining room, and the one in back served as a cellar. Above these functional areas were a parlor, a schoolroom, a reception room, and a printing office. On the third story, there were 12 living spaces, separated by partitions of cotton cloth hung from wires. An interior square in the center of the 12 "tents" became a common sitting room.[10]

With the addition of a two-story wing in 1849, the Mansion House served the community until 1862, when financial success permitted a more elaborate, brick Mansion House. This structure was a Victorian Gothic creation, the multistory segments of which surrounded an inner quadrangle. By 1870, the interior of the Mansion House included a reception room, a parlor, and a library on the main floor and a second story consisting of a museum and the main meeting hall. The meeting hall held more than the community's total membership and hence was suitable for the evening meetings, which nearly all attended, as well as for concerts, lectures, and other entertainment. The south wing served as a new children's house, where the young and their attendants maintained separate facilities.[11] The community living quarters were in the north wing, where individual sleeping rooms had replaced their tentlike predecessors. Writing of the upper-story sitting room in the brick Mansion House, one member noted, "it is the room of all others in which the true home feeling finds the freest play."[12]

Architectural developments at Oneida largely reflected pragmatic considerations. Perfectionist ideology failed to articulate any formal linkage between architecture and proper behavior. Still, several elements linked the structure of the Mansion Houses to the practices of community life. First, housing the entire membership in a single building assured frequent interaction, as befitted a close community. By providing extensive public space (including a hall large enough to accommodate everyone) and by rendering such areas more amenable than private rooms, the community served the same goal. This arrangement reinforced solidarity and encouraged behavior to take place in the public eye, and hence to be subject to community control.

Still another connection between architecture and social practice concerns the use of individual apartments for adults and the maintenance of separate children's quarters. This arrangement seems more suitable for a system that limited its members to temporary sexual relationships and that required communitarian childraising than for the nuclear family. However, the same physical structure was also compatible with other social forms. After the community had broken up and become a joint stock company, many members continued to reside in the Mansion House, which then operated as a large boardinghouse.[13]

The Oneida Community constructed or purchased a variety of other buildings in addition to the Mansion House. These included the Tontine, a large multipurpose structure originally used for washing, the manufacture of travel bags, and printing; an animal trap factory and a nearby dormitory for those who worked there; a summer recreational cottage on the shore of Oneida Lake; and other shops, stables, and barns. The design and setting of these buildings were generally based on functional considerations. The community also maintained well-ordered productive farmland and landscaped lawns with ornamental trees, the latter revealing that the Perfectionists' pragmatism was tempered by a sense of the aesthetic.[14]

THE HUMAN AGGREGATE

One could hardly imagine a group more ideally suited to form a Perfectionist community led by John Humphrey Noyes than the small collection of families that began the Oneida experiment in 1848. They were committed coreligionists and loyal to Noyes (some were members of his family). Many had participated in the previous communitarian effort at Putney. Their suitability is shown by the longevity of their participation in community life. Of the 19 adults at Putney in 1845, 16 stayed at Oneida until their own deaths or the breakup of the community in 1880. Subsequent members of the community lacked the specific Putney experience; however, their backgrounds did include some commonalities. Most were young or middle-aged adults from nearby regions of New England and New York. Most had been affiliated with some Protestant denomination before turning to Perfectionism, and almost all had substantial knowledge of Perfectionism before arriving at Oneida.[15]

As regards their previous occupations, the Oneida members varied considerably. The community included the practitioners of numerous crafts—farmers, carpenters, machinists, shoemakers, blacksmiths, millers, a painter, a gunsmith—as well as some professionally trained lawyers, teachers, and clergymen. Regardless of the specific trade practiced, the Perfectionists had had at least moderate success in their past endeavors. Oneida's communism was no haven for "the wretched of the earth." As one community source noted, "the main body of those who have joined the Association at Oneida, are sober substantial men and women, of good previous character and position in society."[16]

Oneida's population grew rapidly in its first years, from 87 in 1849 to 205 in 1851. However, from that point on, the membership expanded extremely slowly, reaching just over 300 in 1878. Part of the reason for this limited growth was economic. The community avoided having children to prevent its population from increasing faster than its revenues. Another significant factor involved Oneida's rigorous examination and criticism of potential recruits. Essentially, Oneida desired as new members only those deeply committed to its religious values; all others were screened out and rejected.[17]

Notwithstanding the lengthy and serious examination made of potential members, newcomers often encountered difficulty adjusting to community life. It must be remembered that more was demanded of the Perfectionists than that they acknowledge a theoretical theological position. They also had to live their doctrine in practice and do so willingly without reluctance or bitterness. Thus, Estlake observed:

> There were those who had been readers of the Community publications for
> many years, and who had corresponded with one or more of the members for a
> long while, but who knew so little about themselves, that while their great
> anxiety had been lest their wives should be unable to adapt themselves to the
> new relations, it turned out that they were themselves the first to become jeal-
> ous and dissatisfied with the circumstances they had pleaded so hard and long
> to get into.[18]

As Oneida's businesses prospered, the problem of evaluating would-be
members increased. Not only did the community have to sift out those attracted by the sexual freedom of their life style, they also had to detect
those seeking the economic benefits of membership. The time needed to
process new applicants became a burden on the community's resources.
Therefore, with the advent of stirpiculture and the prospect of producing
additional members through scientific breeding, Oneida closed its doors to
recruits from the outside.

Social stratification, according to caste or class, was virtually unknown
at Oneida. Similarly, subgroup organization appears to have been minimal.
A variety of factors account for the absence of such distinctions. The relatively homogeneous background of the membership precluded differences
based on racial or national characteristics. Economic equality eliminated
another possible source of status differentiation. The fact that the community's members tended to be managers supervising nonmember employees,
as well as the frequent rotation of occupation, reduced identification with
specific productive sectors and increased loyalty to the overall community.

There were, however, three factors that did divide the Oneida membership into loosely organized but distinguishable strata: level of spiritual
achievement, age, and sex. As regards the first factor, members were
evaluated according to their spiritual capabilities. This criterion defined the
community's elite—Noyes and the central members—and it resulted in
special privileges concerning access to decision making and opportunities
for sexual relationships. However, once one moved below the central members, spiritual achievement ceased to classify the community into
categories. Of course, a member's level of spiritual development could
change as he underwent criticism and improvement.

Secondly, the young members, primarily the young males, had experiences, outlooks, and rights in the community that proved divergent from
those of their elders. To begin with, young members, having been born in
the community or brought in as children by their parents, had never made
the deliberate decision to join Oneida as had their elders. Neither did they

undergo the rigorous scrutiny reserved for adult applicants. Thus, they avoided both the processes of self-selection and community examination that guaranteed the intense religious enthusiasm of the older members. The young did receive a thorough education in the community's beliefs and practices, but the openness of their educational experience, particularly the time they spent studying outside the community, exposed them to other intellectual forces as well. As a result, while still maintaining loyalty to the community as an institution, the young often found themselves unable to embrace the basic elements of Perfectionist theology. The epitome of this dilemma occurred when John Humphrey Noyes's son, Theodore, whom he recommended as his successor, admitted to being agnostic.[19]

In addition, the community's leadership was convinced that spiritual advancement should be considered a function of accumulated wisdom and experience, the perquisites of age. The young thus found themselves literally defined as lower on the spiritual scale. As a consequence of that inferiority, they could not face their elders on an equal basis in intracommunity debate. Moreover, they were virtually excluded from entering into sexual relationships with other members of their own age, such liaisons being the prerogative of those more spiritually advanced.[20]

In the context of 19th-century America, the question of stratification based on sex reduces to the issue of social equality for women. Oneida's policies in this area were progressive for their time. Community doctrine clearly stipulated that motherhood was not the "chief end of woman's life." Women shared in productive labor, management, and education. Communization of household duties and child rearing, combined with the at least occasional assignment of males to such sectors, relieved women of much of the drudgery that filled the lives of their contemporaries.

Women's rights to participate in decision making and criticism were formally recognized. Also, women were sexually emancipated in the sense that they were free to initiate or refuse relationships, that their sexual satisfaction was accepted as legitimate, and that they could refrain from childbearing if they chose. The doctrine of ascending fellowship and the requirements of stirpiculture restricted women's sexual preferences; however, these restrictions applied to all in a position of spiritual inferiority and were no less a burden to the community's young males than to its females.

The expansion of women's opportunities did not imply a recognition of their equality with males. Women were seen to possess uniquely feminine qualities, which had their own special value and which were encouraged to develop fully, but which nonetheless remained inferior to masculine attributes. The male theological claim to superiority was reflected in the workings of community decision-making. Although women attended the general meetings, they were less aggressive in their participation than men. Similarly, while men predominated in the annual business meetings, women held separate meetings that focused on child rearing, kitchen work, and other housekeeping duties.[21]

Our discussion of the background of the Oneida Community's members indicated the enormous variety of skills that the membership already had or learned subsequent to joining the community. Oneida enjoyed unusual good fortune in meeting some of its needs for expertise. For example, an architect and a stonemason fortuitously arrived just as work began on the first Mansion House. However, for the most part, the community achieved success in its building projects and businesses through the ingenious and thorough use of all available talent and the dogged acquisition of new skills when they became necessary. Oneida's members became silk makers, trap makers, accountants, and machinists, performing their functions in a thoroughly professional manner. Testimony to the quality of their workmanship was provided by the marketability of their products and their consequent economic prosperity.

ORGANIZATIONAL STRUCTURE AND FUNCTIONING

Government

Although the Oneida Community determined the lives of some 200 persons for 30 years, it never enjoyed the legal status of a government. The implications of this situation were twofold. First, the community's leadership could exert only minimal power over the membership. Indeed, only in cases in which contractual relationships between members had been formally or informally stipulated could the leadership demand compliance, and even then it was dependent upon state authority for the exercise of power. For example, in the single case in which a member was forcibly ejected from the community (literally thrown out of an open window), the injured party brought suit, eventually achieving a settlement in his favor.[22] Thus, the community's leadership had to elicit voluntary compliance with their decisions.

A second implication of the community's lack of political standing was its vulnerability to the dictates of local, state, and national authorities. From their point of view, the Perfectionists sought only to live and let live. However, the governments in whose jurisdiction they resided had demands

to make of the strangers in their midst. The greatest difficulty the community encountered involved cases in which local citizens sought to bring the
Oneida Community's marital relationships into agreement with contemporary moral standards.

Another potential conflict concerned the use of conscription for the
Northern armies during the Civil War. Fortuitously, no serious difficulties
materialized. The community had resigned itself to the fact that several of
its men would be called; however, because of an administrative oversight,
the community was left off the local draft rolls. Further, as the war took on
the complexion of a moral crusade, the Perfectionists identified with the
Union cause and voluntarily contributed financially to local military-sup-
port efforts.[23]

There is little doubt that the community exerted significant power
over its membership. Innumerable aspects of one's personal life—the type
of work one performed, one's standard of living, one's relationship to one's
sexual partner or to one's child, one's personal habits, and the development
of one's personality—were determined through community decision-making procedures. The nature of those proceedings were amorphous and hence
are difficult to systematize. The Perfectionists acknowledged the Bible as a
written constitution, but Noyes argued that the scriptures could not be
taken literally but required interpretation.

Noyes recognized that hierarchical rule was logically derivative from a
belief in the divine inspiration of his teachings. The membership agreed
that they did not serve the arbitrary whim of an individual but rather the
dictates of divine power. They would write, "If this was a despotism, it
was a glorious one. . . . Christ was just as much of a despot as this." [24]

Although Noyes often exerted control over minor aspects of member's
lives, he made no attempt to supervise personally the behavior of every
community member. He remained content to indicate the principles upon
which activity should be based. He delegated authority to a clique of central members, which consisted mainly of a group of older individuals upon
whose spiritual qualities he could rely. Many important community decisions were made in consultation between Noyes and these trusted followers.

A network of committees was designed to oversee individual sectors of
activity. Nearly everyone participated in the management of community
life. Indeed, participation was unavoidable, considering the number of
committees in relation to the population. Nordhoff reported the existence
of 21 standing committees and 48 departments, each with its own administration, among a community of some 200 adults. Most of the committees
assumed responsibility for economic areas, but others regulated education,

culture, and family relationships. Noyes or one of his substitutes appointed committee members, thereby assuring central direction of the committees' functions. Committee membership was often perceived as burdensome and undesirable; young members usually had to be pushed forward into accepting the obligations of holding office.[25]

Another mechanism of political decision-making at Oneida was the evening meeting. These sessions, which took place in the main hall and were attended by the entire membership, included two types of governmental activity. The first of these was "home talks," in which Noyes developed points of Perfectionist theology and discussed their relationship to daily life. These statements were more like sermons than like legislation, but in a theocratic society, the establishment of a moral code also constituted the establishment of a social code.

In addition to "home talks," the evening meeting discussed committee reports. If an issue was unusually significant, it might be placed before the entire membership for resolution. Formally, every member could freely participate in these decisions; however, the degree of substantive democracy was more apparent than real. In most cases, the majority simply accepted the position supported by Noyes and the central members. Should opposition appear, the meetings served the purpose of resolving conflict without threatening community stability. By presenting a proposition before the entire membership, the leaders could determine whether their position might lead to dissension. They also had the opportunity to seek a compromise agreement through discussions predicated on the principles of Perfectionism.[26]

As a final method of government in the Oneida Community, one must consider the Perfectionists' system of mutual criticism (see below, pp. 84–86). Mutual criticism involved an intense examination of a member's character and behavior by Noyes or those selected by Noyes. Criticism of the individual's failings were put forward in an unfalteringly candid and sometimes harsh manner. The political potential of this mechanism is obvious. It provided the community leadership with extensive knowledge of each member's actions, as a criticism session was deemed an appropriate occasion for other members to make public any information they possessed about the person under examination. Criticism also permitted the leadership to apply social pressure toward restructuring the personality of an individual.

While committees and home talks enabled Noyes to establish the economic structure and the moral code of the community, criticism served as a means of legislating individual motives, feelings, and actions. The use of criticism also reflected and maintained the spiritual hierarchy among the membership. Noyes never received criticism from others, although on occasion he did criticize himself. Central members stood relatively immune to criticism from those below them. They might, however, be criticized by Noyes, a procedure that enabled him to dominate his potential rivals. For the others, criticism existed as a profound and powerful experience that markedly shaped their lives.[27]

The Oneida Community acknowledged that criticism constituted a means of government and that it operated to maintain the authority of John Noyes. The members' faith in the religious basis of Noyes's influence caused them to accept their subordination as legitimate. In a remarkably revealing section of their *Second Annual Report,* the Perfectionists explained:

> Anyone who will take the trouble closely to examine the mechanism of our Association will find that the secret of the power which harmonizes it and constitutes its government lies not in any code of laws, nor in the commanding influence of any men, or set of men, but in our *system of Free Criticism.* . . .
>
> Here is the whole mystery of government among us. Our government is democratic, inasmuch as the privilege of criticism is distributed among the whole body, and the power which it gives is accessible to anyone who will take pains to attain good judgment. It is aristocratic, inasmuch as the spirit of truth alone can give the power of genuine criticism. The whole secret of the stupendous despotism which J. H. Noyes is said to exercise . . . lies in the simple fact that he has proved himself to be a good *critic;* for what other means has he of controlling men? He has no military, or political, or pecuniary power; no authority from ecclesiastical antiquity, or from public opinion. *Confidence, secured by manifestation of good spiritual judgment,* is the only possible basis of the despotism he wields. Nothing else could give him power for a moment over such a mass of minds as exists in the Oneida Association.[28]
> [original italics]

An overall evaluation of the various governmental processes at Oneida reveals a thoroughly elitist political system. Noyes and the central members dominated every decision-making procedure. Further, rank had its privileges. The spiritually advanced escaped many of the rigors of criticism. A consideration of the fundamental values of Oneida indicates that democratization would have been impossible. Oneida existed as an exercise in religious commitment, a commitment focused upon the theology of a single individual. If at any time Noyes should be questioned or disputed, then the entire raison d'être of the community, and all of its beliefs and practices, also would have come into question and dispute. Considering his premises, Noyes's defense of despotism was perfectly logical. Democracy is predicated on the assumed absence of revealed divine wisdom. If Noyes's beliefs had been reduced to the level of democratic opinion, then Oneida would be transformed from the Kingdom of Heaven to a community of men. In a sense, this was precisely what eventually occurred.

Economy

The Oneida Perfectionists initially attempted to base their economy on agriculture. They were, in fact, diligent and talented farmers. However, it soon became apparent that such pursuits could at best produce some food for the table and earn small amounts of outside income. They could not meet the financial demands of an expanding community. Consequently, the community turned to commercial and industrial ventures as sources of income.

The Perfectionists attempted an astonishing number of enterprises, including fruit preserving, peddling, sawing lumber, blacksmithing, and the manufacture of furniture, slippers, wheel spokes, mop handles, travel bags, chains, rustic seats, silk, sleigh shoes, and so on. In addition, while finances were low, the community met many of its own requirements for products and services rather than purchasing them from outsiders. Oneida's membership performed their own cooking, cleaning, building construction, teaching, bookkeeping, tailoring, sewing, farming, gardening, and dentistry. They also designed some of the equipment in their manufacturing plants and published a newspaper, *The Oneida Circular*.[29]

However, all of their work, creativity, and capital might not have been sufficient to assure their solvency had they not developed an industrial product that could be marketed on a mass scale, the Newhouse animal trap. Sewell Newhouse, a local backwoodsman of legendary skill and prowess who had joined the community in 1848, had invented and produced on a limited scale a new type of animal trap markedly superior to competitive models. It was not until 1854, however, that the Oneida leadership considered the possibility of large-scale manufacturing of these items. After long and arduous experimentation, community members developed procedures for the mechanized mass production of traps without sacrificing their quality. A factory employing water power was established; it soon began to require larger and larger numbers of workers as orders exceeded normal output. With the success of trap manufacture, the community enjoyed a relatively prosperous future as a business enterprise.[30]

Oneida's many money-making activities, as well as their production for home consumption, were managed by committees, essentially one committee for each function. Originally, a committee assignment lasted a single year. However, as the community's manufacturing enterprises increased in complexity and required long-term planning, their foremen continued in the same position until some "good reason" arose for making a change. Positions of high responsibility were often held by two individuals so that one would always be available in case the other became incapacitated.

Coordination between committees was maintained at weekly or biweekly business meetings at which department heads (or others) discussed the special needs, problems, or proposed projects in their area. Annual meetings of the department heads and of the finance committee determined long-range business policy and monetary appropriations. At irregular intervals, women's business meetings took place to consider diverse housekeeping decisions. Business management was facilitated by the gradual development of a sophisticated accounting system. [31]

Everyone at Oneida worked, including women and children. Noyes himself labored as a blacksmith and a farmer. Although all jobs were considered equally honorable, some organizational device was needed to assure the efficient allocation of labor to each community activity. A committee was charged to carry out this responsibility. Several principles guided the committee in its decisions. There was a firm belief in the value of job rotation in assuring the enthusiasm and satisfaction of workers at their tasks. The extent to which this was practiced varied with the job. A highly skilled position might rarely be affected, while undesirable tasks, such as kitchen work, were frequently rotated. One might expect such a policy to interfere with the effective use of skilled personnel, but the community avowed that rotation improved productivity. [32]

As has been implied above, women performed many jobs that had generally been considered the prerogative of males, and men often took assignments at housekeeping. To borrow Muncy's words, "At Oneida, men learned to sew with the women and women learned to hoe with the men." [33] Women worked at bookkeeping, silk manufacture, printing, dentistry, traveling-bag manufacture, teaching, library work, trap manufacture, packing and shipping, and numerous agricultural tasks. They also served on managerial committees, including those supervising manufacturing establishments. Still, men dominated the decision-making structures of the community, and full equality in job assignment was never remotely approached. [34]

Oneida's economic activities were designed to earn revenue for the community. They were also charged with the mission of contributing to the religious and social life of the settlement. Noyes argued that the true purpose of business was education and development. The Perfectionists employed several strategies to keep the money-making aspect of their businesses in a subordinate role. One approach was to emphasize the spiritual aspects of labor. At Oneida, everyone worked, but because of inspiration rather than regulation. It is true, however, that the community's system of criticism ensured that sloth would not be tolerated. The community also directed attention to the spiritual effects of particular jobs. Work in the horse barn was deemed to be brutalizing, hence those who worked there, especially the young, were rotated frequently. Peddling, which kept men away from the community for extended periods and disrupted their spiritual life, was entirely abandoned.[35]

Another priority that the Perfectionists imposed on their economic actions was a concern for the satisfaction of their fellow workers. Oneida's primary device for handling long, dreary jobs was to have a large group of persons work together until some distasteful job had been completed. Such events, known as *bees,* reduced the time any individual worker would have to spend at the undesired labor and assured him of companionship as he worked. Also, work tended to be broken up by periodic recesses during which community members might hold light conversation, dance, or take turns reading the Bible. An additional mode of making work more satisfying involved bringing men and women together on the same projects. "Loving companionship in labor, and especially the mingling of the sexes, makes labor more attractive," Noyes had stated. In the flirtatious atmosphere of Oneida's complex marriage system, his expectation was undoubtedly realized.[36]

With economic prosperity, there were too few community members to perform all the tasks required by their many enterprises. Thus, they adopted a policy that substantially modified their work lives: the hiring of outside labor. The community's employees initially performed tasks relatively similar to those carried out by the membership. However, as business expanded and more workers were hired, the members came to hold almost exclusively supervisory positions, leaving the more menial tasks for their hired hands. By 19th-century standards, the Perfectionists acted in an exceptionally generous manner toward their workers. Oneida paid top wages, provided schools and housing for many workers, and reduced the number of work hours. Although the community did employ child laborers, it sought to mitigate the difficulty of their working conditions and exercised concern for their moral welfare.[37]

The distribution of economic resources among the membership was basically egalitarian. Members lived in similar rooms in the same building and ate at a common table. Their only private property consisted of clothing and "incidentals" (which generally referred to personal jewelry). Living standards at Oneida varied with the success of the community's enterprises. Economic resources were scarce in the early years of the settlement. In fact, for the first 10 years of its existence, the community constantly courted financial disaster. It survived only because it employed significant amounts of capital contributed by new members. A major shift in the community's fortunes occurred with the development of trap manufacture and the abandonment of several of the economically destitute branches.[38]

While the general trend of the community's finances indicated increasing wealth, an analysis of the settlement's finances on a yearly basis reveals significant variation in income. Oneida's economy, as a business, could not avoid dependence on the state of the national economy. Thus, the community's earnings were decimated in the financial panic of 1857. In 1866, the need for cash proved so severe that all unnecessary capital was liquidated, as Noyes proclaimed "Everything for sale except the soul." In 1873, another national economic slowdown caused delays in payment for goods the community had sold, forcing them into another liquidity crisis. Still, Oneida survived each economic threat and continued to increase its aggregate assets through its remaining years as a community.

In a discussion of the details of Oneida's economy, it is possible to lose sight of the general form of the economic structure that gradually developed. The Perfectionists called themselves Bible communists, yet Oneida acquired free capital (through contributions, loans, and earnings), invested in productive equipment, made use of technological innovation, employed free labor, and sold goods on the open market. Thus, in order to prosper in a capitalist economy, the community functioned as a capitalist enterprise. Of course, many of their other practices—including their distribution of earnings, group marriage, and mutual criticism—were communistic in nature. Yet, when the final ideological crisis of the late 1870s occurred, it was the economic structure that survived and the communist utopia that perished.[39]

Family

In a sense, the Oneida community resembled an enormous family, for the system of complex marriage required that each man be the husband of every woman and each woman the wife of every man. Early in his career, Noyes had become disenchanted with the normal Christian attitude toward monogamy, and group marriage had been attempted at Putney on a small scale. Despite the furious opposition of most clerics, Noyes offered a theo-logical defense of his position. The New Testament states "in the resurrec-tion they neither marry, nor are given in marriage." This, the Oneida leader insisted, demonstrated that monogamy did not exist in the Kingdom of Heaven, and in communities under his influence, the Kingdom of Heaven reigned on earth. Also, group marriage seemed a logical correlate of economic communism; if there was no private property, why should there be private marital relationships? Estlake argued that the willingness to accept group marriage was "the crucial test" of man's love for his fellow-man: "without that love he was unfit for community life." [40]

Complex marriage at Oneida cannot be reduced to a simple preference for "free love." For one, it defined a form of marriage, not merely a pattern of sexual relationships. Men and women in the community were committed to their fellow members at least as intensely as men and women in monoga-mous relationships. They provided mutual economic support for each other and accepted the responsibility of raising the children produced by their union.

Secondly, complex marriage functioned according to a definite mode of organization. Each man or woman was a potential mate for every member of the opposite sex. Those who joined the community as a married couple had to accept the cessation of their exclusive relationship. However, the selection of mates was expected to follow the principles of ascending and descending fellowship. According to this doctrine, each individual could be evaluated spiritually. Sexual activity should ideally take place be-tween someone shown to be spiritually inferior and someone who was spiri-tually superior, that is, as ascending fellowship. Of course, every ascending relationship logically had to be a descending relationship for the superior party; however, this defect was allegedly made tolerable by the fact that the superior person could withstand the impact.

The most spiritually advanced people at Oneida were generally the older founding members, with Noyes himself the most advanced of all. Thus, sexual activity often took place between older men and young women and older women and young men. Young persons rarely had the opportunity of sexual contact with each other. Noyes himself usually ac-cepted the burden of initiating virgins into the marriage system. While such a doctrine clearly involved some frustration for the young, it had sev-eral advantages for the community. The fact that young males usually began relations with women past menopause helped avoid unwanted preg-nancies, and the privileges afforded the older men permitted them an ex-tended sexual life. [41]

One very significant rule of complex marriage was the prohibition against exclusive relationships. Each member of the community was married to every other member of the opposite sex. To attempt a continuing relationship with a single mate would be an act of withdrawal from all others, an act of selfish possessiveness. Thus, individuals were expected to change partners frequently in a pattern of "perpetual courtship." When exclusive relationships did occur, they were dealt with firmly. For example, guilty individuals were subjected to rigorous community criticism, had their jobs changed, or were transferred to another branch of the community.[42]

Several factors attracted Noyes to some notion of population control. He had been deeply affected by the suffering of his wife in giving birth to four stillborn children. Also, women burdened by unwanted pregnancies could hardly achieve the equality and development he advocated for them. More pragmatically, a community that practiced complex marriage might find its economic resources overwhelmed unless it limited its population. To legitimize this predilection, he literally turned conventional Christian morality on its head. The community's first annual report insisted that "Dividing the sexual relation into two branches, the amative and propagative, the amative or love relation is first in importance. . . . God made woman . . . for social, not primarily for propagative purposes." [43] Thus, erotic love was given precedence over reproduction.

Noyes endorsed the practice of male continence as a method of birth control. This required the male to exercise sufficient restraint to prevent ejaculation during intercourse. The combination of male continence, with the recognition at Oneida that sexual activity should be satisfying to both participants, led to the female orgasm's being the "ultimate objective in every sexual encounter." Male continence was required conduct at Oneida; no one was entitled to employ a different form of birth control. Enforcement was accomplished through mutual criticism and by the fact that the community women, desiring to avoid pregnancy, rejected those who failed to master the technique. Oneida's members apparently practiced male continence regularly and successfully. Between 1848 and 1869, there were only 31 accidental conceptions in the community.[44]

In 1869, Oneida modified its commitment to birth control by beginning a program of selective breeding. The term *eugenics* had yet to appear, so the Perfectionists employed their own title for the experiment, *stirpiculture* (from the Latin *stirps*, meaning "stock" or "root"). Noyes provided the initiative for the development. He had read Darwin and Galton and concluded that scientific breeding of humans would be another logical step forward in the community's quest for improvement.

No one was required to participate in stirpiculture; however, 53 of the community's women and some 30 of the young men formally acknowledged to Noyes their willingness to do so. A special committee, headed by Noyes, organized and supervised the stirpiculture program. Generally, couples first decided to mate and then presented themselves before the committee; but in about one fourth of the cases, the committee took the initiative in recommending a mating. The extent to which the older members dominated the procedure can be discerned from the fact that the mean age of male participants was 41 years compared to a mean age for women of 30. Noyes himself fathered nine live children (one stillborn), his son fathered three, and the rest of the participants one or two.

During the stirpiculture period (1869–1879), 58 children were born to 44 women (Carden claims, however, that 13 of these were unplanned births). The sample was much too small and the experiment too short-lived to permit systematic analysis of the Oneida attempt at scientific breeding. Sporadic reports indicate that the children suffered no unusual handicaps and enjoyed unusual longevity. But the only result proven by the experiment was that the extended practice of male continence did not reduce subsequent fertility.[45]

There was a significant number of children at Oneida prior to the advent of stirpiculture. A few had been planned; the rest had been "accidental" or had joined when their parents became members. These youngsters were raised collectively rather than by their mothers (it was usually impossible to determine who was the father in complex marriage). The rationale for this system consisted of a desire to avoid fragmenting the community into distinct mother–child units. Equally important was the wish to avoid having intense affection for children interfere with the degree and openness of relationships among adults. Economic reasons supplemented social ones; a central child-rearing facility would require fewer resources—particularly labor—than a system of family units.

In the Oneida framework, children were weaned by their mothers and then transferred to the children's house, where their lives were focused for the next 12 years. In this area, which was architecturally distinct from the rest of the community, they were supervised by those deemed most competent in child care. While the children spent their days in their own section, they often spent nights in the rooms of adults, although they never spent a lengthy period with any single adult.

Once a child entered the children's house, his mother could still maintain contact with him. She might visit him there, bring him to her room, or take an assignment as a child-care worker. The details of community norms regulating the extent and nature of this continuing relationship varied over the years, but their general impact remained consistent. Much as the community sought to prevent special and exclusive love from occurring between adults, so it attempted to restrain affection between mother and child. If excessive relationships began to develop, they were dealt with by criticism or by a forced limit on contacts. While there was occasional distress on the part of parents and children over their separation, there is no evidence of any large-scale difficulty with, or opposition to, the child-rearing system.[46]

Education

One can hardly underestimate both the practical and ideological significance of education for the Oneida Community. According to Perfectionist beliefs, all aspects of life should be educational in nature, contributing to human development. The only "legitimate object" of labor was to secure leisure for social, intellectual, and artistic development. Moreover, the community's educational system had the responsibility of ensuring that future generations had both the technical expertise to maintain Oneida's industries and the religious and moral commitment to continue the community's spiritual and social practices.

Despite its importance, education at Oneida lacked theoretical coherence and was organizationally diffuse. Part of the problem had economic roots. Although children and adolescents worked as a normal part of their education, situations did occur in which extraordinary demands for labor caused them to delay or reschedule their schooling. Also, education at Oneida was necessarily limited to fields in which some member of the small community had expertise. Other skills had to be learned in places outside of community control.[47]

Oneida's educational processes involved several levels, geared for students of different ages and needs. The basic education of children had begun with the arrival at Oneida of the first members and initially took the form of readings from the Bible. Various forms of pedagogical organization were later attempted, involving numerous changes in school location, curriculum, age group, teachers, and hours of study. The community generally preferred to keep its youngest children in a nursery, where they received little or no formal teaching. From 7 to 12, the children underwent primary education, combined with play and some participation in community chores. At this age, children also received instruction in Perfectionist beliefs and in the norms of community life. Children engaged in mutual criticism among themselves, and they had work bees, similar to those of their elders.

Although adolescents and young men had greatly expanded work responsibilities, the community endeavored to provide them with further education. When possible, young men aged 14–26 would meet on a daily basis for systematic schooling. Courses included arithmetic, algebra, and Latin, as well as more esoteric subjects such as zoology, phrenology, and "man's future victory over death." Teachers were often older men who had attended college. The community maintained an extensive library (4000 volumes in 1880), which its youth were encouraged to use. No attempt was made to limit the library to books in agreement with Perfectionist thought, and members were free to follow their own interests.

Certain forms of higher education and technical training were obtained from outside sources. For example, when the community became interested in silk manufacture, it sent a few of its youth to factories and a dye house to learn the trade. Many of the more intelligent young men were offered the opportunity of university education. More than a dozen entered Yale, where they received professional training in medicine, law, architecture, and mechanical engineering. Thus, Oneida's young were taught the ways of their elders but were also permitted to see beyond them.

Adult education was strongly encouraged by the leadership, and the community's members responded with enthusiasm. Nearly everyone participated in one course or another. While some of the fields of study related to the community's business concerns, the vast majority constituted education and self-improvement for their own sake. No one ever developed a consistent or coherent program of adult study, but participation in these courses certainly contributed to the general intellectual alertness and cultural standards of the community.[48]

A BEHAVIOR SETTING: THE DINING HALL

As the community expanded its financial base, produced new buildings, and grew in population, the physical structure of its dining facilities underwent modification. In 1849, the dining hall consisted of a single long table that extended through the room. By 1855, more tables were added, but they still could not accommodate even half of the community's 170 members. In 1868, the dining hall could serve 110 persons: 8 at each of eight oval tables and 46 at two central long tables. The Perfectionists designed their own round tables with revolving disks at the center that could be turned to bring each dish before the diners. Two years later, the dining hall was moved from the old Mansion House into the Tontine.

With the addition of an adjoining room four years after that, the community newspaper announced that everyone could be fed at a single sitting: "After twenty-five years we have for the first time hit on a plan which makes practical the long cherished idea of a 'Family Dining-Room.' " [49]

Dining practices involved some regulations but much informality. Meals were served by waiters. This function was originally deemed so attractive that it was performed by volunteers; however, the positions were later filled by young women appointed by committee to serve for limited periods. Each member entering the dining hall was required to accept the next available seat, regardless of his preferences for mealtime companions. Children dined in the same room as adults but at a separate table, unless invited to join the older members at one of their tables. Manners in the dining hall demonstrated neither vulgarity nor rigid decorum. Although youths were occasionally criticized for failing to maintain "quiet decorum," their elders also stipulated, "A stiff, formal silence at the table is not what is wanted, but rather a free flow of conversation promoting a genial sociable spirit—pleasant conversational buzz is good music while eating." [50]

The times and manner in which food was served, and the contents of the community menu, ranged from a normal level of flexibility to deliberate and more radical variation. Even while at Putney, Noyes had declared that the practice of eating three hot meals a day was "a requirement of custom and not of nature" and hence could be dispensed with. Exactly what constituted a proper diet and mode of eating became a much-discussed issue at Oneida. The community tried to avoid habit by experimenting with different arrangements. For example, the community attempted replacing waiters with a buffet, giving up hot meals twice a day, observing a semifast in which meager fare was passed from member to member, and other variations.

SOCIAL CLIMATE

Personal Ideals and Value System

Noyes and his Perfectionists created Oneida to further the development of an ideal human type. One cannot understate the seriousness of that quest. The ideal did not stand as a distant vision, useful for sermons but irrelevant to daily practice. Rather, active efforts at the realization of "perfection" permeated every aspect of community life. Should the commitment to such a pursuit weaken or vanish, then the form of Oneida's organization might still be maintained, but it would be rendered devoid of higher meaning.

Most important in the Oneida ideal was pure faith in God and obedience to His word, that is, complete salvation from sin. Not all members of the community could claim to be without sin. However, the Perfectionists argued, "A sinless life is the *standard* of the community, which all believe to be practicable, and to which all are taught to aspire." [51] Sinlessness constituted an "inner" state, achieved through religious experience or spiritual contact with God. Although not achieved through "outer" action—action in the world—sinlessness nonetheless affected "outer" behavior. Further, it was the obligation of the Perfectionist to strive constantly to bring his flawed "outer" life to a level commensurate with inner being.

The effort to better oneself consistently was the second element in the Perfectionist ideal. Members were expected to improve themselves in every possible way. Development should take place in their work, in their moral behavior, and in their intellectual activity. Although the community approved of balance in improvement—a member should not excel in business at the expense of moral progress—it did not conceive of improvement as having an end point. Regardless of the level of accomplishment, Perfectionism defined the act of improving oneself as praiseworthy. In addition, self-development was to be a joyous process, not a burdensome striving for endless goals. The ideal was very much taken to heart at Oneida; one might encounter members in their 80s happily beginning the study of algebra or Greek.

Another major aspect of Oneida's ideal was the commitment to community service. Members were to relate to their fellows in a spirit of love, thinking less of themselves and more of the needs of the group. As has already been noted, possessiveness of persons and property was strongly prohibited. In fact, the Perfectionists employed special terminology to describe individual desires to be avoided in excess: *amativeness* (love of the opposite sex), *alimentiveness* (love of food), *philoprogenitiveness* (love of children), and *diotrephiasis* (love of preeminence). The Oneida members exercised self-control and sought to replace egoism with "the community spirit."

In the practical effort to realize the ideal model, the latter two values—improvement and community service—sometimes came into conflict. This conflict often concerned the relationship between the economic requirements of the community's business and the interest of the young in developing through education. Business, or community service, generally received the higher priority. Thus, one winter the young men's schooling was canceled to provide additional labor for community industry. Similarly, although young men had the opportunity to pursue professional training, they could do so only in fields relevant to community needs.[52]

Personal Relationships

Cohesion. The Perfectionists tried to maintain an intense degree of cohesion among their members. The very structure of the community encouraged cohesion. Members lived in a common home, shared a common table, adopted a common faith, obeyed a common leader, and even shared common mates in complex marriage. In addition to this homogeneity of experience, community activities promoted interaction and feelings of fellowship. Daily evening meetings brought the entire membership together to participate in discussion and decision making. Estlake observed the strength of solidarity manifested at these sessions:

> The day's work done, with sighs of relief all sought renewing of life by drawing together in the evening meeting where, with all hearts beating in unison, there was such an outpouring of power for all, that can only be imagined by those who went in, tired physically and spiritually, and came out refreshed and rested.[53]

Community values also emphasized cohesion. Selfishness and possessiveness were denigrated, while service to the group resulted in moral approbation. Moreover, affection and loyalty were directed to the entire membership rather than to any part thereof. Exclusive or selfish love was not tolerated; cohesion required a commitment of each member to every other member. Even mutual criticism exerted a cohesive influence. Not only did members develop that bond that arises from a shared ordeal, but they received, through criticism, an opportunity to correct wayward tendencies, permitting them to regain full family approval.[54]

However, cohesion was seriously, indeed fatally, shattered in one area. The conflict between generations—exacerbated by differences in status, privilege, and ideology—combined with other difficulties and eventually brought about the community's collapse. The disputes that arose between the young men and the older men of the Oneida Community involved much more than the fact that a son rarely holds a view of the world identical to that of his father. At Oneida, age had significant political and social implications. Because it generally required extended years to achieve spiritual superiority, the community's older males enjoyed the highest status, the greatest roles in decision making, and the greatest access to the youngest and most attractive females. As for the young, they could only await their gradual rise in the hierarchy, a situation that, according to Fellman, they experienced with "smoldering resentment."

This problem was compounded by the inordinate role of religion in legitimating this inequality. It was Perfectionism as interpreted by Noyes, rather than any pragmatic argument or secular rationale, that accounted for the privileges of the elders. Yet, the young males constituted that segment of the community membership to which religious belief and the literal interpretation of the Bible had become least meaningful. This was particularly true of those who had received training in law or medicine outside the community. Without divine sanction, the rule of the central members became less and less tolerable.[55]

Support. As a community, Oneida attempted to meet the material as well as the spiritual needs of its members. Everyone received food, clothing, shelter, and medical care as a matter of right, regardless of his or her particular contribution to the collective economy. However, two factors limited the quality of the life style thus provided.

One factor was self-imposed. The Perfectionists distributed goods and services to the membership according to a theological conception of what was best for the individual, rather than on the basis of personal desires. In terms of consumption standards, this meant an absence of luxury regardless of the success of the community's industries. In the area of health care, the limit was more serious. Oneida's leadership considered many illnesses to reflect spiritual failings and hence assumed that patients could best be cured through religious rather than medicinal means. Robertson observed:

> 'The Community people were normally kind and sympathetic characters, but both their circumstances and their religion recommended fairly spartan attitudes towards the weaknesses of the flesh. . . . An epidemic of influenza among the children was met firmly with criticism in which the children themselves were expected to join. . . . The dentist—a member—admitted that it was good to pull teeth without pain but he though that "a little spunk" would be better. . . . A member who complained of sleeplessness was advised to rise above his dependence on sleep into fellowship with the unsleeping energy of God.'[56]

Still, the health of the membership was at least as good as that of their contemporaries. When the community's own young men completed training as physicians, the willingness to use "external remedies" increased.

A second limit on the ability of the community to provide support for its members was the availability of financial resources. As has already been noted, the Perfectionists experienced many lean years prior to the commencement of trap manufacture. In one of the worst, Oneida's total income amounted to less than $2000, a situation that required a drastic reduction in the expenditure for food and lodging. Even after the community's industries began to expand, Oneida's solvency remained vulnerable to instability in the national economy. Several financial panics drastically reduced community income, causing temporary reductions in the standard of living.

Spontaneity. Although Oneida was a deeply religious community, the life style of its membership was not solemn, rigid, or puritanical. On the contrary, they endorsed "inspiration" and "fits of unitary enthusiasm" as opposed to "legalism" or formal regulations. Spontaneity received firm theological approval. Moreover, a spontaneous and vital existence could and should be enjoyed. Sport and amusement were not the private domain of the irreligious. Rather, they should be available to those who could make best use of them, the seekers of Christ. Hence, the community resolved to give "the playful action of life," as distinguished from "more weighty pursuits," a greater role in community activity.[57]

The Perfectionists sought to bring their practice in line with these values. For example, they frequently changed their avocations, the order of their evening meetings and amusements, and even their meal hours. In addition, they abandoned the use of a bell to announce evening meetings, allowing members to enter and leave as they pleased, and they sought to assure a highly flexible agenda for such sessions. Some members felt that even more extreme measures were needed to assure the triumph of spontaneity. In 1864, the *Circular* reported:

> Our evening meeting last Wednesday, instead of beginning with the usual singing, was introduced by a few remarks from Mr. B., in which he deprecated routine as stagnation and death. Immediately upon Mr. B's sitting down, there entered upon the stage a trio with *fife and drums* which filled the room with the rhythmical vibrations of martial music. The next evening at the same time, C. gave us on the tenor drum a representation of a battle, with its confused noises of musketry, roar of cannon, and battery broadsides. Friday evening Mr. A. opened with a declamation, and Saturday evening Mr. C. gave us an oratorical impromptu. Sunday afternoon, in the place of the usual exercises, we had an impromptu concert, music by the orchestra, songs etc. We are out upon routine and bores, and are set upon learning to shift our sails for the breeze of inspiration.[58]

Still, one must understand the context in which the Perfectionist devotion to spontaneity took place. Oneida was a religious and moral community. Its members valued spontaneity only to the extent that it proved compatible with their faith and values. Morality need not be dull or joyless, but one had no choice but to be moral, regardless of one's impulses. Everyone had the obligation to abide by the community's ethical code, and the system of mutual criticism stood ready to correct any deviation from the norm. In addition, Oneida, in values and in practice, affirmed communalism, the importance of group welfare over individual preference.

Both of these influences—religious values and communalism— resulted in substantial restrictions on a member's freedom of action. While some flexibility existed in job selection, private choice in consumption was virtually nonexistent. Interpersonal relationships were strictly regulated. At a community gathering, members might spontaneously begin dancing, but one had best not spontaneously decide to have too many dances with the same partner. Sexual activity was a legitimate object of community control. Communal norms determined to some extent with whom one had relationships (ascending fellowship) and the method of birth control (male continence). Furthermore, numerous other personal characteristics or aspects of behavior might be deemed in need of improvement and subject to criticism.[59]

It must be emphasized that whatever regimentation existed at Oneida was voluntarily accepted by the membership. The community could not coerce anyone into doing anything, with the possible exception of leaving the settlement. Every adult member was free to "secede" if he so chose. In actuality, it was the members' religious faith that predisposed them to tolerate the community control over their lives. Even here, they had had a choice. The adult members had generally not been raised as Perfectionists. Rather, they had selected that faith and then determined to enter a community organized according to its premises.

System Maintenance and System Change

Having witnessed the destruction of one Perfectionist community (Putney) by hostile outsiders, Noyes recognized that the survival of Oneida depended on its ability to defend itself against intolerant neighbors. Several tactics were employed to accomplish this. First, the community limited the amount of information made public concerning its practices. It soon became apparent that rumor was proving more damaging to the Oneida image than the truth could ever be. Hence, the Perfectionists decided to open their small society to visitors.

In addition to welcoming guests, the Perfectionists attempted to demonstrate that they were stable and responsible citizens who posed no threat to others. They were scrupulous in ensuring that their business and personal dealings with nonmembers met the highest standards of ethics and fairness. They also contributed to local charities. These efforts produced an immediate, favorable response. Subsequently, as Parker observed, "Outside criticism of the Community's conduct was most effectively silenced by its expanding business." [60] As a market for goods and a source of capital and, most important, as a major employer, Oneida came to be a vital part of the local economy. Nearby residents were loath to attack a group that contributed so heavily to the area's prosperity.[61]

Clarity. Oneida possessed no formal statute book or community code of regulations. Nevertheless, for the most part, members knew the society's rules and expectations concerning personal behavior. Several factors account for this ability to disseminate information on community norms without a bureaucratic apparatus.

To begin with, Oneida's regulations were largely based on Perfectionist theology, and entrants into the community usually possessed considerable background in that doctrine. Correspondence with and visits to the community provided them with a more detailed understanding. Thus, they were clearly aware of the general principles behind community rules. Second, Noyes presented "home talks" at evening meetings to introduce new points of doctrine or to elaborate on the application of theology to action. Most members heard these reports regularly.[62]

Finally, mutual criticism served as a means of informing members as to the rules by exposing their imperfections. Criticism was especially useful in directing the attention of members to those community norms that they were either unaware of or, more usually, were having difficulty abiding by. The community could thus easily communicate to a member both how they desired he should act and how his actual behavior compared with the expectation.

Social Control. Oneida had no police, courtrooms, or jails. On the contrary, the community maintained social control over its members almost exclusively through its system of mutual criticism (the Perfectionists also cited religious influence and education as means of assuring proper discipline). Noyes had employed criticism at his first community in Putney, Vermont. The entire membership served as "critics" of the individual under examination. But at Oneida, a much larger colony, it was felt that many members did not know others well enough to be their critics. Thus, criticism was usually administered by committees whose members were selected by Noyes. On special occasions, however, the entire Oneida community participated in a criticism session. Individuals often requested criticism as a means of acknowledging that they were having difficulty living up to community ideals but were sincerely struggling to do so.[63]

A criticism session was a simple and straightforward affair. While the

subject of the meeting sat in silence, those doing the critizing would enu-
merate, in a totally candid manner, all the flaws they perceived in his character or behavior. Their knowledge of these faults derived either from personal interaction with the subject or from an investigation of the subject's
performance. According to Nordhoff, by 1874, the Perfectionists, presumably as a result of much experience, were quite adept at offering criticism.
He noted that they spoke with "practiced tongues": "There was no vague-
ness, no uncertainty. Every point was made; every sentence was a hit." [64]

An examination of records of criticism sessions reveals that almost all
forms of human error, no matter how trivial, were considered suitable for
observation and correction. Members might be chided for having too much
self-esteem, or too little self-respect, for being careless or nervous, for talk-
ing too much, for lacking purpose, for being too intellectual or too legalis-
tic, for being apologetic, or inefficient, or reckless. In one case, the Perfectionists found a young woman to be:

> remarkably outspoken and impulsive, and so her faults are decided and well
> known. . . . The elderly people criticize her for disrespect and inattention.
> She will fly through a room, on some impulsive errand of generosity perhaps,
> leave both doors open, and half knock down anybody in her way. . . . She has
> a touch of vanity,—likes to look in the glass, and plumes herself on her power
> of charming. She indulges in unfounded antipathies, and whims of taste,
> while she is likely to be carried out of bounds by her attractions. . . . We
> must cure her of her coarseness, and teach her to be gay without being rude,
> and respectful without being demure." [65]

There is no evidence to indicate that more serious crimes, such as theft or
assault, occurred at Oneida, so most criticism focuses on these more subtle
aspects of character.

To most of the Perfectionists, undergoing criticism was an excrutiat-
ing experience, literally enough to make strong men sweat. However, once
the ordeal had ended, the subjects reported great exhilaration and happiness, a feeling of being cleansed. Thus, the community observed:

> J., after criticism so mortifying and severe that to the outward eye it seemed
> impossible to bear, showed a countenance so unmistakably the reflex of a
> happy heart that we wondered at her. "Why," said she, "I am happy; after my
> criticism I felt relieved just as I think Christian did when the burden rolled off
> his back." [66]

Similarly, one man who failed to join after a probationary period reported,
"Today I feel that I would gladly give many years of my life if I could have
just one more criticism from John H. Noyes." [67]

Of course, the purpose of criticism was not simply to inform members

of their faults or to provide a cathartic experience but to cause them to initiate change for the better. After criticism, members usually vowed to
improve; subsequent sessions served as a check on the intensity of that commitment. Should a member persistently fail to alter his or her behavior
despite repeated criticism, he or she might be asked to leave the community. Once, and only once, a member who refused to withdraw as requested
had to be physically thrown out of the Mansion House. Such an act stands
as the most severe penalty Oneida ever imposed.[68]

Innovation. Always a rebel and inventor, Noyes built Oneida as a
genuinely experimental community, in which new ideas and techniques
were welcomed and often acted upon. His interpretation of Perfectionist
theology clearly sanctioned progressive changes. To Noyes, both Christianity and human social existence demanded constant improvement, which
in turn required a willingness to abandon tradition in favor of novelty.
There were numerous innovations in a wide variety of areas during the
community's 30-year history. As noted above, Oneida abandoned agriculture in favor of commerce and industry and then tried out dozens of economic projects before focusing on trap manufacture and a few others. The
Perfectionists also applied themselves to the development of technological
improvements to render their industries more profitable.

Aspects of social life were likewise open to modification. In addition
to such major social experiments as stirpiculture and birth control through
male continence, the Perfectionists varied meal hours in an effort to improve digestion and explored faith healing, only to decide that scientific
medicine was more effective.[69]

However, Oneida would not tolerate innovation on the question of adherence to Christianity. Perfectionist theology could be flexible in employing modern science as a tool. Noyes himself was well read in many areas of
current scientific interest, and he had no hesitation in applying scientific
methods to resolve technical problems. But such actions were still based on
the ultimate validity of religious truth. If one suggested that science could
serve as a substitute for Christianity, one had moved beyond the limits of
permissible change at Oneida.[70]

This fundamental belief, along with several other factors, accounted
for the dispute and instability that finally resulted in the breakup of the
community. Primary among these factors was the community's deep reliance on one man, John Humphrey Noyes. Members directed their respect,
loyalty, and faith toward Noyes, as an individual, rather than toward any
abstract role or position of community leader. The unique relationship they
had developed with him could not easily be transferred to others. Through-

out the 1870s, the aging Noyes found it increasingly physically burdensome to maintain his status as community director, and he attempted to
delegate his powers to central members. These efforts resulted in confusion
and a general loss of confidence, as the new leaders differed among themselves and lacked an organizational means of reaching decisions that had
once simply emanated from the unity of one man's mind. In 1877, Noyes
stepped down and designated his son, Theodore, as his successor. Theodore
proved unsuited to direct what was still basically a religious community,
and by 1878, Noyes resumed practical direction of community affairs. But
at this point, not even he could prevent the disintegration that was developing.[71]

A second significant factor in the collapse of the community was a
marked decline in the intensity of the religious convictions of the membership. Robertson observed:

> the chief general cause of the fatal change was a gradual loss of the religious
> faith which was their original reason for being, the cement which had held
> them together through so many vicissitudes. When they lost this, they began
> to lose everything—their security, their agreement, their selflessness, their
> happiness.[72]

While some lessening of belief occurred among the older members, the
major deterioration in religious faith took place among the young adults.
Oneida's educational system proved insufficient to cope with the secular
influences that the community's young men encountered at the universities
in which they pursued advanced technical training. Of particular consequence was the fact that Noyes's son, Theodore, succumbed to agnosticism.

A final element in the community's breakup resulted from a shift in
Oneida's normal recruitment procedure. The community normally accepted
applicants only after long examination and deliberation concerning their
commitment to community norms and practices. However, in 1874, the
community accepted 12 new members at once, former members of an
abandoned "free love" colony. One of the 12, James W. Towner, a former
minister, a civil war veteran, and a lawyer and judge, was an imposing
individual with leadership qualities and ambition to match. When he entered into Oneida with 11 loyal supporters, the basis was laid for the formation of a dissident group capable of opposing the authority of John
Noyes.

With the stage thus set, the only question remaining concerned the
details of the drama to unfold. The inflammatory issue concerned the fact
that Noyes himself, or one of his delegates, had always assumed the role of
introducing Oneida's virgins into sexual experience. Towner and another

member objected, other members chose sides, and soon the Townerites and the Noyesites were in open conflict for control of the community. As the dispute became increasingly bitter, Noyes's supporters warned him of his legal vulnerability. Many of the Oneida women had begun sexual activity with Noyes before reaching the legal age of consent. It was possible that the Townerites might bring criminal charges against the aging patriarch. Apparently, Noyes found the argument persuasive, for in the night of June 19–20, 1879, he fled Oneida for the sanctuary of the Canadian border.[73]

Following Noyes's flight, the breakup of Oneida as a utopian community proceeded rapidly. In light of the pressure from outside clergy, and also as a result of continued dissension over the allocation of sexual rights and privileges, the Perfectionists abandoned complex marriage. Such an act seemed a signal to all that the communal basis of the society had ended. Muncy noted, "When the private families shut themselves up in their separate domiciles and out from the community at large, communism took a backward step at Oneida and never regained its footing. When husbands refused to share their wives, they ceased sharing all things." [74] Soon, members were demanding a return to private property. By September, 1880, the adult membership had signed an "Agreement to Divide and Reorganize," which transformed Oneida into a joint stock corporation that continues to this day.

REFERENCES AND NOTES

1. Parker, R. *A Yankee saint.* New York: Putnam, 1935, p. 15. See also pp. 15–117.
2. Robertson, C. N. *Oneida Community: An autobiography.* Syracuse, N.Y.: Syracuse University Press, 1970 (hereafter *Autobiography*), p. 3; Carden, M. L. *Oneida: Utopian community to modern corporation.* Baltimore: Johns Hopkins Press, 1969, p. 23.
3. Robertson, op. cit., p. 34; Parker, op. cit., pp. 17–18.
4. Estlake, A. *The Oneida Community.* London: George Redway, 1900, p. 5; Fellman, M. *The unbounded frame.* Westport, Conn.: Greenwood Press, 1973, pp. 43–44.
5. Carden, op. cit., pp. 11–17.
6. Ibid., pp. 17–23; Robertson, op. cit., pp. 11–12; Parker, op. cit., pp. 89–104, 119–142, 160–165.
7. Parker, op. cit., pp. 164–166; Robertson, op. cit., p. 30.
8. Robertson, op. cit., p. 30; Nordhoff, C. *The communistic societies of the United States,* New York: Hillary House, 1960, p. 277.

9. Robertson, op. cit., pp. 51–52; Parker, op. cit., p. 214; Nordhoff, op. cit., p. 262.
10. Robertson, op. cit., pp. 13, 32–33; Parker, op. cit., 171–176.
11. Carden, op. cit., p. 43; Robertson, op. cit., pp. 28, 34–35, 39–41.
12. Robertson, op. cit., pp. 44–45, 85; Carden, op. cit., p. 43; Nordhoff, op. cit., p. 278.
13. Muncy, R. L. *Sex and marriage in utopian communities.* Bloomington: Indiana University Press, 1973, pp. 177–178; Carden, op. cit., pp. 117–118.
14. Robertson, op. cit., pp. 36–37; Nordhoff, op. cit., p. 278.
15. Carden, op. cit., pp. 20, 25; Robertson, op. cit., pp. 23, 98; Parker, op. cit., pp. 167–168; Nordhoff, op. cit., pp. 263–264; Estlake, op. cit., p. 10.
16. Carden, op. cit., p. 26; Nordhoff, op. cit., p. 263; Robertson, op. cit., p. 98.
17. Robertson, op. cit., pp. 23, 90–91; Muncy, op. cit., pp. 167–168; Parker, op. cit., p. 176.
18. Estlake, op. cit., pp. 33–34.
19. Robertson, op. cit., pp. 89, 98; Estlake, op. cit., p. 10; Fellman, op. cit., p. 58; Carden, op. cit., pp. 94–96.
20. Parker, op. cit., pp. 263–264.
21. Robertson, op. cit., pp. 74, 310, 345, 353; Carden, op. cit., p. 49; Nordhoff, op. cit., p. 288.
22. Parker, op. cit., pp. 221–224.
23. Robertson, op. cit., pp. 71–73; Parker, op. cit., pp. 210–211.
24. Carden, op. cit., p. 85.
25. Robertson, op. cit., pp. 118, 214–215; Nordhoff, op. cit., p. 279.
26. Parker, op. cit., p. 231; Carden, op. cit., pp. 46–49, 85–86.
27. Carden, op. cit., pp. 71–77.
28. Robertson, op. cit., p. 134.
29. Nordhoff, op. cit., pp. 261–262; Parker, op. cit., pp. 212; Robertson, op. cit., pp. 20–21, 68–69, 212–213, 218; Carden, op. cit., pp. 39, 41–42.
30. Parker, op. cit., pp. 205–210; Carden, op. cit., pp. 41–42; Robertson, op. cit., p. 36.
31. Kanter, R. *Commitment and community.* Cambridge, Mass.: Harvard University Press, 1972, p. 11; Robertson, op. cit., pp. 14–15, 74, 221, 224–225, 235, 252, 259–260; Nordhoff, op. cit., pp. 279, 280, 286.
32. Robertson, op. cit., pp. 28, 47, 86; Estlake, op. cit., pp. 68–69; Nordhoff, op. cit., pp. 261, 280–281; Kanter, op. cit., p. 11.
33. Muncy, op. cit., p. 172.
34. Robertson, op. cit., pp. 63, 299, 301–302, 304, 308–309; Kanter, op. cit., p. 10.
35. Robertson, op. cit., pp. 47, 55, 125–126, 140, 226–227, 281.
36. Ibid., pp. 47–48, 61–63, 65; Parker, op. cit., pp. 208–209; Carden, op. cit., p. 66; Kanter, op. cit., p. 10; Muncy, op. cit., pp. 171–172.

37. Nordhoff, op. cit., pp. 263–281; Robertson, op. cit., pp. 22, 24, 73, 89–90, 226, 231, 244–245; Parker, op. cit., pp. 212–213; Carden, op. cit., pp. 42, 83.

38. Carden, op. cit., pp. 37–39, 41–42; Parker, op. cit., pp. 201–203; Nordhoff, op. cit., pp. 261–262; Robertson, op. cit., 49–50, 85–86, 229–232, 241, 254, 256, 261–262.

39. Robertson, op. cit., pp. 104, 213–214, 232, 236, 262–263.

40. Carden, op. cit., p. 16; Estlake, op. cit., p. 35; Muncy, op. cit., pp. 169–170; Robertson, op. cit., pp. 279–280.

41. Carden, op. cit., pp. 52–53; Parker, op. cit., pp. 182, 186, 263; Fellman, op. cit., p. 53; Muncy, op. cit., pp. 176–177; Robertson, op. cit., pp. 281–282; Estlake, op. cit., p. 87.

42. Estlake, op. cit., pp. 87–88; Robertson, op. cit., pp. 21–22; Carden, op. cit., pp. 31, 53–54, 58–59; Muncy, op. cit., pp. 173–176.

43. Robertson, op. cit., p. 269; Muncy, op. cit., p. 184.

44. Muncy, op. cit., pp. 182–183. See also: pp. 180–183; Carden, op. cit., pp. 49–51; Parker, op. cit., pp. 179–181.

45. Parker, op. cit., pp. 259–261; Muncy, op. cit., pp. 189–192; Robertson, op. cit., pp. 22, 347.

46. Nordhoff, op. cit., pp. 281–282; Robertson, op. cit., pp. 14, 75–76, 77, 317–318, 321, 329–330; Carden, op. cit., p. 64; Parker, op. cit., p. 260; Muncy, op. cit., p. 175.

47. Robertson, op. cit., pp. 176–178, 315–316; Carden, op. cit., p. 64.

48. Carden, op. cit., pp. 67–68, 93–94; Nordhoff, op. cit., pp. 284–286; Robertson, op. cit., pp. 123–124, 176–182, 186–187.

49. Robertson, op. cit., pp. 31, 41, 45, 84, 87, 142–143; Nordhoff, op. cit., p. 282.

50. Robertson, op. cit., pp. 31, 84, 140, 156–157; Nordhoff, op. cit., p. 281; Carden, op. cit., p. 64.

51. Nordhoff, op. cit., p. 269.

52. Robertson, op. cit., pp. 51, 58, 100–103, 117, 177; Carden, op. cit., pp. 24–25, 94; Parker, op. cit., p. 112.

53. Estlake, op. cit., p. 60. See also: Carden, op. cit., pp. 46–49; Robertson, op. cit., p. 46.

54. Carden, op. cit., p. 25; Nordhoff, op. cit., p. 277.

55. Fellman, op. cit., pp. 58–60; Parker, op. cit., pp. 261–263.

56. Robertson, op. cit., pp. 152–153. See also: Kanter, op. cit., pp. 9–10.

57. Robertson, op. cit., pp. 109–111.

58. Ibid., p. 75. See also: pp. 59, 66, 82–83.

59. Carden, op. cit., pp. 69–70.

60. Parker, op. cit., pp. 211–212. See also: Fellman, op. cit., p. 58; Carden, op. cit., p. 83.

61. Robertson, op. cit., pp. 66–71, 111–112, 284–286; Parker, op. cit., pp.

187–189; Fellman, op. cit., pp. 56–67; Carden, op. cit., pp. 70, 80–81, 83–84.

62. For a brief summary of the ideas expressed in these "talks," see: Parker, op. cit., pp. 227–240. See also Fellman, op. cit., p. 51.

63. Robertson, op. cit., pp. 15, 54, 71, 129, 132–134; Muncy, op. cit., p. 194.

64. Nordhoff, op. cit., p. 293. See also: pp. 289–290; Robertson, op. cit., pp. 133–134; Parker, op. cit., p. 217.

65. Carden, op. cit., pp. 71–74. For further descriptions of, or excerpts from, criticism sessions, see: Nordhoff, op. cit., pp. 290–293; Robertson, op. cit., pp. 137–149.

66. Robertson, op. cit., p. 147. See also Carden, op. cit., pp. 58–59, 72, 76–77.

67. Carden, op. cit., pp. 73–74.

68. Carden, op. cit., pp. 79–80; Parker, op. cit., pp. 221–226; Robertson, op. cit., p. 143.

69. Nordhoff, op. cit., pp. 285–286; Robertson, op. cit., pp. 20–21, 92,- 228–229; Carden, op. cit., pp. 14–15, 65–66; Parker, op. cit., p. 240.

70. Parker, op. cit., p. 262; Robertson, C. N. *Oneida Community: The breakup.* Syracuse, N.Y.: Syracuse University Press, 1972 (hereafter *Breakup*), p. 30.

71. Robertson, *Autobiography,* op. cit., p. 357; Robertson, *Breakup,* op. cit., pp. 48–66; Carden, op. cit., pp. 92–93, 96–98.

72. Robertson, *Autobiography,* op. cit., p. 357. See also: Robertson, *Breakup,* op. cit., pp. 22–40; Parker, op. cit., pp. 277–279; Carden, op. cit., pp. 97–98, 111.

73. Parker, op. cit., pp. 212–283; Carden, op. cit., pp. 98–102; Robertson, *Breakup,* op. cit., pp. 110–122.

74. Muncy, op. cit., p. 195; Parker, op. cit., pp. 284–285, 287–290; Carden, op. cit., pp. 103–104. For a detailed discussion of the dissolution and reorganization of Oneida, see: Robertson, *Breakup,* op. cit., pp. 110–316.

CHAPTER 4

The Israeli Kibbutzim

The kibbutz is a form of intentional community whose roots date back to the years shortly before World War I, when Dagania A, the first cooperative Jewish settlement in Palestine, was established. In subsequent decades, through the period of British authority over the region, the number of kibbutzim grew. By 1948, the year of Israeli statehood, the kibbutz represented the normal living arrangement of over 50,000 people. Following national independence, kibbutz membership continued to increase at a reduced rate until the mid-1950s, when it stabilized at a population of some 80,000 distributed among approximately 230 settlements.[1]

Our analysis of the kibbutz as an experimental utopia confronts several difficulties of method. To begin with, the kibbutz is a living society undergoing constant change as it evolves and interacts with its environment. The situation at any one time can be made comprehensible only in terms of a concrete past and an expected and planned future. To satisfy this requirement, we must trace the development of many aspects of kibbutz life from the earliest days to the present. Second, the kibbutz movement is not a homogenous entity. Each kibbutz has its own local environment and its own specific inhabitants distinct from those of any other kibbutz. There are also significant patterns of organization and outlook that divide groups of kibbutzim from each other. In fact, the kibbutz movement has a right and a left wing, indicating the separation between the more conservative and the more radical communities. We shall stress common features of the kibbutz. Where this is not possible, we shall focus on the practices of the more progressive left-wing settlements.

ECOLOGICAL DIMENSIONS: GEOGRAPHICAL AND ARCHITECTURAL FEATURES

All kibbutzim are located within the same relatively small geographic area. Bordered by Egypt and the Mediterranean Sea to the west, Lebanon to the north, Syria and Jordan to the east, and the Red Sea to the south, Israel stands at the juncture between Africa and Asia. Topographically, the state can be divided into four major regions: a coastal plain along the Mediterranean, a central portion composed of rugged hills, the Negev Desert in the south, and the Jordan River and Arava Valleys to the east. Climatically, the area falls within the Mediterranean zone, characterized by winter rains and summer droughts. Temperatures are generally high, with summer peaks in the vicinity of 104 degrees Fahrenheit.[2]

Israel's geographic environment does not permit man to survive without struggle. When the first kibbutzim were founded, conditions were even less conducive to human habitation than they are today. Centuries of neglect, deforestation, and primitive agricultural methods, in combination with heavy winds and rain, had resulted in extreme erosion, which limited soil productivity. Also, water was in short supply. The Negev was arid or semiarid; other regions had erratic rainfall and streams that ran only half the year. Without man-made systems—wells and irrigation—the quantities of water necessary for cultivation could not be obtained. As an additional problem, much of the land was swampy, especially those parcels cheap enough to be acquired by the first Jewish settlers. And with the swamps came malaria, sometimes in epidemics severe enough to force the abandonment of a settlement. Finally, there was the general harshness of the climate: cold, wet winters and intensely hot summers. One reporter cited the comment of a resident in a border kibbutz to the effect that the heat was worse than terrorist attacks; the latter came and went but the heat always remained.[3]

Against this geographic situation, the founders of the early kibbutzim had few defenses other than their will. Capital was scarce; settlers often lived in tents and relied upon rudimentary agricultural technology. Yet even under those circumstances, the obstacles posed by the physical environment were not insurmountable. With courage and perseverance, grains and fruits could be grown and flocks of sheep and goats maintained. Once modern equipment became available, intensive agriculture provided increasing yields from the limited arable land. Thus, the kibbutzim survived and prospered, and as they prospered, they transformed their environment to meet the needs of their members. Swamps were drained, forests replanted, and irrigation systems installed. Today, barren regions of the past have been replaced by a fertile successor. Even those unpleasant features of the environment that could not be modified have had their impact mitigated. The cold rain and hot sun remain, but they can be avoided through well-heated housing, fans, and swimming pools.[4]

In addition to the natural aspects of its geographic location, the kibbutz is affected by political and ideological factors as well. First of all, it cannot be overemphasized that to the members of the kibbutz, the land of Israel is very different from land of comparable quality elsewhere in the world. As Jews and Zionists, they believe that this is their land, the land inhabited by their ancestors centuries ago and the only land where they can enjoy dignity and security as a people. Second, the state of Israel is not composed solely of kibbutzim. Thus, within their own country, kibbutz members must deal with people and institutions distinct from, and sometimes opposed to, the kibbutz way of life. Finally, the land of both the kibbutz and the state of Israel is contested. Both those Arabs who once dwelled in Palestine and fled during the war of 1948 and those Arab nations that border Israel have maintained hostility toward the Jewish state. Thus, the kibbutzim have been under military attack four times in the past 25 years.

Architecturally, the kibbutz is a designed community, whose framework primarily reflects functional considerations. In most cases, kibbutz settlers selected previously unoccupied sites so that no existing buildings would interfere with a rational construction plan. Richard Kaufmann, an innovative architect, produced the blueprints for some of the early communities, and his perspective has been copied extensively.

In general, Kaufmann "considered the functional relationship of structures and groups of buildings, but also suited the basic plan to local topography and to the social and economic conditions and special requirements of each village."[5] One of his fundamental principles was a clear separation between residence areas and farm areas. Since westerly winds are prevalent in nearly all of Israel, the western section of a kibbutz was designated for living quarters. Thus, the inhabitants could enjoy a fresh sea breeze and avoid noxious farmyard smells. Trees and lawns might also be planted to reinforce the separation between these two areas.

The communal dining-hall is usually placed in the center of the residential zone, with a good road leading to the kitchen section to permit easy transport of provisions. Other buildings in this region may be libraries, museums, and auditoriums. Clothing depots and laundries are set in that part of the residence zone nearest to the farmyards to facilitate contact with

water and power lines. Large kibbutzim may have a distinct group of
buildings set aside for the use of the settlement's children; these include
nurseries, dormitories, and schools. As a rule, children's quarters are given
priority in terms of building materials and location to ensure security
against the climate and possible hostile attack.

The type and layout of kibbutz housing has varied, depending on the
capital available for construction. Funds allocated for residences were deliberately kept low as housing construction constituted expenditure for private
consumption, while kibbutz ideology emphasized priorities for production
or communal activity. Thus, the original settlers lived in tents. Once wood
and brick became available, a common housing design consisted of a one-
story, elongated building with three to eight living units that opened on a
common veranda. Variations on this design might be linked to climatic or
social considerations. As examples of the former, homes in the Kinarot and
Bet She'an valleys—where temperatures are high—have shaded porches
around them and ventilation gaps below the windows. On the high ridges
of Upper Galilee, however, roofs are built of reinforced concrete to withstand severe winter storms. As regards the latter, the common veranda
might be replaced with adjacent units having their entrances on opposite
sides of the building to ensure greater privacy.[6]

In the early stages of kibbutz existence, an apartment included only a
single room. Bathrooms were communal and, in fact, served as meeting
places where members gossiped and discussed local problems. In modern,
"luxury" kibbutz housing, an apartment may have one or two rooms, a
kitchenette, and a private bath. This change in housing structure reflects a
growing desire among kibbutz residents for privacy and personal comfort.
On the other hand, the existence of more comfortable personal space encourages private living and reduces time spent in communal interaction.

THE HUMAN AGGREGATE

The kibbutzim developed historically as part of a larger social movement, the Zionist settlement of Palestine. Throughout this century, Jews
from many parts of the globe have journeyed to Palestine with the hope of
creating a homeland for their widely scattered people. The men and women
who have joined the kibbutzim have been a subgroup of this larger migra-
tion.

For the most part, the pioneers of the early kibbutzim began their
exodus to a new land from Russia or Eastern Europe. Since the vast major-

ity had reached adolescence before emigrating, they had spent sufficient time in their former homelands to be deeply influenced by their experiences there. The culture and social structure of the communities they had lived in constituted one powerful influence. Many settlers had been raised in a rural Jewish village, known as a *shtetl*. Life in these communities was parochial and restrictive. Families had close emotional ties but were also rigid and authoritarian. The father was a patriarch before whom his wife was submissive, and both parents dominated their children. Intense and orthodox religious convictions served as an additional restraint on novel behavior. Social values were largely petit bourgeois; the pursuit of knowledge and/or property led to high personal status, whereas work with one's hands and physical labor were less esteemed.

A second influential factor in the settlers' background was membership in a youth movement. Groups of youths joined together in associations dedicated to exploring new ways of life distinct from the prevailing culture. While these movements varied among themselves, many of them emphasized the value of community as opposed to individualism, the benefits of a return to nature, the satisfaction of physical labor, and a revolt against traditional institutions and norms. Jewish youths formed associations of their own, adding Zionism and socialism to this general outlook.[7]

In the years following the founding of the first kibbutz settlements, the movement grew in population and number of communities. By 1920, there were 40 collective groups encompassing 650 people; in 1931, 58 kibbutzim supported 4391 members. In 1948, the year of Israeli statehood and the apex of kibbutz strength in terms of the proportion of Jews in the country who lived on the collective farms (7.9%), there were 149 settlements with a population of 54,200. During this period, the kibbutzim relied primarily on recruitment of new adherents for the expansion of the movement. Admission to a kibbutz required acceptance of the principles on which the community was organized; these varied from religious kibbutzim to Marxist ones.[8]

Jewish immigrants to Palestine constituted the source of new members for the kibbutzim. Historically, these immigrants arrived in relatively distinct waves, called *aliyot* (plural), which can be categorized according to the predominant country of origin and the social characteristics of its members. The first *aliyah* (singular), begun in 1882, numbered at most 30,000 persons. Largely consisting of Russian Jews seeking to escape pogroms (anti-Semitic riots) in their homeland, it was responsible for the establishment of numerous agricultural settlements in Palestine. While members of this group successfully adjusted to the new environment, they

did not constitute a force for changing it. In 1904, the second *aliyah*
began. Also primarily Russian, but much smaller than its predecessor
(perhaps 10,000 people), it exerted a profound dynamic impact on Palestine and the Zionist movement. It was this group, future-oriented and
ideologically radical and experimental, that brought forth the *halutz* (the
pioneer) as a cultural ideal type and that founded the first kibbutzim.

The third *aliyah* (1919–1923) included many youths who were committed to Zionist and socialist ideology and determined to serve as pioneers
in a new Jewish homeland. They were active in forming both kibbutzim
and labor organizations. The fourth *aliyah* marked a change in the pattern
of Jewish immigration. Most of the 82,000 members of this group were
Polish; they tended to have middle-class roots and included larger numbers
of merchants and fewer intellectuals than the second and third *aliyot*. A
substantial number chose to reside in towns and enter commerce. The fifth
and largest *aliyah* began in 1932 and continued through to the achievement
of Israeli statehood. Partially a response to the rise of Naziism, it included
many German and Central European Jews.[9]

Following the foundation of the state of Israel, Jewish immigration to
the area has continued to be a major source of population growth. However, the kibbutz movement has had increasing difficulty in attracting new
recruits. Indeed, despite efforts to encourage immigrants to join kibbutzim, the communal settlements have, since 1948, accounted for declining
percentages of the Israeli population.[10]

As the background of recruits has shifted, and as the kibbutz has undergone internal development, the composition of subgroups among its
membership has changed. In the early years, when immigrants joined a
kibbutz, they became part of a relatively homogeneous society. Not only
did the pioneer settlements lack a pattern of stratification, they avoided any
substantial degree of social differentiation. The family constituted a weak
and often hidden social unit. Efforts to achieve sexual equality called for the
minimization of differences between men and women. As opposed to occupational specialization, everyone was assumed capable of performing any
job.

In subsequent periods, however, greater and greater degrees of differentiation have occurred, and various distinguishable subgroups have appeared. One mode of differentiation that has accompanied the passage of
time is age. As the first settlers married and raised children, they produced
a new generation whose experiences and outlook were distinct from their
own. What the first generation achieved through toil and sacrifice was
matter-of-fact reality to the second. In addition, the first generation kib-

butz members could be segmented according to the amount of time actually lived on the kibbutz. Groups formed on this basis roughly correlated with membership in different *aliyot*. Thus, the distinction between those who founded the kibbutz and those who subsequently joined it was reinforced by differences in national origin.[11]

Increasing economic and technological complexity in the kibbutz has given rise to occupational specialization. The requirements of efficient production, competitive with the external economy, made some division of labor a virtual necessity. When jobs have required significant amounts of skill and training, these divisions have tended to become permanent. Further, long-term members of a branch of the kibbutz economy may socialize with each other and develop an interest in the special needs of that particular sector. Even managerial positions have been affected by this pressure toward efficiency. Thus, while rotation of high positions remains a kibbutz rule, those rotated often come from a small segment of the total membership.[12]

Finally, despite formal professions of sexual equality, there is a growing divergence in status between men and women. The primary basis for this disparity is a definite sexual division of labor. In the early days, everyone was engaged in productive labor. More recently, a shift in work assignments has developed, resulting in the employment of men in productive areas (primarily agriculture) and women in service occupations (teaching, child rearing, kitchen work, and laundry). These assignments produce status differences, since it is the productive agricultural jobs that are given high prestige in the kibbutz's norm structure. As an added problem, more women than men lack a regular job assignment and, consequently, are rotated from one undesirable and unskilled position to another. Furthermore, sexual inequality in the distribution of positions of authority is apparent. Women participate on decision-making committees, but they generally serve only on those related to their occupations. Those holding general leadership positions or managing major economic sectors are almost exclusively male.[13]

ORGANIZATIONAL STRUCTURE

Although it includes numerous organizations, some of them highly complex, and although it requires long-term policy decisions, the kibbutz is not a "planned society" in the same sense as Skinner's Walden II. The first settlers did not arrive in Palestine with a fixed plan for a new society.

This is not to say that they lacked a general vision; in fact, they were already committed to Zionism as a fundamental mission and to several other distinct political and economic principles, particularly equality and democracy. However, they did not possess a detailed outline of how to organize a government, or an economy, or an educational system. Those forms that did emerge developed through experience and interaction with the environment. Because there was no guiding blueprint, the kibbutz has been free to experiment. Its organizational forms are continually changing; they are dynamic rather than static.

Government

Before analysis of the specific features of kibbutz government, it must be emphasized that the kibbutz is not a sovereign entity. Kibbutz government is subordinate to the laws of the state of Israel. This formal subordination results only rarely in direct control of kibbutz members' activities, such as the requirement that kibbutz youth must perform military service. It is more significant in the sense that outside forces set policy for political and economic institutions with which the kibbutz must continually interact. Still, the kibbutzim have proven themselves capable of resisting considerable pressure from the central government. Their refusal to help provide employment for new immigrants by hiring nonmember workers is an example of this relative autonomy.

In order to exert influence on its political environment, the kibbutz maintains organizational links to the national Israeli political system. Many kibbutzim are joined in federations that function as elements in Israeli political parties. The substance of the kibbutz role in these parties has changed over the years. The left wing of the movement originally considered themselves a vanguard that would exert a revolutionary influence on the rest of the society. Now, while maintaining their commitment to socialist principles, kibbutzim have lowered their expectations and perform in the give-and-take of parliamentary coalition politics.

Since its inception, the kibbutz has had a strong commitment to direct democracy. In one settlement, decisions were originally made by informal group discussions without chairmen or agenda. The general meeting now exhibits a greater degree of structure. More important, it has reluctantly delegated its authority to a set of officials and committees who carry out much of the business of government. Spiro's analysis of a left-wing kibbutz in 1950 revealed the following decision-making positions (economic committees are discussed below). The general secretary was the central administrative officer of the kibbutz; his functions included chairing general meetings, maintaining official correspondence, and serving as liaison to the kibbutz federation. He was responsible for the satisfactory execution of noneconomic policy. A central executive committee, of which the general secretary was a member, shared this concern with the overall welfare of kibbutz society. In addition, there were several committees with specialized functions, including a nominating committee, an education committee, a welfare committee, and a security committee.[14]

Because of their interest in preserving political equality, kibbutz members employ a variety of procedures to prevent office holders and committee members from becoming a ruling class or an elite. First, those nominated for office must be ratified by a vote of the general meeting. Second, there is a strict rotation of office with short terms of tenure, usually of only two or three years. Third, each committee has limited powers and is relatively independent in relation to other communities. Thus, no single position provides total political power. Finally, there are virtually no economic incentives for holding office. In fact, most officeholders are not excused from their regular jobs; they must put in a normal full day's work and then attend to their committee responsibilities on their own time.

Of course, formal safeguards do not guarantee that an elite stratum will not appear. However, in the case of the kibbutz, empirical evidence indicates that there are few existing tendencies toward elitism. With rare exceptions, nomination to office is designed to encourage wide participation and representation. Tenure in office is kept brief. In one kibbutz, the average continuous tenure in a primary committee or office was 1.9 years. The high ratio of positions to be filled to the overall population reduces the possibility of elitism. In a small kibbutz, 30–40% of the membership may be on a committee. When this ratio is combined with rotation requirements, it is clear that a substantial part of the membership plays some role in kibbutz government.[15]

One factor that discourages elitism is the balance between the rewards and the costs of holding office. Officeholders receive some material advantages. While they do not get extra pay, they do have easier access to kibbutz institutions and may get better service. They have more opportunities for travel, and they receive a small additional personal allowance when they work outside the community. There are also nonmaterial benefits. Holding office gives the individual an opportunity to acquire prestige. This, however, may be a dubious advantage. Prestige is not attached to an office but rather to the way a person fulfills the duties of an office. Thus, accomplishments may bring praise, but failure results in condemnation. One of the most common reasons given for withdrawing from a kibbutz office is the desire to avoid constant criticism.

Compared with these rewards, the personal costs of holding office may seem disproportionately high. One of the major hardships is the loss of leisure time. As noted above, committee work is usually done on one's own time, and a disturbance in one's relationships with family and friends may thus occur. Also, the officeholder may undergo a loss of acceptance in the community. Those in positions of responsibility must often act in an authoritative manner, decide between conflicting claims, and reach decisions that disappoint some members. Thus, Talmon reports that "Many of the most competent office holders, who are accorded high esteem and approval are not liked." [16] In a kibbutz, where social relationships are confined to a small, inclusive group, this interference with friendships can be a serious penalty.

A proof that the cost of holding a governmental post is greater than the rewards is the genuine reluctance of many kibbutz members to accept such positions. Often a potential officeholder insists on limited tenure and the right to return to his former occupation before he agrees to serve. In some cases, public opinion and informal pressure must be put on an obstinate holdout who adamantly rejects the entreaties of the nominations committee.[17]

There is more to political life in a kibbutz than the formal organization of government. Particularly in the left-wing kibbutzim, questions of ideology and politics are taken quite seriously, and informal debates rage constantly. These arguments can facilitate decision making. Spiro observed, "long in advance of town meetings, most people have made up their minds on issues to be presented; on the basis of these informal discussions, lines are drawn and partisans are prepared with arguments. And long after the meetings have been held, the discussions continue unabated." [18]

From the viewpoint of individual liberty, however, there is serious question as to the extent of the boundaries within which discussion can take place. In the left-wing kibbutzim, debate can take place freely up to a point, and no further. Because of the intensity of their members' political convictions, these kibbutzim cannot tolerate the risk of having small political disagreements degenerate into full ideological schism. Hence, they practice "ideological collectivism." Every member must accept a majority decision of his kibbutz, his federation, and his party. Before a decision is made, debate is open. But once the vote has taken place, all members must yield to and, if necessary, work for the implementation of the majority directive.

In one case a pro-Arab kibbutz member was refused readmission to his kibbutz (see below). One participant in the general meeting offered the following view of freedom of expression: "A man has a right to his own opinions, a right to speak them openly—we all believe in a free exchange of opinions, but the exchange must be made among members of the same family. . . . A member of Rakah [the Israeli Communist Party] is not one of our family. . . . A man who does not believe in Israel is not one of our family." [19] To the extent that this position reflects kibbutz norms, it indicates an inability of the kibbutz to tolerate criticism of its basic values.

Economy

Every working day, the kibbutz demonstrates that a communistic economy can function effectively, albeit not without its problems. This communist structure dates back to the early days of the first settlements. At that time, both conviction and necessity encouraged collective economics. Pioneers from Eastern Europe, particularly those who had been members of youth movements, were already favorably disposed toward the principles of communal living. Reinforcing their beliefs were the difficult conditions in their new homeland, which required cooperation and sharing.

The basic features of the kibbutz economy established then continue to this day. The means of production—buildings, tools, livestock, and all other fixed capital—are owned by the community as a whole. The land on which the kibbutz rests is owned by the entire nation; it is rented to the kibbutz on a long-term renewable lease. Economic resources for consumption are allocated according to the dictum: From each according to his ability, to each according to his needs.[20]

Productive activities in the kibbutz are primarily agricultural. Kibbutz farmers cultivate field crops, vegetables, fruit orchards, and fodder crops; maintain dairies and fisheries; and raise sheep and goat flocks and poultry. Unlike many other types of agricultural enterprise in Israel, the kibbutz employs several distinct methods of farm organization. First, kibbutz agriculture is usually highly diversified. This practice serves several objectives. In terms of its ecological effects, mixed farming permits profitable use of crop rotation, reduces the threat of disease, and provides wastes from animal herds that can be recycled into the soil. From an economic perspective, it enables the community to use its labor force on a more consistent basis than if a single seasonal crop were raised. Diversification also serves the ideological goal of kibbutz self-sufficiency.

Second, kibbutz agriculture relies on mechanization. Because their lands are generally larger than those of single-family farms, kibbutzim can economically invest in expensive labor-saving machinery. Finally, kibbutz settlers, recognizing the limited amount of arable land in their nation, are proponents of intensive agriculture. Every effort is made to glean as much produce as the supplies of land and water will yield.

In addition to farming, kibbutzim also provide necessary services for the welfare of their community: cooking, laundry, education, sanitation, health, maintenance and repair shops, and so on. More recently, the settlers have sought to diversify their economic base by beginning the operation of light industry. In 1965, the Kibbutz Industries Association reported a total of 151 nonagricultural enterprises operated by the communal settlements; these accounted for about 5% of Israel's total gross industrial production.[21]

Despite its socialist principles, the kibbutz faces the rest of the Israeli economy (and indeed, the world economy) much as a business does. The kibbutz exports a certain quantity of goods and services, consumes a quantity of goods and services produced elsewhere, and must achieve a profitable balance between the two. Moreover, there are additional practical and ideological reasons for the kibbutzim to emphasize high productivity and efficient operations. Once the period of pioneer asceticism had passed, kibbutz residents began to desire many of the consumer items available to others in Israeli society. The productive facilities of the kibbutz must increase revenues to establish a standard of living comparable to that attainable elsewhere, or the community risks losing members. Second, kibbutzim are part of a movement that seeks to expand collective agricultural settlement in Israel. To provide assistance for new struggling communities, older established settlements must be capable of achieving a significant economic surplus.

How well has the kibbutz economy managed to accomplish its objectives? Performance fluctuates over time and between communities. There are also disputes over the proper mode of economic evaluation to be employed. As regards increasing productivity, however, there is little room for doubt: the kibbutzim have proved to be enormously successful. Indeed, for the period 1949–1960, it is estimated the agricultural productivity of the kibbutzim increased at an annual rate of over 10%. Although the profitability of the kibbutzim is in some dispute, there is no doubt that the settlements can maintain themselves economically.[22]

Economic decisions are made by a set of officials and committees that are organized similarly to the kibbutz's political decision-making apparatus. Among the major officials are the general economic manager and the work-assignment chairman, who seek to balance the manpower demands of the various productive units with the members' desires for particular types of work. Economic committees include an executive committee, long-term and short-term planning committees, a work assignment committee, and a construction committee.

At the operational level, each branch of the kibbutz economy has a foreman responsible for its administration. These persons may be elected by the members who work in that branch or by the general meeting, depending on whether the work force of the branch is permanent or transitory. It is the foreman who determines how many workers and how much machinery are needed to complete a specific task. In some branches—for example, laundry, kitchen, and clothing room—the job of foreman is so intensely disliked that members must be strongly pressured to take the position.[23]

All members of the kibbutz who are physically able must work. Even high school students must devote some time to labor. It is the expectation of the community that each will work to the best of his ability; shirkers are subject to intense social disapproval. In addition to requiring that all of its members work, the kibbutz desires that all of its work be done by its own members. This attitude is based on the socialist conviction that the hiring of outsiders would transform the community into a class society of employers and employees. It is a position that has caused the kibbutz difficulty for several reasons. First, the Israeli state has faced a chronic problem of finding employment for new immigrants. The kibbutz has refused to help in this regard, unless the newcomers are willing to become full members. Second, many kibbutzim suffer from severe labor shortages. This shortage has caused some kibbutzim to yield and hire ourside personnel to work in a new factory or in the fields at harvest time. Third, the requirement that all work be done by members makes it very difficult for a kibbutz to afford having a member work outside its boundaries.[24]

A community that demands that everyone work must devise some procedure for determining what specific task each will perform. If the community is also egalitarian and antiauthoritarian, this can be a difficult problem, since the supply and demand of jobs and job seekers may not (and in fact do not) match. Too many people want to work in some areas, while no one wants to work in others. As a further complication, the basic imbalance between jobs and job seekers has become a conflict between generations. Many popular jobs are held by first-generation kibbutz members. This was historically inevitable: the second generation had not yet appeared in the manpower pool when the placements were made. Yet, as long as these persons are capable of performing adequately, they cannot be removed from their jobs. This leaves the second-generation kibbutz worker with a much smaller real set of job possibilities than the set he is theoretically entitled to choose from.[25]

Kibbutz organizations struggle to resolve these dilemmas of job placement. One device employed is rotation of especially unpopular job assignments. Thus, everyone must have a turn working in the kitchen or in the laundry. Also, the kibbutz tries to be as flexible as it can, allowing members to change jobs and to move into a preferred specialization whenever possible. In recent years, there has been an increasing tendency to allow members with special skills to work outside the community. However, on some occasions, all mechanisms fail, and an individual's desires for employment cannot be satisfied. In such cases, the worker must subordinate his own wishes to the needs of the collective. If a worker refuses to accept a job to which he is assigned, he can be expelled from the community.[26]

As a basic principle, the kibbutz distributes its resources in an egalitarian manner. No one receives a larger share of the community's wealth because of his job, status, family, or ethnic background. This ethic is modified, however, by another value: each should receive according to his needs. If someone has an unusual requirement—for example, a need for special training because of a speech defect—he may be allocated a greater share of the community's resources.

In practice, the application of these principles of economic distribution is a source of continuing tension. First, some kibbutz members have access to outside sources of income and thus enjoy a level of personal possession higher than that of most of their comrades. Second, certain products cannot be allocated on an egalitarian basis because the kibbutz cannot afford to distribute them to everyone at the same time. The best example in this category is housing. New residences—which are constructed slowly—must be allocated according to some set of priorities. Usually, the basis for preference in housing is seniority: a new apartment goes to the member who has been working in the kibbutz the longest. Other products of this nature may be allocated by lot.[27]

Third, the kibbutz is experiencing an increase in expectation regarding the appropriate level of consumer goods. This results in part from a decline in the ascetic ideology of the original settlers. It also results in part from the visible prosperity and levels of personal wealth available in the nonkibbutz sectors of the Israeli economy. Whatever the cause, the kibbutz cannot ignore these new expectations without risking the loss of members. However, yielding to demands for more consumer goods produces conflicts with egalitarian principles. An increase in the number of large consumption items means a concomitant increase in products that, like housing, cannot be distributed to everyone at once. The difficulties the kibbutz has had implementing the equal distribution of consumer goods has led many members to demand greater personal choice in consumption decisions or to begin semilegitimate or nonlegitimate efforts to acquire personal goods. Both of these practices can result only in greater economic differentiation and greater competition for consumer items among members.[28]

Family and Education

As in its economic and political relationships, the kibbutz has developed a communal pattern for family relationships and the socialization of its children. Early kibbutz settlers strongly opposed the practices of the bourgeois family. Their feminist perspective led them to criticize middle-class norms for defining women as inferior beings and for relegating them to menial household tasks. The family, with its strong affective ties, was criticized as a dangerously exclusive social unit, a group whose members would maintain commitments to each other rather than to the kibbutz as a whole. Environmental pressures demonstrated the practical advantages of these attitudes. Compared to centralized communal institutions, separate households were wasteful of scarce resources. The community could not afford to have all of its women "keeping house" for individual men when it could simply allocate a few people to perform tasks of that nature for the entire collective.

Opposition to bourgeois norms did not automatically provide an acceptable alternative mating arrangement. However, as the great majority of the early settlers were young and single, they were free to attempt a variety of sexual practices, including polygamy (both polygyny and polyandry). They eventually adopted a pattern of informal monogamy. A single male and a single female joined together as a couple, but they maintained the relationship only as long as the original affective ties remained strong. To become "married," a couple simply requested a joint room; divorce was accomplished by a return to separate rooms. The community had no formal power either to approve or to disapprove of the commencement or termination of a relationship.[29]

As time passed, initial patterns were modified in the direction of greater family cohesiveness and an increased family role in kibbutz life. Several factors may account for this shift. Communal values in general are less vigorously adhered to. The appearance of strata based on occupation and age have removed from the family the onus of being that single group that might interfere with kibbutz unity. Perhaps most important, the appearance of a second generation has served to strengthen family ties greatly. The impact of these forces is readily observable. Marriages are more stable; divorce is less frequent. Weddings are celebrated as significant events and spouses openly acknowledge their relationship.

In seeking to achieve a satisfactory framework of family life and a stable balance between family and community loyalties, the kibbutz must deal with the relationship between parents and children as well as those between men and women. Pioneer settlers in the kibbutz rarely brought children with them to Palestine. Moreover, many of them neither desired to have children nor had any plans for their care. This attitude may be understood if one recalls that early kibbutz life was a struggle for survival. Children could not assist in that struggle; in fact, the time and material necessary to their care reduced the resources available for production and defense. Despite these attitudes, however, children did appear, and some decisions had to be made regarding their welfare. Those settlers who had participated in European youth movements were ideologically predisposed to adopt a system of collective child-rearing. Environment reinforced ideology: every mother could not be spared from productive work to care for her offspring. Thus, the kibbutz commitment to communal education was born.[30]

Children enter the collective socialization process by being placed in a communal infants' house as soon as they are brought back from the hospital after birth. From that point on, contact with their parents is restricted to certain designated periods. Children are generally breast-fed by their mothers and weaned by six months. During this period, they are not permitted in their parents' apartment, nor are their parents allowed to spend the night with them. After six months, they begin participation in the "children's hour," a period of an hour or two each day reserved for interaction between parents and children. Parents and children are eager to spend time with each other, and the relationship of the children's hour to the overall socialization program virtually ensures that this time will be as pleasant as possible. All learning, discipline, and other difficult aspects of child rearing take place in the children's quarters and in school. The hours spent with parents are thus completely free for affection and play.

A third point of contact between parent and child occurs when children are permitted to sleep in their parents' room. Most kibbutzim allow this from time to time, perhaps more often for a particularly nervous child who has difficulty sleeping in the infants' house. In many cases, however, parents allow their children to spend the night with them more often than formal kibbutz policy permits. Because it is felt that sleeping arrangements will have an effect on future generations' communal attitudes, this issue has become a point of controversy. Talmon's surveys indicated that 42% of kibbutz respondents endorsed the principle of children's sleeping in their parents' room, while another 42% opposed it. This divergence of opinion reveals the extent to which the family's role in kibbutz life remains an unsettled question.[31]

The limitations on the parents' role have definite implications for the values, attitudes, and feelings of kibbutz children. For one, the child is relatively secure from undesirable parental influence; indeed, there is little opportunity for any single maladjusted adult to have a fundamental impact on a child's development. Second, the child learns that it is the kibbutz and his comrades on whom he must depend. The family may be a source of love and concern, but it is the community that can translate concern into action to meet his needs. Finally, it has been suggested that the lack of a sustained intimate relationship between the kibbutz child and his parents, or between the child and any adult, reduces the ability of the child to develop intimate relationships when he matures.[32]

Having established that child socialization takes place in communal institutions, we must now examine the way in which these institutions operate. One can hardly overemphasize the importance of the function they perform. If a society with definite structures and ideals is to survive, it must acquire new members committed to these forms and values. The kibbutzim initially relied on outside recruitment to meet this need, but the number of recruits has recently declined. The kibbutz must rely on its own children to perpetuate its existence. Thus, the system of education must produce a generation willing and able to carry on the kibbutz life-style.

Kibbutz education combines formal schooling with socialization into the basic norms of the community. These activities initially take place in a series of houses in which the children live. A newborn spends his first year in the infants' house, where nurses attend to his needs. He is then transferred to the toddlers' house. At about the age of four, there is another move—to the kindergarten. Activities that take place here are approximately equivalent to those in an American nursery school. Following kindergarten is primary school. At this point, the child is introduced to formal academic training and to social responsibility and work. In addition to schoolwork, which is informal, without grades or exams, the child has chores to perform—cleaning the house or working in the garden—for about an hour a day.

With the completion of sixth grade and entrance into high school, the life of the kibbutz child changes abruptly. At previous levels, he was pampered and largely permitted to enjoy himself. In high school, however, he faces a more rigorous academic program and an increased role in the productive work of the community. The high school curriculum is similar to that of a European gymnasium, providing a broad background in the liberal arts. Originally, the completion of high school usually constituted the end of formal schooling, as the kibbutz was reluctant to finance higher education for its youth. More recently, increased pressure by young sabras (native-born Israelis) for education has caused kibbutzim to modify this position and to permit larger numbers of students to receive university training.

During the time that they are in school, children are not full members of the kibbutz. The community wishes them to make a voluntary commitment to join at an age when they understand what they are doing. In fact, it requires that they have some experience of nonkibbutz life before they make their choice. Prior to the formation of the state of Israel, high school graduates spent a year working in the city before becoming candidates for admission. The three years of required military service is now deemed to serve the same purpose.[33]

Throughout the educational process described above, children in the kibbutz are learning more than academic subjects, technical skills, and the rules that govern their society. They are also learning what it is like to live in a cooperative fashion with one's fellows. The vehicle for this "instruction" is the peer group. Beginning with his first days in the infants' house, a child in the kibbutz is never alone. His cribmates will later become his companions in the toddlers' house, and they will eventually become part of a self-conscious group that completes much of its education together. Throughout the changes in buildings, nurses, and teachers that mark the child's life, his peer group, his comrades, remain a secure feature. They work and study together, providing mutual assistance when necessary. It is thus that the kibbutz educational system teaches its most important lesson, the value of solidarity among the community's members.[34]

BEHAVIOR SETTINGS

Although the kibbutz is a collective settlement, there are only a few occasions on which the entire membership interacts. Two of these situations have been selected for our discussion of behavior settings: the communal meal and the "town meeting."

Communal Meals

In its physical design, the kibbutz dining room is simple and practical. It is essentially a large room with numerous tables (formica in a modern kibbutz). It is usually spacious enough to accommodate the entire
membership and guests.

Meals are organized in an informal manner. Breakfast and lunch are
fast and businesslike, taken during breaks on the job. Dinner is only
slightly slower, but it is a more social meal, with families often eating
together. Yet, what is most striking about the meal is its lack of gra-
ciousness and comfort. Observers stress the general hustle and absence of
manners. Diamond, for example, wrote, "eating is regarded as a basic
physical necessity, little value is placed on the careful preparation of food,
meals are consumed in a hectic and unceremonious atmosphere." [35] In addition, kitchen work has a low status and is usually disliked, so personnel
are unlikely to have high morale or a strong commitment to their jobs.

The crude and careless manner in which the dining hall is operated
stands in marked contrast to its symbolic importance for the kibbutz. The
dining hall was the center of the early settlers' lives. It was often the best-
constructed building in the kibbutz and served as a social, ceremonial, and
political center (it is still often the location of general assembly meetings).
These functions, in combination with the fact that it is the one place where
a kibbutz member is likely to interact with most of his comrades on a daily
basis, make it the communal institution par excellence.

Because of a growing disparity between the role of the dining hall in
ideology and in practice, it has become a controversial issue in kibbutz life.
Initially, eating in the dining hall was a significant communal experience,
compatible with the community's norms. When a person entered the hall,
he took the next available vacant seat, thus inviting interaction with any
comrade. In recent years, however, partially as a result of poor food and service, this communal behavior pattern is no longer maintained. Kibbutz
members often eat the evening meal with family and friends when in the
dining hall; they have also begun to serve themselves at home. In some
cases, a vicious circle occurs, in which a poorly operating staff drives potential diners to their private rooms and then proceeds to provide even worse
service because the hall is so rarely attended. [36]

General Meetings

The general meeting is the fundamental decision-making entity in the
kibbutz, the site of the community's sovereignty. As such, it is open to

every member who wishes to attend. These meetings decide on the annual
budget, on the election of officers, on major changes in the kibbutz economy, and on other matters of similar importance. They also deal with less
significant matters. Because kibbutz members prefer pure democracy and
distrust bureaucracy, they decide in general meetings questions that elsewhere would be left to administrative discretion or to a legislature. In addition, as the kibbutz is like a family in some respects, the general meeting
may discuss issues that might be considered a family affair. Thus, for example, there might be debate whether a disturbed child should be sent to a
psychiatrist. There has been a tendency recently for these personal matters
to be resolved by the kibbutz secretariat rather than in open meetings of
the entire membership.

General meetings are usually held in the dining room. They occur
frequently, perhaps once every two weeks. Their format is democratic. An
official presents the agenda and acts as chairman. As each issue is reached,
there is a brief statement of relevant background information; then the
question is thrown open to the members who may come forward and
present their opinions. No one is required to attend or to participate in a
general meeting. In the early days, most members attended and argued intensely. More recently, attendance has dropped to 50% or less, with a concomitant fall in participation. A disproportionate share of those who do
come regularly are older kibbutz members. Still, the general meeting serves
as an important mechanism for imparting important information about the
community and for focusing the attention of the membership on areas outside their normal routines.

An example of how a specific issue was resolved in one kibbutz may
serve to clarify the workings of a general meeting. A member who was
extremely unpopular because of his pro-Arab (or at least anti-Israeli-expan-
sionist) views, and who had left the kibbutz for a substantial period of time
without permission, requested that he be allowed to return. An official
committee interviewed the would-be returnee prior to the general meeting
and recommended that the individual be reaccepted. During the meeting,
several people argued as to whether the individual had indeed changed his
views. Some insisted that the kibbutz must maintain an atmosphere of
freedom of political conviction. Then one member delivered an emotional
speech opposing the returnee and his beliefs. No further speakers stepped
forward, and a vote was therefore taken. The results showed 75 for acceptance, 91 for rejection, and 121 abstentions. While this incident reveals
the limits on political expression in the kibbutz, it also indicates that the
general meeting is sufficiently open and unstructured to permit decisions

that go against basic kibbutz norms and the opinion of the community's leadership.[37]

SOCIAL CLIMATE

Personal Ideals and Value System

Those who founded the first kibbutzim sought to create a new social reality in accordance with their revolutionary vision. Many of the values cherished by the early settlers were embodied in the ideal of the *halutz,* the Zionist pioneer. Fundamentally, the *halutz* was a revolutionary in that he sought to tear down one culture and build another. Instead of a model to be emulated, he saw the tradition he had come from as an obstacle to be overcome. In its place, he would build a new Jewish state, and a new Jew to live within it. Thus, he challenged the physical passivity and intellectualism of the *shtetl* Jew with an adulation of physical labor, particularly agricultural work. Rather than seek wealth, he would practice asceticism, living lean and tough. He did not advocate hardship for its own sake, however, but rather as a necessary means to create a new social order. In fact, the image of *halutzim* was also an elitist vision: the kibbutz settlers saw themselves as a vanguard accepting the burden of colonizing and defending the frontier and setting a model for the rest of their brethren.

Politically, the values of the kibbutz settlers were essentially democratic, egalitarian, socialist, and Zionist. They opposed private property as an institution and preferred communal life to individualism. In some cases, their political views were formally Marxist, and their socialist orientation included a commitment to solidarity with the Soviet Union and the Communist world. Since the advent of Russian diplomatic and military support of the Arab cause in the Middle East, however, kibbutz members have found it difficult to maintain a pro-Soviet stance, although they have not abandoned their local and national commitment to socialism.[38]

With the achievement of Israeli statehood, members of the kibbutz movement began a long process of evaluating their progress toward the accomplishment of their goals and of evaluating the meaningfulness of further efforts in such directions. The formation of the state of Israel constituted the achievement of the greatest Zionist goal. Nonkibbutz sectors of Israeli society accepted this as the culmination of their revolutionary ambitions. Like other Western populations, they devoted their energies to the quest for prosperity, security, and personal success. Whereas the kibbutz member had once been admired as one of an elite, a member of a pioneer vanguard, he is now often seen as the representative of a parochial, overly ideological life-style. The former pioneers are no longer young and vigorous. Many are weary of continual effort and sacrifice while much of the rest of the nation enjoys comfort and ease.

Recent years have thus witnessed numerous modifications in the system of kibbutz values. Physical labor is still respected, but there is growing recognition of the role technical skill must play in the kibbutz economy. Family life has become more important to the membership and communal activity less so. Also, much of the rebellious fervor of kibbutz morality has lapsed. There is less of a sense of mission, of being a vanguard—a change that reflects the unwillingness of nonkibbutz Israeli society to continue to perceive the communal settlements as guides or models. Perhaps the greatest value change, however, has been a move away from the spirit of asceticism and self-sacrifice. Kibbutz members increasingly demand more and better consumer goods as well as greater personal choice in consumption patterns. They also accept and desire amounts of personal private property that would not have been tolerated decades ago.

These attitudes also prevail in the sabras. The second generation still believe in equality and social justice, but they do so as a matter of routine conviction. They remain loyal to the kibbutz as a way of life, practicing kibbutz socialism and cooperating and sharing with their comrades. Yet, they also wish the kibbutz to meet their own needs and those of their children. Hence, they desire a reasonable standard of living and improved educational opportunities. In addition, the second generation have largely demythologized work; they recognize and value it as a necessity, but they see no reason why it should be more difficult than necessary. When technology can effectively replace physical labor, the sabra has no reluctance about accepting the innovation. In brief, the desire to establish a new man as a personal ideal has been replaced with the wish to improve the life of the one who lives in the kibbutz today.[39]

Personal Relationships

Cohesion. The kibbutz has always emphasized the development of high cohesiveness among its members. Kibbutz socialism involved more than economic equality: in addition to sharing resources, the pioneers shared experiences, living closely together in as many ways as possible. A major objective of the community's educational system has been to orient future generations toward a life style of comradeship and mutual support. To a great extent, the kibbutz has been able to translate this value, communal living, into social reality. Levels of interpersonal interaction are high; members depend on one another for the satisfaction of their physical, emotional, and social needs. The kibbutz is a society of comrades. However, the level of cohesion achieved is not without conflict and strain.[40]

Several factors account for the difficulty in maintaining the kibbutz as a cohesive communal society. Demands for constant interaction with one's comrades make the pursuit of solitude a difficult undertaking. Keeping to oneself may be interpreted as a rejection of one's fellows. Constant social interaction renders the kibbutz an open society in which each is revealed to the community. There can be no secrets. The feeling of constantly being "naked" before the group may be a severe psychological strain. Finally, interpersonal disputes do occur. The cause may be jealousy over the allocation of consumer goods or perhaps competition for prestige at work. The problem is compounded because it is almost impossible for the antagonistic parties to avoid each other. Overt conflict is recognized as dangerous to the stability of the community; aggression is expressed through complaints and gossip, the latter being particularly prevalent.[41]

Cohesion in the kibbutz reflects the relationship between members of subgroups as well as the relationship between these members and the community as a whole. Since the family and the peer group are socializing agents, internal harmony within these groups is particularly significant. As family relations have become more important for the personal stability and collective cohesion of kibbutz members, they have become of greater concern to the community. Work and vacation schedules, for example, are adjusted so that husband and wife can spend free time together. Moreover, kibbutz norms now oppose both adultery and divorce. Either situation may result in extreme bitterness and jealousy among people who must maintain close contact with each other.[42]

Relationships among members of a peer group provide a foundation for future community cohesiveness among second- and third-generation kibbutz members. It is in these associations that the young experience a continuing lesson in sharing, cooperation, and mutual concern. Essentially, the training is successful. Sabras retain a commitment to cooperative living after they complete their education. Moreover, commitment to the peer group is generalized into a commitment to the kibbutz as a whole.

If relations within subgroups of the kibbutz are relatively harmonious, the same cannot be said for relations between subgroups. Periodic tensions occur between occupational and ethnic groups. However, the conflicts that are particularly persistent and disturbing are between different age and sex groups. Much of the problem of the aged results directly from the kibbutz's own value system. Founded by young pioneers, the kibbutz tends to glorify youth, strength, and vigor. The major basis of prestige is one's contribution to the work force, with the highest value placed on physical labor. To make matters worse, once a kibbutz member stops working, his dependence on his comrades cannot be experienced in a detached sense, as in the receipt of a pension check. Rather, he is in daily contact with those who work to support him, while he makes no economic contribution in return. Considering the above, it is hardly surprising that older kibbutz members hold onto their jobs as long as possible or that they have trouble adjusting to leisure when retirement can no longer be put off.

In addition to feeling that they comprise a subgroup whose problems do not receive sufficient attention, older kibbutz members also have strained relations with their opposite subgroup, the young. Part of this antagonism is structural. Since jobs in the kibbutz are allocated according to competence, there are no vested positions, and even long years of service in a production branch cannot long delay replacement if there are others more capable of performing the task. For the aged, this means that continued work in the branch of their choice is threatened by competition from stronger, and often better-educated, younger members.[43]

Conflict between the sexes in the kibbutz is evident in the discontent of women with their lot. One aspect of the kibbutz woman's unhappiness concerns the status of the family. Family life in the settlements was initially almost nonexistent. First-generation women who had been socialized in Europe found adjustment to such arrangements more difficult than did their male comrades. It was they who had to abandon their traditional social role and learn to perform jobs to which they were unaccustomed. Perhaps because of the impact of family models from outside the kibbutz, the image of deeper family relationships continues to be a disturbing influence. Many women resent the separation from their children required by the communal education system. Women are responsible for the expanded role of the family in kibbutz social life. Indeed, a prominent reason why women leave the kibbutz is their desire to devote more attention to the development of a full family life.

Family relationships are only part of the explanation. Status differentials and occupational restrictions also reduce women's satisfaction with kibbutz life. Kibbutz women may find themselves performing the same type of tasks as bourgeois housewives—only for 300 people rather than a single family. Often these jobs in the kitchen and the laundry are dreary and menial, offering little challenge or intrinsic reward. In addition, working conditions in the service sectors, where women predominate, are among the worst in the kibbutz, as allocations for innovations and labor-saving machinery are based on an ongoing set of priorities that favor the productive sectors.

Women's responses to their situation range from withdrawal to pressure for change. Most of the tension and almost all of the resignations arise from their dissatisfaction. Also, much of the pressure for more privacy, more private property, and higher consumption levels comes from women who seek to achieve in a private life gratification that they are denied in a communal one.[44]

Support. The kibbutz provides extensive economic security for its members. Whether they are old or young, more or less productive, healthy or ill, the community endeavors to satisfy their economic needs. It should be recognized, however, that the absolute level of security, the extent to which the kibbutz actually can guarantee to meet those needs, depends on the settlement's viability as an economic entity. In the early years, because of acute resource shortages, the standard of living in kibbutzim was uniformly low. Substantial progress has been made since that time, but the availability of consumer goods and physical comforts still requires an efficient productive base and thus varies with the economic capabilities of the community.

In addition to economic security, kibbutz life furnishes emotional and social support. A member always belongs to an ongoing social group. Even if his immediate family should die, he is still among comrades who can offer understanding and solace when needed. He has a legitimate status and will never face the isolation and anomymity that may occur in Western capitalist society. Of course, this does not mean that he can assume acceptance of anything he might do or say. However, as long as he stays within the boundaries of his community's norms and rules, his place is assured.[45]

Spontaneity. One might expect that the men and women who founded the kibbutz would place great value on personal freedom and political liberty. The ideology of their youth movements had emphasized spontaneity over planning in personal life. They had broken with the restrictions of their families, culture, and class and had adopted democratic, egalitarian, and socialist principles. In point of fact, the first efforts at settlement reflected just such an inclination. Kibbutz members opposed all form of authoritarianism; they saw formal organization itself as restrictive. Social and sexual mores became objects of innovation and experiment.

There were two serious flaws in this spontaneous approach to pioneering. First, it proved incompatible with communal living. An ongoing

group with collective objectives cannot function very long without discovering that the sum of spontaneous individual impulses does not always
coincide with communal needs. At some point, a man or a woman will be
required at the irrigation works when he or she would rather relax in the
sun. Every member must be willing to sacrifice his desires for the welfare of
his comrades; otherwise the group ceases to be a communal enterprise and
is reduced to a collection of individuals in the same geographical area.

Second, a fully spontaneous life-style could not meet the demands of
the physical environment. Farming cannot be performed according to one's
whims; it requires a set routine. In a harsh, inhospitable region, the necessary routine permits little margin for laxity. Furthermore, as agricultural
production becomes more intensive and complex, it requires greater organization.

In order to survive as communities, the kibbutzim accepted organization and collective self-discipline. Indeed, through the years, kibbutzim
may have undergone a sociological process akin to that described by Max
Weber as the "routinization of charisma." The basis of activity changed
from emotional fervor and moral resolve to rules and structure. Political
meetings, which once lacked chairmen and agenda, now exhibit both. Economic decisions are made through formal managerial offices and committees. Hours for work and dining become set, and the allocation of resources
is standardized. In brief, will is replaced by regulation, and spontaneity by
order. [46]

Restrictions on personal activity in the kibbutz economy occur in both
the productive and the distributive sectors. All members must work, sometimes at a job not of their own choosing. Specific occupations have their
own organizational requirements, for example, beginning at set hours and
demanding the performance of special tasks. In addition, because the kibbutz must regulate its labor supply, a member must receive formal permission before he can legitimately take time off from work and temporarily
leave the community. On the other hand, the kibbutz attempts to permit
flexibility and choice where possible. Managerial positions are rotated to
prevent authoritarianism, and workers actively participate in making decisions regarding their production sector. [47]

First-generation kibbutz members derived their normative commitment to observe community regulations from their social ideology and their
recognition of the environmental necessity of cooperation. Socialization of
second-generation members must include training in the subordination of
individual preferences to the needs of the community. In fact, one can
argue that the living experiences of kibbutz children now constitute a con-

stant repetition of such instruction. Children are taught that toys belong to the collective and must be shared, that the work responsibilities of their age group must be fulfilled, that once collective decisions are made they must be followed by all. These teachings are supported by the authority of adult instructors, youth-group leaders, and child-care workers and by the intense social pressure of the peer group.[48]

System Maintenance and System Change

Clarity. While some kibbutz regulations are unquestionably clear and well understood, there are large areas of behavior the propriety of which either remains in doubt or changes over the years. The root of this ambiguity lies in the fact that the kibbutz often operates on the basis of social norms rather than a codified legal system, with enforcement operating through relatively informal social processes. Violators may be subject to acute negative criticism from their comrades; however, the definition of an infraction depends upon a community decision as to its values. To the extent that these values are unclear, or disputed, or changing, the parameters of acceptable behavior are uncertain.

For example, one of the most basic principles of the kibbutz is that everyone must work. Even if a member receives a job assignment he does not like, he is still required to perform it. While this seems straightforward enough, there is some room for flexibility. A member is free to protest an unwanted assignment, and if he complains long enough and loud enough, he may very well secure a transfer. On the other hand, if no change is available and the member adamantly rejects performance of the assigned tasks, he will almost certainly be expelled. As another example, one observer cites the case of a couple who requested a leave of absence at the general meeting but were turned down. Despite the negative vote, they announced their determination to take the leave anyway. When it became apparent that they would carry out their stated intentions, they were expelled.[49]

Although the norms noted above were strictly enforced, there are numerous instances of violations of kibbutz values that go unpunished. In the kibbutz that he studied, Spiro observed two "flagrant" examples of the acquisition of private property: one member inherited an automobile; another couple received a refrigerator as a gift from relatives. At the time these events occurred, however, pressures for new consumption patterns were rising, and the norms concerning private property were in contention. In such a context of normative uncertainty, strict adherence to the older values cannot be maintained.[50]

From the perspective of maintaining the kibbutz as an ongoing community, lack of clarity may be beneficial. It permits flexibility in the face of changing environmental pressures, such as the rise in living standards in the rest of Israel. It prevents members from being forced out of the community for relatively trivial infractions. Perhaps most important, it permits the community's norms to evolve without destroying the unity of the settlements in the process. Members of a kibbutz may disagree on an issue; some may disagree enough to feel justified in violating a norm. Yet, as long as the issue is not pushed to the limit of decision, as long as a rigid position is not defended and enforced, both groups can continue to live in the same community until a new, enforceable consensus is reached.

Social Control. Kibbutzim are voluntarily created societies of equals: men and women joined together for the purpose of cooperation and mutual support. Therefore, their objectives of social control are distinct from those common to stratified societies in which elites must struggle to maintain their privileges. There is little preoccupation with the prevention of serious antisocial conduct, for the basic level of interpersonal trust and commitment among the membership renders such behavior almost inconceivable. Rather, kibbutz rules are essentially oriented toward encouraging members to be "good" comrades: individuals who participate in communal activity, accept their work responsibilities, and abide by collective decisions.

It is a normal expectation in the kibbutz that individuals will dutifully follow community regulations with no other incentive than conscience and commitment. After all, every member chose to join the community and is free to leave if he finds it no longer meets his needs. Still, infractions do occur, and mechanisms of social control, both formal and informal, attempt to counteract them. Informal pressures are usually the first to be directed at an offender, the basic method of transmitting social criticism being public opinion. Since kibbutz members have limited privacy, they are open to observation and judgment by their peers. Furthermore, candor in social intercourse is a kibbutz norm. Thus, those who violate a rule are quickly noticed and quickly receive harsh and public comment from their fellows.

If informal processes are unsuccessful, the offender may be threatened with having his case brought before the general meeting, where he would be subject to the criticism of the entire community. This is considered a serious sanction by individuals whose social relations are essentially restricted to that small group. If the individual persists in his behavior, the threat is carried out and the entire issue aired in public discussion. If the general meeting agrees that the acts in question are unacceptable and the individual persists in refusing to comply, then the kibbutz may impose its most severe penalty, expulsion.[51]

Innovation. The kibbutz itself is a social experiment. It has undergone innumerable innovations since its inception. There is simply no question that kibbutzim are open to modification and change. In almost every critical situation, new programs have been devised to counteract destabilizing tendencies.

Women's dissatisfaction with kibbutz life has been a major target of social innovation. New fields designed to provide new occupational options for women have been established. Expanded opportunities for extra training have permitted the professionalization of jobs generally held by women, thus increasing their status. Increased mechanization has liberated many women from long, tedious hours of physical labor. Where a job remains distasteful despite efforts at improvement, it may be filled by rotation so that the burden is spread among the membership. Progressive change is also taking place in other aspects of kibbutz life relevant to women. Attempts are being made to equalize representation by sex on decision-making committees. In addition, greater flexibility in child-rearing arrangements, permitting closer contact between mothers and their children, as well as a general increase in the social acceptance of family interests, constitutes an effort to enrich the personal lives of kibbutz women.[52]

Innovations have also been applied to the problems of the aged. Since retirement is often resisted by older members, kibbutzim have sought to locate or create employment suitable to their capacities. Jobs are specially analyzed for their appropriateness for older workers. In some cases, tasks are subdivided so that they provide an independent function that an older member can perform without taking orders from a younger one. Kibbutzim have developed flexible retirement regulations so that specific cases can be handled according to individual needs. For those members who have given up work, the kibbutz promotes a variety of leisure and cultural activities. Kibbutzim are also beginning experiments with new forms of dwellings for the aged. Some settlements place the elderly in small apartments next to the quarters of their children; others are considering segregated areas where services designed for the aged can be economically furnished.[53]

As a final example, we consider the development of kibbutz industry, a single innovation that has contributed to the resolution of several problems confronting the settlements. Although kibbutz productive sectors are predominantly agricultural, there has been a substantial increase in the diversification of the kibbutz economy through the addition of small industrial plants.

Since industry is more profitable than farming, it brings in the new revenue needed to satisfy the members' rising expectations. Also, industry provides additional forms of employment, some of which are particularly suited to meet the desires of the kibbutz work force. Women and older workers can find income-producing tasks in the factory that do not require extended physical exertion. Younger members are able to receive assignments involving technical sophistication; these jobs may also serve as a functional rationale for the provision of expanded educational options. Another impressive aspect of kibbutz industry is that it has been structured so as not to interfere with the fundamentally egalitarian relationships among kibbutz members. The kibbutzim in general have been quite successful in transferring their techniques of managerial rotation and worker participation from the agricultural fields to the factory.[54]

In light of the above evidence, the kibbutzim must be credited with successfully employing innovation to cope with disequilibrating forces in their social system. However, if one focuses on the impact of innovation on the kibbutz value system, the results are less sanguine. With the adoption of new structures and procedures, many of the principles that the first settlers considered crucial to their vision of a better society have been compromised. The kibbutz member is no longer fundamentally a communal being; family life and private interests account for significant and expanding amounts of his time and interest. Private property in consumer goods, once anathema, now exists and expands, although the means of production remain firmly under collective control. Particularly in industry, but also in agriculture, the kibbutz has resorted to hired labor. Over half of all industrial workers are employees from outside the community.[55]

In brief, the kibbutz movement has accepted innovations designed to ensure the continuity of the settlements at the cost of yielding some of its ideological convictions. Only time will tell whether this position constitutes expediency or wisdom, whether it forebodes the decline of utopia or represents a necessary feature of the struggle to realize utopia.

REFERENCES AND NOTES

1. Kanovsky, E. *The economy of the Israeli kibbutz.* Harvard University Press, Cambridge, Mass.: 1966, pp. 19–21, 147.

2. Orni, E., and Efrat, E., *Geography of Israel.* Jerusalem: Israel Program for Scientific Translations, 1966, pp. 3–126.

3. Infield, H., *Cooperative living in Palestine.* London: Kegan Paul, 1946, pp. 20–22. See also: Cohen, R. *The kibbutz settlement: Principals and processes.* Israel: Hakibbutz Hameuchad, 1972; Gorkin, M. *Border kibbutz.* New York: Hart,

1971, p. 201; Rokach, A. Land and water. In J. Ben-David (Ed.), *Agricultural planning and village community in Israel*. Belgium: UNESCO, 1964.

4. For a brief description of the development of kibbutz and Israeli agriculture, see: Rokach, A. The development of agriculture in Palestine and Israel. In J. Ben-David, op. cit., pp. 21–30.

5. Orni and Efrat, op. cit., p. 232.

6. Ibid., pp. 232–233. See also: Spiro, M. *Venture in utopia*. New York: Schocken Books, 1956 (hereafter *Venture*), pp. 64–65.

7. Spiro, *Venture*, op. cit., pp. 39–50. See also: Bettelheim, B. *Children of the Dream*. London: Collier-MacMillan Ltd., 1969, pp. 20–22; Eisenstadt, S. N. *Israeli society*. New York: Basic Books, 1967, p. 238; Talmon, Y. *Family and community in the kibbutz*. Cambridge, Mass.: Harvard University Press, 1972, pp. 3–4.

8. Kanovsky, op. cit., pp. 17–20.

9. Orni and Efrat, op. cit., pp. 171–183; Eisenstadt, op. cit., pp. 7–33; Stern, B. *The kibbutz that was*. Washington, D.C.: Public Affairs Press, 1965, pp. 4–22.

10. Curtis, M. Utopia and the kibbutz. In M. Curtis and M. S. Chertoff, *Israel: Social structure and change*. New Brunswick, N.J.: Transaction Books, 1973, p. 108. For a broader discussion of the changing characteristics of immigrants to Israel following independence, see: Matras, J. *Social change in Israel*. Chicago: Aldine Publishing Co., 1965, pp. 53–85.

11. Kanovsky, op. cit., p. 61; Spiro, *Venture*, op. cit., pp. 60–63, 78, 108; Talmon, op. cit., pp. 2–6, 10, 118–119, 166–180.

12. Spiro, *Venture*, op. cit., p. 28; Leon, D. *The kibbutz: A new way of life*. Oxford: Pergamon Press, 1969, pp. 70–71. For an example of competition between productive branches in the kibbutz over relative profitability, see: Kanovsky, op. cit., pp. 46–47.

13. Spiro, *Venture*, op. cit., pp. 221–235; Talmon, op. cit., pp. 18–20. For an analysis of the causes of women's discontents in the kibbutz, see: Keller, S. The family in the kibbutz: What lessons for us. In Curtis and Chertoff, op. cit., pp. 115–144.

14. Spiro, *Venture*, op. cit., pp. 94–96; Stern, op. cit., pp. 137–149.

15. Talmon, op. cit., p. 186–187.

16. Ibid., p. 199. Also see: pp. 196–200.

17. Ibid., pp. 188–189; Leon, op. cit., p. 72.

18. Spiro, *Venture*, op. cit., p. 93.

19. Gorkin, op. cit., pp. 229–230. See also: Spiro, op. cit., pp. 198–200.

20. Bettleheim, op. cit., pp. 20–22; Cohen, op. cit., pp. 288–289; Infield, op. cit., pp. 12–15; Spiro, *Venture*, op. cit., pp. 19–23, 43–48.

21. Spiro, *Venture*, op. cit., pp. 71–74; Leon, op. cit., pp. 37–39, 47–51; Kanovsky, op. cit., pp. 52–64; Cohen, op. cit., pp. 69–231.

22. Kanovsky, op. cit., pp. 31–41, 74–125; Cohen, op. cit., pp. 20–57; Leon, op. cit., pp. 34–35, 56–62.

23. Spiro, *Venture,* op. cit., pp. 78–83; Kanovsky, op. cit., pp. 24–25. Also see: Ben-David, J. The kibbutz and the moshav. In J. Ben-David (Ed.), op. cit., pp. 54–55.
24. Bettelheim, op. cit., p. 224; Talmon, op. cit., p. 119. For further discussion on the motivations of kibbutz workers, see: Spiro, *Venture,* op. cit., pp. 82–90; Leon, op. cit., pp. 77–78.
25. Bettelheim, op. cit., pp. 163–164. Also see: Talmon, op. cit., pp. 118–124; Kanovsky, op. cit., pp. 37–41.
26. Talmon, op. cit., pp. 45–46; Spiro, *Venture,* op. cit., pp. 77–78; Cohen, op. cit., p. 306.
27. Spiro, *Venture,* op. cit., pp. 19–23, 106–107; Leon, op. cit., pp. 32–33; Talmon, op. cit., p. 208.
28. Talmon, op. cit., pp. 206–213. For additional discussion of collective consumption on the kibbutz, see: Leon, op. cit., pp. 79–91.
29. Spiro, *Venture,* op. cit., pp. 110–124; Infield, op. cit., pp. 19–20.
30. Bettelheim, op. cit., pp. 18–19; Spiro, *Venture,* op. cit., pp. 126–127.
31. For statistics cited, see: Talmon, op. cit., p. 85 (Table 13). Discussions of parent–child relationships in kibbutzim can be found in Talmon, op. cit., pp. 84–86; Spiro, *Venture,* op. cit., pp. 124–130; Bettelheim, op. cit., pp. 70, 73–78, 109–116, 131–135.
32. Bettelheim, op. cit., pp. 100–109, 187; Leon, op. cit., pp. 104–106; Spiro, *Venture,* op. cit., pp. 121–122, 275–277.
33. Spiro, *Venture,* op. cit., pp. 128–135, 139, 277, 280–283; Bettelheim, op. cit., pp. 159–165, 208, 223–226, 242, 335–336; Leon, op. cit., pp. 97–104.
34. Spiro, *Venture,* op. cit., pp. 133–136; Bettelheim, op. cit., pp. 85–92, 115–116, 127–130; Leon, op. cit., pp. 110–111. Two studies that focus on childhood in the kibbutz are: Rabin, A. I. *Growing up in the kibbutz.* New York: Springer, 1965; Spiro, M. *Children of the kibbutz.* New York: Schocken Books, 1965 (hereafter *Children*).
35. Diamond, cited in Bettelheim, op. cit., p. 227. See also Talmon, op. cit., pp. 80–81; Spiro, *Venture,* op. cit., p. 69. For photographs of a kibbutz dining-hall, see: Leon, op. cit., Figs. 8 and 9.
36. Bettelheim, op. cit., pp. 26, 27, 73, 151–153; Talmon, op. cit., pp. 74–76, 80–82; Gorkin, op. cit., pp. 60–61; Stern, op. cit., pp. 64–66. For a pessimistic view of the prospects of the communal dining-hall, see: Stern, op. cit., 140–142.
37. Spiro, *Venture,* op. cit., pp. 91–92, 211, 268–269; Gorkin, op. cit., 48–51, 220–232; Leon, op. cit., pp. 64–65.
38. Spiro, *Venture,* op. cit., pp. 10–38, 258–260; Stern, op. cit., pp. 69–83.
39. Talmon, op. cit., pp. 203–243; Spiro, *Venture,* op. cit., pp. 236–239, 249–250, 263–268, 278–280; Leon, op. cit., pp. 143–144.
40. Spiro, *Venture,* op. cit., 29–32, 53–56; Bettelheim, op. cit., pp. 85–92, 160, 250–251.

41. Spiro, *Venture,* op. cit., pp. 30–31, 103–107, 204; Gorkin, op. cit., pp. 134, 177, 186. For a discussion of the psychological cost of enforcing cohesion in the community, see: Bettelheim, op. cit., pp. 248–251, 259–261.

42. Spiro, *Children,* op. cit., pp. 347–349; Bettelheim, op. cit., pp. 237–239. For a structural–functional explanation of kibbutz marriage patterns, see: Talmon, op. cit., pp. 139–165.

43. Spiro, *Venture,* op. cit., pp. 219–220, 255–256, 279, 289–290. See: Talmon, op. cit., pp. 166–181.

44. Talmon, op. cit., pp. 37–39; Spiro, *Venture,* op. cit., pp. 221–235. See also Keller, S. The family in the kibbutz: What lessons for us. In Curtis and Chertoff, op. cit., pp. 115–144; Leon, op. cit., pp. 128–136.

45. Bettelheim, op. cit., pp. 174–175, 248.

46. Infield, op. cit., pp. 19–20; Talmon, op. cit., pp. 2–3.

47. Talmon, op. cit., pp. 43–44; Spiro, *Venture,* op. cit., pp. 204–205; Bettelheim, op. cit., pp. 216–220; Leon, op. cit., pp. 84–88.

48. Bettelheim, op. cit., pp. 211–213, 232–235. See also: pp. 125–131, 181–184, 231; Leon, op. cit., pp. 97–104.

49. Spiro, *Venture,* op. cit., pp. 77, 103.

50. Ibid., pp. 207–208.

51. Ibid., pp. 94–104; Bettelheim, op. cit., pp. 50, 229–230; Leon, op. cit., pp. 75–77.

52. Talmon, op. cit., pp. 42–48; Spiro, *Venture,* op. cit., p. 287.

53. Talmon, op. cit., pp. 176–180.

54. See: Rosner, M. Worker participation in decision-making in kibbutz industry. In Curtis and Chertoff, op. cit., pp. 145–158; Leviatan, U. The industrial process in Israeli kibbutzim: Problems and solutions. In Curtis and Chertoff, op. cit., pp. 159–172. For additional data on kibbutz industry, see: Stern, op. cit., pp. 35–51.

55. For discussions of the problem of hired labor on the kibbutz, see: Kanovsky, op. cit., pp. 64–67; Stern, op. cit., pp. 104–117.

CHAPTER 5

The New Town of Columbia, Maryland*

INTRODUCTION

The United States of America has become an urban nation. Since 1920, when a census first showed that more of the population was living in urban than in rural areas, the trend toward urbanization has transformed American life. By 1970, 74% of the population lived in cities of more than 2500; 69% in one of the 243 "standard metropolitan statistical areas" (consisting of a core city of at least 50,000 plus contiguous urbanized counties). These megalopolises—263 as of 1972—for the most part exhibit a now familiar pattern: an inner city of older buildings, high in density, whose shrinking population consists increasingly of the black, the poor, and the old; and a spreading suburban ring, defended by zoning, of low-density housing occupied mainly by middle-class whites, many of whom commute to jobs in the city.[1]

Few believe this sociological and economic cleavage to be healthy—for the suburbanite or for the inner-city dweller. The cities, losing their most taxable citizens, are left with a bitter and dependent population. And the suburbanite finds long commutes wearying and the cultural life less than stimulating. Both life-styles lack what some observers have struggled to define as a sense of "community," of belonging and relatedness. Yet, given a choice between the two, most Americans have been opting for suburbia;

---

* This chapter is co-authored with Constance Hellyer.

127

80% of the total population increase in our metropolitan areas has occurred in the suburbs.[2]

Suburban growth has occurred in the absence of any national policy or program, as has the development of individual suburbs. "Our cities grow by accident," observed James Rouse, a Maryland mortgage banker and developer who founded the new city of Columbia:

> A farm is sold and begins raising houses instead of potatoes—then another farm. . . . kids overflow the schools—here a new school is built—then a church. . . . Traffic grows; roads are widened; service stations, Tastee Freez, hamburger stands pockmark the highway. Traffic strangles. Relentlessly, the bits and pieces of a city are splattered across the landscape. By this irrational process, non-communities are born—formless places, without order, beauty or reason; with no visible respect for people or the land. Thousands of small, separate decisions—made with little or no relationship to one another, nor to their composite impact—produce a major decision about the future of our cities and our civilization—a decision we have come to label "suburban sprawl."[3]

Rouse felt the results of such helter-skelter development to be "anti-human":

> The vast, formless spread of housing, pierced by the unrelated spotting of schools, churches, stores, creates areas so huge and irrational that they are out of scale with people—beyond their grasp and comprehension—too big for people to feel a part of, responsible for, important in. The individual is immersed in the mass. What nonsense this is. What reckless, irresponsible dissipation of nature's endowment and man's hopes for dignity, beauty, growth.[4]

Feeling strongly that there was a better way to accommodate to America's growing population and its taste for suburban amenities, Rouse set out to create a development in which that elusive "sense of community" would be fostered: the new city of Columbia, Maryland.

The "New Towns movement," as a utopian—or at least reformist—effort at creating an alternative and superior form of city life, owes its recent impetus to the work of an Englishman, Ebenezer Howard (1850–1928). In the England of Howard's day, industrialization had created a rearrangement of the population, which, while somewhat different from that in contemporary America, still represented a drastic and unplanned change. People swarmed from the countryside to the industrial centers, aptly described by Howard (a Londoner) as "crowded, ill-ventilated, unplanned, unwieldy, unhealthy cities—ulcers on the very face of our beautiful island."[5] As the key to the evolution of a "higher and better form of industrial life," Howard put forward his far-reaching and audacious proposal: the creation of clusters of wholly new "garden cities," where, through careful and unified advance planning, a balance could be achieved between the urban and the rural, agriculture and industry, individual well-being and community life.

The specifics of the plan advanced by Howard related mainly to the physical layout of the new city. (He had flirted with but abandoned the idea of a "cooperative commonwealth" in which businesses would be owned by the public, choosing instead what he called "social individualism." [6]) His plan began with the acquisition of about 6000 rural acres by a group who would oversee the financing and planning of the city. Only 1000 acres would be taken up by the city proper, the surrounding green area being retained for agriculture and parkland and serving as a physical barrier to expansion. Population and land increase would take place by the establishment of additional towns, so that the population of each could continue to enjoy a "healthy, natural, and economic combination of town and country life." Economic balance would be achieved by the proximity of farms to markets and by the establishment in the city (on its periphery) of industries, warehouses, and the like. The city center would contain a large market and commercial establishments, as well as a park and cultural institutions.

Residences for the city's population of 30,000–50,000 (which should represent all classes) would be divided into at least six "wards" (or neighborhoods), each with a school and a store to serve daily needs, and all within walking distance of the city center and of the peripheral industries and the greenbelt.

Howard was attacked as both utopian and impractical. The Marxist weekly, *Justice,* for one, sniffed that "towns are not created; they grow," to which Howard replied, "towns have grown: ours shall be built." [7] Howard himself went on to participate in the founding of Letchworth (1903) and Welwyn (1919–1920) garden cities. His proposals were revived, some years later, with the New Towns Act of 1946. Through this and subsequent legislation, more than 25 New Towns, with a projected combined population of nearly 2 million, have been planned in Great Britain. [8]

James Rouse, the founder of Columbia, Maryland, shared with Ebenezer Howard a utopian vision: "Our cities are for people. . . . We should begin our total plan and program with the first and fundamental purpose of making a city into neighborhoods where a man, his wife, and family can live and work and above all else grow—grow in character, in personality, in love of God and neighbor, and in the capacity for joyous living." [9]

Rouse was, however, an atypical utopian, for he had no very fixed social structure or institutions in mind for achieving this kind of community—other than the assumption that the American-style nuclear family would be its basic unit. A practical developer, his first move was to commission a study of the economic feasibility and potential profitability of a city-sized development. Realistically, Columbia could never have come into being without the mobilization of large amounts of investment capital made available in anticipation of a substantial profit.[10] Rouse was not, however, a typical developer either, for the planning process that followed included not only the usual architects, site planners, and engineers, but also a team of experts in the fields of government and local administration, family living, recreation, social structure, economics, education, health and welfare, and community and communications. Rouse urged this team to be, in effect, utopian:

> Let's examine the optimums. What would be the best possible school system in a city of 100,000—the best health system? How might religion be made most effective in the growth of people? With shorter work weeks and increasing wages, what opportunities can be made available for better use of leisure time? . . . Can the relationship of home, school, church and community be such that there is some alternative to loneliness, some relief from fear and hate? In what size community do people feel the most comfortable? In what kind of community the most challenged? The most creative? Don't worry for the moment about feasibility. It will compromise us soon enough. Let's look at what might be and be invigorated by it.[11]

The outcome was not, however, particularly startling. Although "community" was much on the minds of the working group, they were not tempted to any radical departures, such as communal living or dining arrangements. Instead they proposed institutes devoted to the "living sciences" and to "family life"; flexible day-care facilities; preventive health, welfare, and dental programs; an emphasis on public transportation; a comprehensive, all-ages, year-round educational program; a multitude of cultural, recreational, athletic, and nature-study programs; planned teen-age activities; and so forth.

Ultimately, all such utopian or "optimum" proposals had in fact to pass an economic test. For as a 1960s private enterprise development in the United States of America, Columbia had to make money. As Jim Rouse put it with disarming honesty, "Unless Columbia makes an outrageous profit, it's a failure." [12] He was aware that if Columbia became a losing proposition, it would be an unrepeated experiment rather than a prototype for a new generation of sensitively designed cities.

A second constraint on utopian planning was the governmental context. Columbia was to be located in Howard County, subject to its zoning laws, building code, educational system, and public health regulations. Inevitably, some adjustments of the plan were required to meet the fears and objections of that rural county. The Rouse group and the county commissioners were able to work out a "New Town" amendment to the existing zoning ordinance, an amendment that represented a compromise between the desires of each. Agreement had also to be reached with the county board of education on the location and size of the schools—an important issue for Columbia's planners since the catchment area of the local elementary school was to determine the boundaries of the social "neighborhood."

A third constraint on utopian social planning was fundamental. Rouse was not, strictly speaking, in the business of creating communities per se but rather the "shells" for communities: the physical setting, the buildings, the facilities. What would occur between people in those settings was another matter. Although an attempt was made to "preservice" the community with institutions, there were limits to how many the development company could afford to underwrite or subsidize. And so community-building necessarily became decentralized, as different institutions and methods were used.

One technique was to seek out American institutions that were successful examples, or "living answers," to the questions raised and to invite them to move to or to establish a branch in Columbia.[13] Among those enlisted were Antioch College (Antioch–Columbia), Johns Hopkins University (the medical plan), and the Peabody Museum. Other efforts to indirectly shape the social life of Columbia included not only the physical planning but the choice and location of commercial enterprises, some of which were to serve social functions (such as the "Mom and Pop" neighborhood stores). Facilities were built for community centers, teen centers, and so on, with the hope that social cohesion would be facilitated. Even the religious institutions were shaped by the persuasive efforts of Rouse (himself a Presbyterian elder), who brought together local churchmen of various denominations and encouraged them to think in ecumenical terms about the role that the churches could play in the new city.

Columbia thus represents an earnest and self-conscious attempt to create—within the constraints of the American market economy and social system—"the best possible environment for the growth of people."[14] If it is not quite a "new America," it is an ambitious prototype of "The Next America" (as characterized by its promoters). In the words of Morton Hoppenfeld, Columbia's director of planning and design, "it should be a valuable social experiment to observe the evolution of this city whose developers seek to balance social goals and private profit." [15]

ECOLOGICAL DIMENSIONS

Geographic Features

Unlike most utopists, who seek a degree of geographic isolation for their new communities, Columbia's planners sought close proximity to population centers. The reasons were purely economic. As William Finley explained,

> First, the site had to be located in the magnetic field of a growing metropolitan area. It could not be built in an area set apart, because houses cannot be built without jobs nearby. . . . Secondly, it had to be a location where a major highway system already existed or was planned. [16]

Central Howard County, Maryland met these specifications exactly: situated between the expanding cities of Baltimore and Washington, D.C., whose beltways are separated by only 20 miles, it was largely undeveloped but would soon be crisscrossed by several highways, four of them linking the two cities. Thus, when a large parcel of 1039 acres came on the market, roughly halfway between the two cities, Rouse moved swiftly to buy it up and went on to acquire as much of the adjacent land as possible.

The target area was in more than 600 parcels, including some small subdivisions. Rouse was able to piece together 15,200 acres, but large enclaves of non-Columbia holdings remain. In fact, as many as 6000 Howard County residents—20% of its voters—found themselves engulfed by the new city. Internally, then, Columbia is not a cohesive geographic entity, which creates problems not only in physical design but in social and political relationships.

Early in the planning process, proposals were made—and rejected—to define the external boundaries of Columbia by the creation of an encircling greenbelt. But with 20% of Columbia's land already earmarked for open space, Rouse could not afford another 3000 acres for a greenbelt. As a consequence, Columbia may in time find itself engulfed by the waves of uncontrolled development pouring into the gap between Baltimore and Washington.

The land acquired by Rouse was fertile and well watered, but Rouse's company was not interested in the agricultural potential of the land. The new city would draw on the existing American food market. Likewise, the basic utilities, such as electricity, water, and telephones, would be provided by exterior organizations. Sewage would be disposed of through the county's Savage plant on the Little Patuxent River (from whence it eventually empties into Chesapeake Bay) and solid garbage would end up in the county's sanitary landfill.

The early development of Columbia (in the mid-1960s) predated the rise of an "ecological consciousness" in America, and its planning shows it. However, the environment was highly valued as an *aesthetic* resource. The planners were very concerned with preserving the more attractive features of the landscape, which included three major stream valleys and over 3000 acres of woodland. They even created new geographical features, such as the 32-acre Lake Kittamaqundi. Trees were surveyed and stockpiled for future landscaping. And where unattractive commercial areas had intruded, as along U.S. Highway 29, they were purchased only to be demolished.

Architectural Features

Ebenezer Howard's diagram of the "garden city" was arranged in concentric circles, with parks, shopping, and major public buildings at the center, surrounded by a ring of pie-shaped "wards" (or neighborhoods). The next ring consisted of the industrial areas alongside a circular railway, and finally there was the broad outer ring of agriculture and open space, the greenbelt. The model contained the essential elements of a balanced city, where industry, agriculture, residences, commerce, culture, and education each had their appropriate location planned in advance.

This too was the goal of the Columbia planners (with the exception of the greenbelt). Their site, however, lacked physical cohesion. Nonetheless, the resultant plan of the new city is in many respects an organic and free-form version of the Howard diagram—modified in relation to the natural features of the landscape, ownership patterns, and the locations of county roads and highways. Business and major cultural facilities are central, while industrial areas are outlying or along major arteries. And residential areas (subdivided into smaller units around local schools and facilities) lie in between. However, the residential areas are not all contiguous, and the open space, instead of being concentrated in the center (and the periphery), meanders through the city following stream courses and other natural features.

The resulting city plan is irregular and to a degree broken up, but then a "big concentrated city plan" had not been the planner's intent. "Personally," said Rouse in 1962, "I hold some very unscientific conclusions to the effect that people grow best in small communities . . . that a broader range of friendships and relationships occurs in a village or small town than in a city; that there is a greater sense of responsibility for one's neighbor and also a greater sense of support by one's fellow man in a small town than in a city." [17] Accordingly, the residential areas, already to a degree separated, were broken further into subunits, or "neighborhoods" (comparable to Ebenezer Howard's wards), in which the planners hoped the advantages of city life would be combined with the virtues sentimentally attributed to the vanishing small town.

The working group had also been concerned with the problems of scale, but mostly in relation to the educational system. Schools, they felt, should be the focal point of a community, open to community activities and involving people of all ages. Ultimately, the size of the "neighborhood" came to be the catchment area for an elementary school of the size approved by the Howard County school system (optimally 600 pupils, but with a minimum of 510) [18]—larger than the planners had initially hoped but still small enough to be within walking distance of the whole neighborhood.

The "neighborhood" was seen as the locus of "the most place-bound members of the urban community, mothers and young children," and an effort was made to create near the school the kinds of facilities that would be useful to this constituency: a convenience store with a coffee bar (ideally run by friendly "Mom and Pop" proprietors); a "tot lot" (playground for small children); a swimming pool with snack bar; and a community center, consisting mainly of a multipurpose meeting room for neighborhood business and socializing. It was also assumed that the elementary school and its adjacent play areas would be useful to the rest of the community during non-school-hours.

Within the neighborhood (population 2000–5000), social interaction was further encouraged by the arrangement of houses around cul-de-sacs, the absence of fences, and the establishment of group mail boxes. Internal pedestrian walkways were laid out to make it unnecessary to resort to the automobile within the neighborhood. Thus every effort was made in the physical arrangements of the neighborhood to create an intimate community, where people would find it easy to get together. Nonetheless, the family home (or apartment) remained the irreducible architectural unit; Columbia's planners intended to bolster rather than to break up the nuclear family.

The design of individual housing (which includes apartments, townhouses, condominiums, and detached, single-family houses) was left to dozens of commercial homebuilders to whom the developer sold land. The builder's main architectural criterion has been acceptability to buyers in their (above-average) price range. The resulting lack of architectural consistency or distinction in Columbia has been unfavorably compared with nearby Reston, Virginia, another planned community. However, the developers have evolved a procedure for architectural review and control to ensure that the exteriors of the buildings are minimally tasteful. They seem to have succeeded: at least 75% of residents participating in a neighborhood survey felt that their neighborhood was more attractive than where they had lived previously.[19]

In Ebenezer Howard's plan, there had been no intermediate level of organization between the wards or neighborhoods (population about 5000) and the city as a whole (population perhaps 30,000). However, Columbia was to be a city of over 100,000—which its planners felt to be the minimum consistent with a good job base; adequate health, education, and recreation programs; and a sizable market for diverse consumer goods. The planners therefore grouped the neighborhoods, in clusters of two to four, into "villages"—seven in all, each having a population of 10,000–15,000. The villages, like the neighborhoods they embraced, were, in theory, to be centered on schools—the secondary schools whose pupils were to be drawn from the constituent neighborhoods. The village level would also provide an adequate catchment area for the kinds of frequently used shopping and services needed in a small town: a supermarket, a barbershop, a beauty salon, a gas station, a restaurant, a bakery, a bank, a pharmacy, a doctor's office, and a religious center or church. The plan also dictated a village community center and at least one major recreational facility (e.g., skating rink, miniature golf, athletic club, or Olympic-size swimming pool) of citywide utility.

As the neighborhoods are clustered around the village center, so too are the seven villages clustered around the city center or "downtown," where, quite logically, are found the major shopping center—the Columbia Mall—and such urban features as large office buildings, a hotel, a hospital, a cinema, college-level educational facilities, insurance and employment agencies, a post office, and a variety of stores and shops offering such luxury items as "Toys for Men" and rental tuxedos. The city center, which fronts on Lake Kittamaqundi, also contains a major, 40-acre park, where the 5000-seat Merriweather Post Pavilion of Music has been constructed. Other major recreational facilities—such as golf courses, tennis courts, a riding club, and a hunting preserve—are scattered throughout the city.

The Columbia Plan, as it has come to be called, also reserves about

20% of the land area for business and light industry, with the latter spotted about the periphery of the city. One of the goals of the planners was to provide as many as half the resident workers with employment in Columbia, eliminating the geographic isolation between job and home, thus making fathers more available to their families.

A great deal of thought was given to the question of transportation. Within the neighborhood, distances were kept small, so that a child could easily walk to school, the neighborhood center, or a playground, and walkways were provided for that purpose. A Columbia Association neighborhood survey showed that the children do get around the neighborhood mostly on foot but that the adults still use cars rather heavily.[20]

Pedestrianways and bikeways to the village and city centers are not as well developed, but there has been an effort to make public bus transportation available. Utilization of the buses has been low, and the system runs on a subsidy from Rouse's development company. In general, the affluence of Columbia's populace (60% own two or more cars and only 3% own none) makes it easy for them to spurn public transportation in favor of private cars. The heavy reliance on cars (51% of the Columbia neighborhood-survey sample actually said their car use had *increased* since they had moved to Columbia) [21] has been a disappointment to the planners.

Rouse and his colleagues did, however, accomplish a great deal through planning. A heavy investment was made in both space and construction for commercial and recreational facilities and community centers, all in advance of the arrival of residents. Consequently, this allocation of land was made without empirical knowledge of what the actual demand would be for such facilities. Such advance planning is inevitably a kind of gamble, an act of faith, a set of assumptions or hopes as to how people will behave in a given setting. Thus, such planning must be based on certain assumptions as to what people are like. Human behavior is still, however, somewhat unpredictable, and, to complicate matters, the people who came to Columbia were in many respects atypical.

THE HUMAN AGGREGATE

Columbia was initially conceived of as an economically and racially diverse city. In fact, Rouse made headlines when he declared that he would sell to all qualified buyers, despite a recent Maryland vote against requiring open occupancy in public accommodations. Rouse's pledge has been carried out, and over 16% of Columbia residents belong to racial minorities (mainly black). A survey of 63 new American communities and large-scale developments made by the Department of Housing and Urban Development shows this to be an exceptional achievement: every community surveyed other than Columbia was less than 10% black.[22] (Columbia's blacks are solidly middle-class: half of the black families had, in 1973, an income of over $20,000, and only 12.6% earned less than $10,000.[23])

The dream of economic integration has been harder to achieve. Rouse once pledged that everyone who worked in Columbia—from the janitor to the corporation president—should be able to live there. But, in fact, the economic realities of the free-enterprise housing market have skewed the housing opportunities of Columbia, to the detriment of those at the lower end of the income distribution. For if Columbia was to be a profitable enterprise for its developers, it had to be aimed at "that majority segment of the population which is economically viable and in the market." [24] Housing for other groups had to be constructed on the margin of profit or subsidized from without the Rouse organization. At present, only 6% of Columbia's housing is priced for low-income residents.

The shortfall in low-income housing has been blamed variously on a lack of commitment by the Rouse company, lack of funding by the federal government, and zoning limitations by the county. In working out the New Town amendment to the county zoning laws, the Howard County commissioners had indeed been concerned about density, requiring that no less than 60% of the total area of the new city be taken up by open space and single-family detached houses, while attached dwellings (apartments and townhouses) could take up no more than 10%. Since the more land a dwelling occupies, the more it costs the developer, these density limitations have also limited lower-income housing. A request for the rezoning of a tract on which the Rouse company wanted to build cheap housing was recently turned down by the county commissioners.[25]

Not surprisingly, then, Columbia's population is affluent. In a 1973 survey, 68.5% of the families earned more than $15,000 a year, 43.5% more than $20,000, and 12% more than $30,000. The median family income in 1975 was estimated to be over $24,000.[26] As one would expect in these income brackets, most household heads in Columbia—76% according to one survey—hold professional or managerial positions. The balance is made up of other white-collar (12.7%) and blue-collar (11.4%) workers and a few unemployed (4.1%).[27]

Columbia's population consists primarily of young families, which makes it more like a new suburb or a Levittown than a large city. Of its adults, 80% are married, and 66% of the households have children (the average household size is 3.2 persons). The household head is usually a male (84%) and usually employed full time (93.4%). The relative youth of the community is shown by the median age of the household head (34.4 years); only 2% of the household heads are retired.[28]

For such families, however, there is a wide choice of housing in the Baltimore–Washington area. So while Columbia cannot be said to be an intentional community in the usual sense, those who choose to live there are to a degree self-selected. The reasons given by Columbians for choosing that city differ from those given by residents of a nearby control community of similar socioeconomic complexion. (For instance, 47% felt that the overall planning of the community was a plus, while those in the control community found that aspect neglible in their choice.) And Columbians also turned out to be somewhat different sociologically from those becoming residents in the control community, particularly in their higher level of education: 90% of the household heads (usually male) and 63% of the second household adults (usually wives) have at least attended college; more than 40% of the household heads and 15.5% of their mates have studied on the postgraduate level.[30]

Survey results also indicate that Columbians, like their counterparts in other planned communities, are somewhat more liberal and cosmopolitan than the average urban American. They feel more comfortable with people of other races and religions, are more likely to want to live in a foreign country, are less likely to be status conscious, and so forth.[31] (See pp. 149–150).

In sum, the resident population of Columbia is drawn largely from the pool of economically viable home-buyers who populate the suburbs of America. (Given the financial requirements for private developers and home buyers, it could not be otherwise.) However, the Columbia population represents a special subsample of this pool. Given Columbia's unusual degree of planning and of racial integration, prospective residents inevitably sorted themselves out, and those who chose Columbia turned out to be very highly educated, politically liberal, and concerned with community life and interested in community participation. To some extent, their interests and demands took the planners, who had been thinking in terms of more typical 1950s-type suburbanites, by surprise. In addition, the daily population is more mobile and diffuse than anticipated. A large proportion of the approximately 18,000 people who hold jobs in Columbia live elsewhere, and, conversely, the shopping, recreational, business, and educational facilities of Columbia also draw many temporary visitors. These discrepancies between the expected and the real human aggregate has led to some interesting adjustments and even collisions between people and plans.

ORGANIZATIONAL STRUCTURE AND FUNCTIONING

Government

Columbia's government is more properly referred to as governments. For Columbia is not really a discrete governmental entity any more than it is a discrete geographic area. It was established within the confines of Howard County, in the state of Maryland, in the United States of America, and it is subject to all the laws and taxes, and enjoys the services, of each of these. However, the needs of a city of 100,000 go beyond those provided by these governmental entities: even though Columbia was not to be incorporated as a legal municipality, city-level services and functions had to be provided. These range from such urban necessities as public transportation to the facilities and organization for a variety of cultural and recreational activities.

Rouse wanted the facilities and institutions for urban-level amenities to be established as part of the development process. In effect, he wanted to create a network of cultural and recreational facilities with the organizational equivalent of departments of parks, recreation, cultural affairs, and transportation to run them. In addition, it would be desirable for Columbia to have some kind of citywide organization that would remain under the developer's control during the developmental period but that could carry on independently afterwards.

The answer was the quasi-governmental Columbia Association (or Columbia Park and Recreation Association), an extension of the home-owner's association concept but with a broad mandate, a secure financial base, and vast holdings. The Columbia Association, legally a "private, non-stock, non-profit corporation" was established under the general laws of the state of Maryland. It was given broad purposes:

> To aid, promote, and provide for the establishment of any and all utilities, systems, services and facilities . . . which tend to promote the general welfare of its people with regard to health, safety, education, culture, recreation, comfort or convenience to the extent and in the manner deemed desirable by the Board of Directors.[32]

Of course, without funds, such powers mean very little, but the Columbia Association was provided with a large and growing source of revenue: a lien on all taxable property in Columbia, permitting an annual assessment of up to 75¢ for every $100 of assessed valuation.[33] In addition, the Rouse company is deeding to the association about 300 acres of open spaces and land for parks, playgrounds, community centers, major city recreational facilities, and pathways.

The association is thus financially able to support a large professional staff, including financial experts, lawyers, accountants, social workers, day-care professionals, recreational specialists, architects, construction managers, and other specialists. With these kinds of financial and human resources, the association has become the dominant institution in Columbia. It currently owns and operates the recreational facilities and runs teen programs, before- and after-school activities, day camps, nursery schools, and day-care centers. It also operates the ColumBus and Call-a-Ride transportation systems and acts as a clearing house and an advisor and organizer for a multitude of community and cultural activities.

The association has been under developer control, with its seven directors named by the development company. But written into its charter is a schedule for increasing resident participation and phasing out developer control until, in 1981, the board will be composed entirely of directors selected by the residents. The selection process is indirect, with the residents of each village electing one member to an electoral Columbia Council, whose members then nominate from among themselves candidates for the Board of Directors. The board chooses from among these nominees the number of candidates to which the residents are entitled (1 vote per 4000 dwellings). The council can have the deciding vote by nominating to the board only the number to which it is entitled, so that the board has no alternatives among the candidates.[34]

More representative bodies exist in the village associations, which are nonprofit corporations whose membership consists of every household, whether owned or rented (with one vote per dwelling unit). The membership as a whole meets at least annually, electing five directors (the village board) who act as an executive committee and select a salaried village manager. Curiously, given the planners' emphasis on neighborhood relationships, there has been no effort to include the neighborhood as a political or governmental unit. Village board members are typically elected at large, with the single exception of the village of Long Reach, whose residents amended their articles to ensure that every neighborhood is represented on their village Board.

Although the village associations are technically separate from the Columbia Association, the citywide organization provides the village board with its facilities (community center) and a minimal annual budget for its operations. The village associations can raise additional revenue through fund-raising events or voluntary household assessments. The role of the village associations and their boards is largely undefined, although some villages have negotiated contracts with the Columbia Association by which they have assumed responsibility for running their own village centers and programs. Each village is also scheduled, seven years after its founding, to take over the enforcement of architectural restrictions within its boundaries; two villages have already "graduated" to that status.

Village activists have felt that as the only truly representative bodies in Columbia, their boards should have a say on citywide policies. In an effort to increase their influence, a number of boards joined in 1970 to form a combined Villages Board, which has pushed successfully to increase citizen participation in the Columbia Association budget process, to secure majority control of the Childhood Education Board (of the Columbia Association), and to oppose such environmental blights as overhead power lines. This effort to increase resident input into the Columbia Association may cease once the association officially falls under resident control. Certainly the association, with its huge endowment and revenue and its professional staff, is likely to remain a dominant force in city life. If it continues to be responsive to resident desires, it may in effect co-opt the development of any substantial grass-roots or rival organization.

Another factor that may affect the future politics and government of Columbia lies in its relationship with the Howard County government. Columbia may come to exert an increasing influence (or control) over the county government as its proportion of county voters grows (possibly even to a majority). This could, for example, lead to closer cooperation in the planning of social programs (which, except in the realm of education, has been lacking).

Economy

The economy of Columbia was largely predetermined by the fact that Columbia's developers were striving to achieve both economic (profit-making) and social (community-building) goals. But the goal of profitability inevitably came first, especially in the fundamental decisions as to the location of the city, its relation to the regional housing market, and its central commercial establishment.

Its strategic location—in the heart of a growing region—was dictated by the fact that a good return on investment could not be achieved within 15 or 20 years if a settlement was started from scratch in virgin territory (like the kibbutzim and the Oneida Community). The strategy was to jump on an economic bandwagon created by the anticipated rush of people into the Baltimore–Washington corridor. The developers expected to join the competition to house these people, and in fact fully half of Columbia's residents have come from Baltimore and Washington, D.C.[35]

Columbia's commercial center was also designed to be regional rather than local in character. Part of the "economic rationale" of Columbia was the development of income properties—of which the most important would be a central shopping center. It would be an impressive enclosed mall, designed to serve not only Columbia's residents but those of central Maryland. Over 100 stores have leased mall space from Rouse's company, and ultimately a total of 500 is planned. The mall, say its promoters, "is destined to become the retail and commercial heart of the region as well as the shopping core of the new city." [36]

Through its continuing ownership of most of the commercial property in Columbia, the Rouse company inevitably has considerable power in shaping its commercial life. Few regret the imposition of architectural standards on commercial enterprises: the gas stations are relatively inoffensive, and the mall and village centers are more attractive than the usual commercial strips in unplanned suburbs. Centralized planning by the developer has also been of benefit to Columbia's businessmen. The rule is one-to-a-corner for gas stations and, judging from the village store rosters, one-to-a-village of everything else (one liquor store, one barber shop, one grocery store, one fast-food service, one restaurant and so forth). Depending on one's point of view, the Rouse company plan results in either sensible distribution or in monopoly; one thing it does not produce is competition.

In pursuing a high-quality image for Columbia, the Rouse company has favored not only those enterprises that could afford the rent but those that sell the more expensive lines of goods. One explanation is that high-income customers such as Columbians want high-quality goods. The paucity of discount stores in Columbia has, however, been a matter of complaint, and many residents shop for at least some items in discount houses outside Columbia.

There is also some question as to whether such planned shopping areas as the mall and the village centers can ever hope to achieve the kind of commercial interest and diversity enjoyed in older cities. Jane Jacobs has maintained that cities need aged buildings, for the low rents of older buildings make possible the marginally profitable little enterprises that enliven a city: craft shops, thrift and antique shops, secondhand book stores, small art galleries, family restaurants, studios, and so forth. Old buildings can also, she has suggested, serve as "incubators" of new, chancy enterprises: "Old ideas can sometimes use new buildings; new ideas must use old buildings." [37] Although the development company has attempted to diversify Columbia's commercial life through the institution of a weekly flea market, its established businesses must still be able to afford the high overhead of a new and exclusive shopping-center location.

These basic decisions about the future economy of Columbia—that it would draw on regional as well as local demand for housing and shopping facilities and that it would contain major income-producing commercial facilities under continuing Rouse company control—were largely predetermined by the development strategy. The impact of social-planning considerations on economic planning for Columbia is more evident in the push to create an industrial base for the city.

In the social-planning sessions of the work group, a vision emerged of a city that would "provide an opportunity for the people who live in the community to work in the community." [38] It was hoped that fathers would not have to commute to work but would be able to play a greater role in family life, while children would have more contact with the work world than they could gain in the typical bedroom suburb.

Accordingly, the physical plan provided for a number of "employment centers," including not only the shopping areas but a "downtown" of large office buildings and four industrial parks. The development company actively sought to enroll businesses to occupy these locations. Although an important goal of the developer was to create local jobs, the best way to do so proved to be to take advantage of Columbia's position vis-à-vis regional and national markets. More than half (52%) of its industrial establishments are warehouse and distribution centers. Columbia has thus become integrated with and dependent upon an economic web that goes well beyond its borders and is ultimately worldwide.

Industrial development in Columbia has been, however, constrained, not only by the county zoning restrictions and governmental pollution regulations but also by the developer's concern with aesthetics. Thus, heavy and polluting industries were excluded in favor of distribution firms, light manufacturing, research and development companies, and administrative offices. These businesses were further restrained by restrictions in their deeds or leases pertaining to the location and type of buildings, usage, setbacks, size and appearance of signs, and so forth (enforced by an architecture and review committee).

A measure of the developer's success in attracting business to Columbia is the fact that over 600 businesses and 100 industries have located there or are planning to locate there. Local employment has already reached 18,000 (in relation to 11,000 dwelling units) and the developers have raised their sights from 30,000 jobs to an eventual 60,000. [39]

However, the hoped-for consequences to the social fabric of Columbia are far from being realized. For, as it turned out, most of those working in Columbia do not live there, while more than three quarters of those Columbia residents who are employed work elsewhere—scattered among at least eight counties in Maryland and Virginia and the two cities of Washington, D.C. and Baltimore.[40] Columbia's jobholders, like its industries, have been operating in a regional rather than a local economy.

The developers express the hope that the proportion of local residents holding local jobs will increase in time. However, progress toward this goal will probably be slow. For one, the price of housing in Columbia has put it beyond the means of many industrial-park and office or retail employees. And the job status of typical Columbian breadwinners gives them a mobility and a degree of specialization that make the local job market somewhat limiting, especially when there are so many alternative employers within commuting distance.

Thus, Columbia has been effectively "preserviced" with an economy, just as it has been preserviced with recreational and community facilities. Certain elements of this preplanning are likely to be enduring, such as Columbia's integration with the larger economy and the involvement of the Rouse company in its commercial life. Others, however, have proved ephemeral, such as the attempt to create on the neighborhood level a commercial establishment (the "convenience store") that would serve an important social function. The failure of this effort at social–economic planning is inseparably bound up with the changing face of the American family.

Family

The basic social and economic unit of Columbia is the family. There was really no question that it should be otherwise, for families of a certain kind and age were the most likely customers for Columbia housing. In deference to the presumed wishes of such customers (and with the sincere conviction that family life is in itself a positive good), Columbia was designed to promote family welfare. This was one of the motivations behind the effort to create employment opportunities within Columbia and was central to the decision to subdivide the residential areas into neighborhoods, each with its own neighborhood facilities.

The neighborhood was designed so that young children could get themselves to school, a playground, or a pool; buy a candy bar; or meet their friends—all by way of protected neighborhood pathways. And their mothers (whose "job" was assumed to be the care of house and children) would also be able to meet their own daily needs for conversation (at a community-center meeting or the coffee bar) or for a loaf of bread (the convenience store) within the neighborhood. The social planners were particularly taken with the potential of the neighborhood convenience store, which they hoped would be more than a source of miscellaneous groceries and candy bars: "It should also be a service center for the neighborhood, providing some managerial and caretaker functions; acting as a communications link out from the neighborhood . . . also a natural meeting place." [41] It soon became evident, however, that small, locally run stores were not financially feasible on the neighborhood level (especially since the nearby large village groceries were open long hours). Some convenience-store facilities are standing empty, and the management of others has been turned over to chain stores.

Also underutilized is the second neighborhood facility intended to serve as a gathering place and focus for neighborhood activities—the community centers—built by the Columbia Association on land donated by the developer. Some of these buildings have housed day-care programs and have provided meeting space, but it is generally conceded that they are not serving their intended function as a "neighborhood livingroom." [42]

The facilities that are most heavily utilized at the neighborhood level are the elementary school and the pool (the latter run by the Columbia Association), the former focused on the children and the latter heavily utilized by children. In truth, it is for the children that the neighborhood (with its population of 2000–5000) seems to have the most value as a social unit. Their mothers, while appreciative of the advantages of an intimate neighborhood environment for their children, were not, as it turned out, particularly interested themselves in neighborhood-level activities. The kinds of cultural, social, and recreational activities that would attract these educated and affluent women were, as it turned out, better provided at the village or city level than in the neighborhoods. Another unexpected factor was the advent of the women's movement, which legitimized the discontent of many housebound wives, stimulating them to challenge their traditional roles.

Columbia is like the larger society in that the responsibility for homemaking still falls largely on the adult female in each nuclear family. There are indications that Columbian women feel at times burdened or confined by these tasks: 37% said they wished to spend less time (versus 10% more) on homemaking, and 74% expressed interest in an emergency homemaking service. Nearly half (48%) were intrigued by the idea of a food service for the evening meal. And a surprising 24% expressed interest in housing designed for a multifamily or group-living situation. [43]

The main drive of Columbia women has been to increase the involvement of extrafamily institutions in the care and education of children. This arose in part because of the need of both employed and unemployed mothers to spread the burden of round-the-clock child care (a burden not easily shared with the typical commuter father) and also from a desire to provide their children with the maximum educational and cultural opportunities.

One need that the planners did anticipate was for family or marital counseling, and a Family Life Center was established as part of the institutional preservicing of the new city. The center is a private, nonprofit, mental-health service organization that provides a wide range of group and individual counseling programs. These include parent-effectiveness training, family and marriage counseling, and educational workshops. Three quarters of the problems for which clients are seeking counseling are associated with marital conflict, and it is most often the wife who takes the initiative in seeking counseling.[39]

The Women's Center is another supportive organization, but unlike the Family Life Center, it developed spontaneously out of the need for a place women could "talk to each other." It has provided not only a place for socializing but a series of ongoing morning programs during which women can explore issues relevant to personal growth (e.g., sex roles, the nuclear family, open marriage, conformity, aggression, the experience of being single again, and so forth).

While most families in Columbia are intact in the sense of having both parents, 16% of the households are "headed" by females, many with children. The relatively advanced child-activity program of Columbia is a help to these women, most of whom are compelled to work full time. Divorced and single mothers tend, however, to be financially handicapped, so that even the relatively modest costs associated with child care, recreation, and education in Columbia can be a barrier to full participation. Parents Without Partners has an active chapter in Columbia, but single parenthood in Columbia is, as almost everywhere else, a lonely and difficult undertaking.

In general, however, Columbia seems—despite the discrepancies between the expected and actual needs of Columbia families (especially Columbia mothers)—to have created an environment supportive of (nuclear) family life. In one survey, 39% of the respondents reported that their family were doing things together more often than before, probably partly because of the wealth of recreational facilities.[44] Nonetheless, a majority (56%) of respondents in a second survey were less than completely satisfied with their family life. But then, only 21% were completely satisfied with their lives as a whole, even though 67% felt that the quality of their lives had improved on their moving to Columbia! [45] Columbians are not, it seems, by nature complacent.

Education

Education was considered of high importance by Columbia's planners. One reason was, quite simply, that good schools attract buyers. At the very least, such schools should be up-to-date and comparable in quality to the school systems of other communities in the area. But the second reason was that the planners became quite excited by the potential importance of a good learning environment as "the basic foundation for a healthy community." [42]

The proposals that Christopher S. Jencks, the work-group expert on educational policy, put forward in his report were comprehensive and imaginative, involving basic changes in the structure and scale of the public school system.

Understandably, the Jencks proposals, with their implication that conservative Howard County was still, educationally speaking, in a dark age, was quite a shock to the county school establishment. There were inevitably some defensive reactions and counterattacks, but ultimately, the county officials launched a reappraisal of their own and began to incorporate into the county's new schools many of the progressive trends in contemporary American education. [46]

These trends are reflected in the design and teaching methods of the 14 Columbia schools (9 elementary, 3 middle, and 2 high schools). The traditional "egg-crate" design has been abandoned in favor of more flexible, "open-space" arrangements. At the core of each school is a "media center" containing not only books but filmstrips, recordings, slides, globes, and so on. Team teaching, individualized programs, and cross-age tutoring are employed. Although others of Jencks's recommendations have not been implemented (e.g., year-round schooling, differentiation of schools, and mechanization through computer-aided instruction), Columbia parents seem on the whole to be satisfied with the county schools within Columbia. [47] Thus, Columbia's developers were successful in influencing (though not controlling) the establishment of a well-regarded, progressive public school system for Columbia children.

The planners had also thought it would be both desirable and efficient if school and community facilities were jointly planned and used. For instance, libraries, auditoriums, and athletic facilities could be used after hours for other community purposes. In order to encourage this sort of interaction and complementarity, the planners clustered the school and community facilities. But the hoped-for coordination did not materialize. Thus, each public school built up its own library without reference to community library needs, while the County Commission complained that no separate provision had been made in the plan of the new city for central library space.

The planners were also frustrated in their efforts to "preservice" the community with prestigious outside cultural and educational institutions, although the results were at first impressive: Johns Hopkins University, Antioch College, Corcoran Art Gallery, and the Peabody Music Institute all established branches in Columbia, and the Washington (National) Symphony Orchestra made Columbia's new Merriweather Post Pavilion its summer home. However, some soon withdrew, in part because their introduction had been premature in relation to the population of Columbia, at least in its early years. Others have changed their approach to become more viable and/or to better meet the needs of Columbia and nearby county residents.[48]

After this initial shakedown, there remain a number of educational institutions, including five colleges, which for the most part cater to the part-time and evening student wishing to brush up or to acquire certain vocational skills, to get a start on an undergraduate degree, to take practical business-oriented courses, or to enjoy some cultural enrichment. For prestigious bachelor's degrees or higher-level professional training, Columbians usually travel to the larger metropolitan centers nearby.

The Columbia Association (and, in some cases, the independently run village centers) has, however, facilitated the development of a flourishing local cultural life, including art exhibits, culture fairs, and courses for all ages in everything from pottery to belly dancing. The association has also become deeply involved in early childhood education, aimed at those children aged two and above who have not yet entered kindergarten. Although initially surprised by the demand for preschool programs, the association responded by running and/or coordinating a number of nursery and daycare programs. It is estimated that over half of Columbia's children aged two to four are enrolled in some such program, whether in a parent cooperative (there are six), a Montessori school (three), the Responsive Learning Center, or the Singer Learning Center.[49]

On the whole, then, Columbia's educational and cultural life represents a particularly rich version of that available in a medium-sized American city or an upper-middle-class suburb. More coordinated than most (but less than the developers had hoped), it is an amalgam of efforts of a variety of public, private, and volunteer organizations and individuals. Each individual cultural or educational activity tends to flourish or decline in relation to current demand and the immediate availability of financing. However, given the values and the considerable income of the typical Columbian, and the fact that the population of the new city is still rapidly increasing, Columbia's educational and cultural life can be expected to grow in level and variety for some time.

SOCIAL CLIMATE

Personal Ideals and Value System

Columbia's residents came to a community that was in part shaped by the personal ideals and values of the developer and his colleagues. These were succinctly characterized by Hoppenfeld as follows: "Two fundamental goals for Columbia were: first to create a social and physical environment which would work for people, nourishing human growth; and second, as a venture of private capital, to make a profit in the land development and sale." [50] The second goal, of profitability, was, in the context of the contemporary economic system and housing market, natural and inevitable. Many of Columbia's residents are themselves concerned about economic values—such as cost, convenience to work, and maintenance of real-estate values. Many also share the developer's ideal of an attractive and supportive environment.

However, Columbia was and is not, in the usual sense, an "intentional community." Although its residents freely chose to live there, they were acting primarily as consumers (albeit impressed by Columbia's attempt to create a superior life-style), rather than as religious devotees or ethnic colonists. The personal values held by the people of Columbia are largely imported, reflecting that part of the larger society—young, affluent, and educated—from which Columbians came (see pp. 136–138).

Themselves high achievers, Columbians are oriented toward employment, education, and achievement. Columbian women, many of whom are less employed and educated than their husbands, are eager to catch up; a large proportion work full- or part-time and many are enrolled, or wish to be enrolled, in school. And Columbians also place a high value on their children's education (with its importance to future achievement).

Columbians are, however, exceptionally liberal in their political attitudes and acceptance of other races and lower-income groups. For instance, over 60% of the Columbians polled felt that low-income white families would not harm the neighborhood (compared to only 23.3% in a control community). Low-income blacks were similarly more welcome in Columbia, with over 60% not considering them a liability (while in a control community less than 20% were receptive). In fact, half the Columbians said they would like to see more money spent in the community for low-income housing (versus 29% in a control community).[51]

The most important difference in the values held by Columbians (as compared to residents of similar socioeconomic class in a less planned "control community": Wheaten–Norbeck) is in their appreciation of *community* values. For instance, Columbians were less house-centered or "house-proud" when deciding to move to Columbia: they paid little regard to the construction of their dwelling or to its layout and space, or even to the appearance of the neighborhood. Instead, they responded strongly to the "overall planning of the community." [52] Accordingly, Columbians have accepted a high degree of control and planning to ensure that the overall aesthetic and environmental quality of the community will be protected.

Organized religion in Columbia also reflects community values, in that sectarianism is deemphasized in favor of interdenominational cooperation. Rouse set in motion a process of consultation, cooperation, and mutual planning for the religious life of Columbia that was quite unusual. Two significant outcomes have been the coordination of ministerial manpower and services through the Columbia Ministry, and the coordination of religious construction through the nonprofit Religious Facilities Corporation. The various denominations—Catholic, Protestant, and Jewish—share village facilities, such as the Interfaith Center, which provide worship space and house such community services as the Women's Center. In addition, the Catholic diocese decided not to build a parochial school in Columbia (which is about one-fourth Catholic) but rather to provide religious education after school in private homes; the result is that Columbia schoolchildren of all religions attend public schools together.[53]

On the whole, Columbians do seem—within the limits of their economy, society, and background—to be striving toward a greater emphasis on community values, whether it is by their concern for and acceptance of controls over the physical features of the community or by their willingness to loosen the bonds of sectarianism in favor of cooperative ecumenism. The evident desire on the part of many residents to foster cohesion within the community is also a manifestation of this community ideal.

Personal Relationships

Personal relationships in Columbia take place within a matrix created by the developer and the planners. There are indications that the physical planning has facilitated the formation of personal relationships. For instance, the arrangement of many of the single-family homes in cul-de-sacs with a shared mailbox has helped bring together immediate neighbors. The approximate correspondence of the boundaries of the residential neighborhood with those of the local elementary school has also created a convenient social unit for young children. The majority of children aged 5–12 have had more friends since moving to Columbia, and these friends are overwhelmingly (93%) within the neighborhood. Among teen-agers (13–18 years old), the circle of friendship extends a little wider, but 63% still have mostly Columbia friends, commonly within walking distance.[54]

Columbia is, it is generally agreed, a friendly place. Most residents feel that it is easy to make new friends, and most have close friends within Columbia, many of whom live within walking distance. This friendliness represents a positive response to the challenge of a racially and religiously heterogeneous population. However, such diversity does complicate the task of achieving a high degree of cohesion.

Cohesion. It is unlikely that Columbia could ever achieve the degree of "cohesion" that can exist in a religious community, a commune, or a kibbutz. For one, there is a matter of sheer size: Columbia's population has reached 36,000 and upon completion is expected to pass 100,000. Second, Columbia as a geographic entity is interpenetrated with non-Columbian lands and, as a result, with non-Columbian residents. A third limiting factor is the economic integration of Columbia with the larger region. Most Columbians do not work in Columbia, and most Columbian workers live elsewhere.

Unexpected sociological developments have also influenced the degree of cohesion within the community, notably the emergence of the women's movement, which (at least in its early stages) has had divisive effects on marital and family relationships. The increasing independence of teen-agers and their involvement in the larger "youth culture" have also served to exacerbate age-group divisions. However, a majority of Columbians reported more interracial friendships and characterized race relations as "close," especially as compared to their experience in their previous communities.[55]

While the developer had hoped that sociological distinctions between neighborhoods would be minimal, he nonetheless welcomed a certain divergence among the villages. Thus, the architectural style of each village center is consistent within itself but different from that of the other villages. As early as 1971, residents noticed the emergence of individual village characteristics beyond those of physical design. Wilde Lake, the first village, is perceived as politically dominated by reformers and liberal Democrats: it also has a strong arts-and-crafts flavor. Harper's Choice contains "the landed gentry": "conservative, League of Women Voters" types. And Oakland Mills has been described as "the conservative middle class, the more typical suburbia." [56] This trend may enhance village cohesion at the expense of citywide cohesion.

Columbians do seem to have—in comparison to other residential communities—a feeling of high involvement and participation: 55% say they "feel a part of what goes on in the community" (versus 41% in a control community), and 75% rate general participation in community life higher in Columbia than in their previous community. Over 33% say that they themselves participate in community affairs more than before.[57]

Whether Columbia will be able to maintain the degree of cohesiveness and participation that has marked its early years is problematical. With the passage of time, housing patterns may begin to exhibit the economic and racial segregation typical of older cities. The city's population will more than double (at present, about 500 new people have to be assimilated each month). And, as population turnover proceeds, older residents will be replaced by new ones who may not feel the same commitment to the "Columbia ideal."

Support. The support system—both physical and emotional—is pluralistic and incomplete in Columbia, as it is in American society at large. Much of the physical support that each individual has depends upon his employment status or that of the breadwinner of the family to which he belongs. Columbia's planners have attempted to supplement the existing "support" system without replacing or changing it. For instance, a prepaid health plan is offered to Columbia residents. Nonetheless, a Columbian who loses his job (as in the recession of 1974–1975) also loses a great deal of security. It would not be long before a person in such a position would have to sell his house and, in all likelihood, leave Columbia.

When Columbia's planners talked of support, however, they were thinking mainly of the emotional, psychological dimensions—of "a more supportive environment for the growth of people" [58] First, an effort was made to provide the stimulus for personal growth by making education (or at least schools) the focal point of the community. Second, they hoped that the personal contacts created by the physical design, the shared community facilities and schools, and the membership in village associations would evolve into supportive emotional relationships. Certainly, the level of contacts is relatively high, and most Columbians feel that these new friendships or acquaintances are potentially supportive. When asked about calling on neighbors for help, 53% of Columbians said they felt it would be easier (versus only 14% harder) than in their previous community.[59] Third, there was an effort to create emotional and psychological resources for those who needed special help and especially for troubled families (through the Family Life Institute).

Additional community organizations have sprung up to serve troubled residents or those with special problems, examples being Faith at Work (church counseling), the Women's Center, Parents Without Partners, Grassroots (a community drug counseling and crisis intervention group), the Howard County Association for the Aged, and the Friendship Exchange.

In general, then, Columbia is not in physical terms much more supportive than the usual American community. Individuals are to a degree economically vulnerable and may sink or swim alone. However, the emotional supportiveness of the community is higher than in those from which its residents come, and many opportunities for growth and help are available. Nonetheless, people may still fail to avail themselves of these opportunities, becoming isolated and "unsupported" to a degree probably not possible in smaller communal utopias.

Spontaneity. In Columbia, *spontaneity* is a word with good connotations: everybody seems to be in favor of it. And there does seem to be more—both in the behavior of individuals and in collective activities—than one usually finds in an older, established community. The residents find it easy to make new friends in the community, and only 16% said they "hardly ever" strike up a casual conversation with others at the neighborhood pool.[60] This kind of spontaneous socializing is a liberating experience for many new residents, especially those who have moved from the defensive atmosphere of an inner city.

People are also allowed to pursue a variety of life styles. With no "old residents" to set a traditional tone, the style of the community is still open. In addition, diversity is fostered by the fact that Columbia's residents tend to be liberal and open-minded. Columbia is, in fact, a city that prides itself on its tolerance of hippies, gays, and youth.

Inevitably, however, there are some constraints on individual spontaneity, even in a new city. The necessity of meeting work responsibilities and conforming to the desires of employers inevitably shapes the life style of many Columbians. In addition, Columbia's subdivision into smaller social and residential units reduces the urban anonymity that fosters eccentricity and deviance, and social controls are not entirely absent. There is also a strong community ethos in favor of racial harmony and community cohesion that must dampen the freedom of expression of those who harbor racist or strongly individualistic views. Religious conservatives and traditionalists also feel that their views are unwelcome.

Spontaneity in collective activities is also high, stimulated by the newness of the community and by the characteristics of its residents, who are "doers." Having already taken the initiative by moving to an experimental community, and with one of their expressed values being "participation," Columbia's residents take an activist approach to collective problems or needs.

Consequently, when the planners underestimated the demand for preschool programs, a number of cooperative nursery schools were formed. And when it seemed to some residents that builders were removing trees unnecessarily, tree preservation became a major issue, spurring the resident-controlled village boards to hire a lawyer and leading ultimately to revised tree-protection regulations. Other examples of spontaneous resident initiatives include the formation of a Columbia organization known as the Friendship Exchange (which tries to welcome each new Columbia family), the formation of a charter bus service to and from Washington, D.C., and the resident-organized annual Columbia "birthday party." The residents of one village (Oakland Mills), frustrated by inadequate management of its village center, persuaded the Columbia Association to allow the community to take over, fielded over 400 resident volunteers, and opened the first all-volunteer post office in the United States.

Such spontaneous resident activity may ultimately decrease as the needed social institutions become established and the excitement of newness dies down. But for the short term, it seems likely to continue, especially as Columbia goes through the transition from developer to resident control.

System Maintenance and System Change

Clarity. The rules and regulations that govern the lives of Columbians are various and fall under a number of different jurisdictions. But a concerted effort has been made to maximize clarity by providing Columbians with the information they need right from the start. A prospective resident sees, as part of his deed or lease, the "covenants" that specify the architectural and maintenance restrictions and that establish the village associations. The bylaws of these associations are, of course, public, as are the articles of incorporation of the Columbia Association, including information on whether and how they may be amended. In addition, the Columbia Association publishes a 68-page *Briefing Book* explaining its own workings and those of the village associations.

Newcomers are also provided with a 64-page *New Resident Handbook,* with information about local regulations and license requirements as well as a guide to services and utilities, schools and preschools, transportation, local newspapers, and so forth. Sources of further information are given, such as a League of Women Voters booklet, *Know Your County Government;* the local library; and the telephone numbers for queries about the county government, taxes, Columbia Association recreation programs, covenant violations, civil liberties (the ACLU), the county police department, and so forth.

The flow of communication and information within the community is facilitated by the listing of the names of wives as well as husbands in the telephone book and by such publications as the village newsletters, Columbia Association mailings, and local newspapers. One in particular, the *Columbia Flier,* is read in 92% of the households.[61]

Despite this high level of clarity about specific regulations and activities within the community, there are indications that some residents had expectations about life in Columbia that have not been realized. These may have been in part stimulated by the missionary fervor of the developer; individual builders and salesmen may also have glossed over the realities in their efforts to secure sales. The tenants' association of one apartment building even brought suit in 1971 against the development company for breach of promise and fraud (charging that their living rooms were smaller than expected and that the building maintenance was inadequate).

And some parents, who had expected their children to attend new, progressive schools in their neighborhoods, were disappointed when their children were sent to older, more traditional schools in Howard County. (Although the developer planned and hoped for neighborhood schools, he could not control the schedule by which the county board of education built them.) Given the inevitable bias of promotional efforts and the high hopes of both the developer and many of his prospective customers, discrepancies between expectations and reality were probably inevitable.

Social Control. In its patterns of control Columbia provides interesting contrasts, for it is relatively high in environmental control and relatively low in behavioral control.

Of course, the larger society imposes some behavioral controls through various laws (e.g., civil, criminal, and tax), requirements as to school attendance, and so on. In addition, a few local stores post signs forbidding bare feet and/or chests. Otherwise, however, Columbians feel that they have considerable latitude in their personal behavior, and tolerance is considered a virtue. While individual Columbians may dislike certain kinds of people or behavior, most try to prevent these feelings from controlling others. Thus, Columbia, a community where marriage is the norm, allows homosexual groups to use community facilities. When feelings against the behavior of youths began to surface, Project Awareness was born. And instead of prohibiting further rock concerts (as the county police department had suggested after a rowdy one), Columbians chose to exert only the most benign and indirect kind of control: "integration" of the mostly youthful audiences by adults.

Interestingly, Columbians have accepted a high level of control over their physical environment. Not only did they choose a preplanned community, but they also accepted, in signing their deeds, a set of highly restrictive covenants, which cannot be amended until 2065! These covenants require proper maintenance of private buildings and grounds and restrict changes in the use and appearance of any property, the type and number of pets, the outdoor hanging of laundry, the erection of fences, the conduct of home industries, and so forth.

Responsibility for enforcing these very explicit and strong covenants is given to village architectural committees, whose members, during the "development period" (the first seven years of each village's existence), are named by Rouse's company. In practice, the development company has allowed community participation, through advisory "resident architectural committees" in each village. And after the development period, enforcement will be officially under resident control. Regardless of the makeup of the enforcing architectural committees, however, Columbia residents are in effect accepting external control over their private property. Challenges by individuals to such controls have been rare: there have been only 15 appeals to the more than 10,000 decisions made on requests for external alternations.[62] After all, the maintenance of overall community attractiveness helps protect private property values, no small consideration to the homeowner.

A second area in which control is relatively high within Columbia is in its commercial life, as the developer's company retains ownership of most business properties. Through the granting or withholding of leases, the developer can determine who shall do business in Columbia. Charges that this power has been abused (to exclude certain businesses illegally or to set prices) were brought by the Federal Trade Commission and settled (out of court). Even within the law, however, the developer will continue to exercise unusual control in this area.

Innovation. In creating the new city of Columbia, the developer and his planners were themselves being innovative. The scale of the project, its planned racial diversity, the involvement of social scientists in the planning process, the coordinated ministry of diverse religious denominations, the attempt to preservice the community with social institutions—all these were to a degree innovative. How much room is there in Columbia for additional innovation?

Certainly, Columbia's residents are receptive to innovation. Many Columbians want not only to try new things but to do new things—to participate in the creative process of community building and problem solving. The role of the Columbia Association—with its considerable resources and its eager attention to anticipated and real needs—is problematical. Some fear that its very presence and effectiveness may stifle grass-roots innovation. But the association has also facilitated the establishment of several new organizations by providing expert staff advice, publicity and scheduling assistance, and facilities. Community sentiment seems to be in favor of more such efforts by the association to foster "third party development." [63]

Despite resident openness and initiative and despite the broad mandate and capabilities of the community association, innovation within Columbia will still be severely constrained. One reason is that Columbia is not autonomous. Innovations in many areas cannot be implemented without the cooperation—or at least acquiescence—of external governments, jurisdictions, or private organizations. Attempts to change family structure may run afoul of laws governing marriage and family relations. Attempts to arrange communal-living settings run counter to mortgaging practices and often to zoning laws. Food cooperatives or "conspiracies" may find their sources drying up as a result of pressure from retailers. Innovations in building design challenge conservative building codes.

These restraints on innovation affect Columbia no less than other American communities and more than some. For, as an unincorporated city, Columbia must look to an external jurisdiction, the county, for the administraton of many functions that an incorporated city controls internally. In addition, Columbia has a legacy of internal controls over the physical aspects of the city that are virtually cast in concrete.

These controls, which were intended to preserve the quality of the environment, also inevitably restrict innovations in land use and in building structures and use. Although enforcement of these restrictions is discretionary, there are conditions that may make it difficult *not* to enforce them. For one, insofar as there may be overlap or conflict between the Columbia covenants and other laws or regulations, the *most restrictive* of these provisions applies. Therefore, a county prohibition against home industries would invalidate a decision by a village architectural committee to allow such activity. Another is that even if the architectural committee were reluctant to enforce a certain provision, any other village property owner is empowered to bring a law suit against another property owner who violates any portion of the covenants.[64] Presumably, a single irate resident could (if supported by the law court) make it impossible for a village to make so simple an energy-conservation move as the installation of permanent clothes lines.

The generally innovative atmosphere of Columbia appears, then, to apply mainly to forms of social behavior or novel social services that do not fall afoul of existing laws and jurisdictions. But when it comes to more fundamental kinds of innovation, Columbia is severely constrained, for it is inextricably embedded in the matrix of the larger society. Major innovation in Columbia is probably impossible unless coordinated with innovation along similar lines in that larger society.

These institutional constraints on innovation in Columbia may at times chafe. However, it is doubtful whether Columbia's residents, despite their apparent innovativeness, will demand much more innovation than that taking place in the larger society. For the people of Columbia are, like its institutions, embedded in the larger society. Most residents have been educated and socialized elsewhere. The children go to county schools and most of the parents work outside the city. And the Columbia population keeps abreast with American culture through television and movies, radio, rock music, and the print media. In fact, a new community such as Columbia is probably unusually susceptible to externally generated cultural influences.

Another reason why Columbians may be expected to have reservations about major innovations is that Columbians are for the most part society's successes. As affluent homeowners enjoying a pleasant environment, they necessarily have a stake in the status quo. They are therefore unlikely to tamper with the fundamental institutions of society. Columbians are more likely to favor reform than revolution.

Columbia is, in sum, a landmark in the history of American private enterprise: a city-sized development designed not only to produce a profit but with an unusual concern for community values and for the preservation of aesthetic standards. Such an enterprise was necessarily costly, so that its residents would of necessity be economically well off (low-income housing could be only a small proportion and required outside subsidies). But the human mix that Columbia attracted is unusual in its racial diversity and in its concern for community values. Thus, Columbia represents something close to the ultimate in community spirit, aesthetic preservation, and racial diversity that is possible in a new city developed under the free-enterprise system.

It was hoped, of course, that Columbia would inspire the development of a new generation of cities for the "growth of people." However, amid the resource shortages and economic constraints of the 1970s, Columbia looks more like an attractive but unrepeatable relic of the energy-intensive, optimistic, affluent 1960s. Without innovations more profound than its institutions and attitudes may allow, Columbia could become not the wave of the future but an attractive anachronism.

REFERENCES AND NOTES

1. *Report on national growth 1972.* Washington, D.C.: U.S. Government Printing Office, 1972, Ch. 1.
2. Ibid., p. 20.
3. Rouse, J. W. The city of Columbia, Md. In E. H. Wentworth (Ed.), *Taming megalopolis,* Vol. 2. New York: Praeger, 1967, p. 839.
4. Ibid., p. 840.
5. Howard, E. *Garden cities of to-morrow.* London: Faber and Faber, 1945, p. 145.
6. Buder, S. Ebenezer Howard: The genesis of a town planning movement. *Journal of the American Institute of Planners,* 35:390–398, 1969.
7. Ibid., p. 394.
8. Osborn, F. J., and Whittick, A. *The New Towns,* rev. ed. London: Leonard Hill, 1969.
9. Breckenfeld, G. *Columbia and the New Cities.* New York: Ives Washburn, 1971, p. 250.
10. Hoppenfeld, M. A sketch of the planning-building process for Columbia, Md. *Journal of the American Institute of Planners,* 33:399–401, 1967. See also: Eichler, E., and Kaplan, M. *The community builders.* Berkeley: University of California Press, 1970.
11. Breckenfeld, op. cit., p. 252.
12. Ibid., p. 261.

13. Brooks, R. O. *New Towns and communal values: A case study of Columbia, Maryland.* New York: Praeger, 1974, Chs. 4 and 6.
14. Laza, A. J. *The planning of Columbia, New Town.* Doctoral dissertation, Boston College, Boston, 1973, p. 71.
15. Breckenfeld, op. cit., p. 399.
16. Laza, op. cit., p. 56.
17. Brooks, op. cit., pp. 150–151.
18. Laza, op. cit., p. 124.
19. Columbia Association and Howard Research and Development Corp. Neighborhood evaluation survey (mimeo). Columbia, Md., 1973, p. 7.
20. Ibid., pp. 13, 30.
21. Ibid., p. 46.
22. New Towns: How are they doing? *Mosaic* (National Science Foundation), Vol. 5, No. 3 (Summer), 1974, p. 4.
23. Columbia Association. Income of household heads (Columbia Demographic Analyses Series, No. 3). Columbia, Md., 1974, Table 111.5.
24. Hoppenfeld, op. cit., p. 399.
25. Richards, B. Reality put damper on Columbia ideal. *Washington Post,* Jan. 13, 1975, pp. A1–A6.
26. Columbia Association, Income of household heads, op. cit.
27. Center for Urban and Regional Studies, University of North Carolina. Columbia, Maryland: Community profile—Spring 1973 (CP Report #1). Chapel Hill, N.C., 1974, p. 2.
28. Howard Research and Development Corp. Columbia today. Columbia, Md., 1973.
29. Center for Urban and Regional Studies, op. cit.
30. Howard Research and Development Corp., Columbia today, op. cit.
31. Lansing, J. B., Marans, R. W., and Zehner, R. B. *Planned residential environments.* Ann Arbor, Mich.: Survey Research Center, University of Michigan, 1970, pp. 30–31.
32. Columbia Association. *The briefing book, 1975.* Columbia, Md., 1975, p. 9.
33. Ibid., pp. 5–8.
34. Ibid., pp. 10–11.
35. Howard Research and Development Corp., op. cit.
36. Howard Research and Development Corp. *Columbia quarterly,* Apr. 1975; and The promise and purpose of Columbia, Nov. 1972.
37. Jacobs, J. *The death and life of great American cities.* New York: Vintage Books, Random House, 1961, Ch. 10.
38. Brooks, op. cit., p. 36.
39. Howard Research and Development Corp., *Columbia quarterly,* op. cit.
40. Howard Research and Development Corp., Columbia today, op. cit.
41. Temple, C. Planning and the married woman with children—A New Town perspective (mimeo). Columbia, Md., 1973.

42. Columbia Association. An analysis of village community centers (mimeo). Columbia, Md., 1974.

43. Stuart, M. A study of women's needs in Columbia (mimeo). Columbia, Md.: Columbia Association, 1974.

44. Columbia Association and Howard Research and Development Corp., Neighborhood evaluation survey, op. cit.

45. Center for Urban and Regional Studies, op. cit., p. 12.

46. Laza, op. cit., Ch. 4.

47. Center for Urban and Regional Studies, op. cit., pp. 4, 7; Columbia Association and Howard Research and Development Corp., Neighborhood evaluation survey, op. cit.

48. Brooks, op. cit., pp. 40–49, Ch. 6; Columbia Commission. *Impact of New Town zoning on Howard County, Md.* (Report to County Executive and County Council). Howard County, Md., pp. 38–39.

49. Howard Research and Development Corp., *Columbia quarterly,* op. cit., p. 10.

50. Hoppenfeld, op. cit., p. 399.

51. Center for Urban and Regional Studies, op. cit., p. 10.

52. Ibid., p. 10.

53. Breckenfeld, *Columbia and the New Cities,* op. cit., pp. 291–294; Laza, op. cit., Ch. 5.

54. Columbia Association and Howard Research and Development Corp., Neighborhood evaluation survey, op. cit.

55. Ibid.

56. Rosenthal, J. A tale of one city. *New York Times Magazine,* Dec. 26, 1971, p. 16.

57. Center for Urban and Regional Studies, op. cit., pp. 4, 11; Columbia Association and Howard Research and Development Corp., Neighborhood evaluation survey, op. cit.

58. Howard Research and Development Corp., The promise and purpose of Columbia, op. cit., p. 5.

59. Columbia Association and Howard Research and Development Corp., Neighborhood evaluation survey, op. cit.

60. Ibid.

61. Howard Research and Development Corp., Columbia today, op. cit., p. 11.

62. Columbia Association, *The briefing book, 1975,* op. cit., p. 24.

63. Ralph, R. Some lessons from Columbia at 33,000. Presented at the Association of New Community Social Planners, Echelon, New Jersey, June 1974.

64. Columbia Association, *The briefing book,* op. cit., Pt. II, p. 22.

CHAPTER 6

B. F. Skinner's *Walden II*

INTRODUCTION

An oft-cited credo in the halls of academe is that a specialist who seeks to extend the application of his discipline to broad questions of social concern treads on dangerous ground. B. F. Skinner, author of the work we are about to examine, is one of those willing to accept such risks. An emeritus professor of psychology at Harvard University, Skinner has been one of the foremost developers and proponents of that school of thought in contemporary psychology known as *behaviorism*.[1] In *Walden II*, he applied behaviorist theory to the formidable task of designing a utopian community.[2]

Walden II, the title of the novel as well as the name of the fictitious community Skinner envisioned, is unquestionably a utopian venture. It promises nothing less than to provide a means for rescuing a society hopelessly caught in a web of seemingly insoluble dilemmas and to thrust it forward into a new "golden age." What makes this claim particularly audacious is that *Walden II*, unlike other modern utopias that offer pictures of the future, takes place in the present. It is the world of 1945, the year in which the novel was written, which Skinner depicts as in a terminal state of confusion and disarray. As Frazier, the fictional founder of the Walden II community, exclaims:

> Our civilization is running away like a frightened horse, her flanks flashing with sweat, her nostrils breathing a frothy mist; and as she runs, her speed and her panic increase together. As for your politicians, your professors, your writers—let them wave their arms and shout as wildly as they will. They can't bring the frantic beast under control.[3]

Fortunately, a science of behavior capable of producing a more perfect social order has been developed. However, this science cannot be directly applied to the existing political and social order, not that there is any flaw in the techniques. The difficulty lies with those who would use them. No group in the postwar United States combines the ability to employ these methods experimentally with the desire to design utopia. In fact, many of the society's problems are caused by those who understand the techniques of reinforcement theory—such as "the charlatan, the demagogue, the salesman, the ward heeler, the bully, the cheat, the educator, the priest"—but employ them immorally or unwisely.[4] Thus, to the question, "What do you do with a runaway?" Frazier replies, "Let her run till she drops with exhaustion. Meanwhile, let's see what we can do with her lovely colt." [5]

The colt, of course, is Walden II. Rather than attempt immediately to achieve social change on a macroscale, Frazier chooses to create a microutopia, a settlement of some 1000 persons. In time, as more and more people observe the superior quality of life in this settlement, others will be established. Walden II communities will eventually cover the nation and possibly the earth. From that point on, the human prospect is virtually unlimited.

ECOLOGICAL DIMENSIONS: GEOGRAPHIC AND ARCHITECTURAL FEATURES

Walden II is located in a rural valley 30 miles from the capital city of an unspecified area, probably somewhere in the northeastern part of the United States. The valley is surrounded on three sides by wooded hills and is fairly close to a river. Beyond that meager description and a few adjectives affirming the "pleasant" character of the region, there is little mention of the area's physical geography.

Surprisingly, in light of the author's commitment to explaining human behavior in terms of responses to external stimuli, there is no discussion of the impact of different physical environments on human social organization. Walden II is developed in an agricultural area, but the reasons for this choice are not explained. A rural farm seems to have been selected as the community's site because it was inexpensive and potentially self-sufficient and because it was remote, minimizing the chances of disturbing contacts with the outside world. Apparently, neither a belief in the salutary effects of rural life on human character nor a critique of the impact of urban or industrial environments played a role in the decision.

Functional considerations have received high priority in the physical design of the community. A central main building is surrounded by farming areas and workshops. Pine groves separate the work places from the living quarters, and a strip of birches keeps the truck gardens and sheep pasture apart and provides firewood. A swamp has been converted to a pond; it is used as a reserve water supply as well as for recreational purposes. Most buildings are production-oriented. These include poultry houses, a piggery, granaries and barns, a textile building, a metal shop, a wood shop, and laboratories.[6]

Walden II's central building includes dining halls, schools and children's quarters, meeting rooms, reading rooms, art studios, and auditoriums—actually rooms for every need the members wish to satisfy in their "home." The structure is elongated, consisting of numerous wings and tiers that follow the slope of the land. All sections are connected to each other so that members never need to go out of doors during inclement weather to reach services or recreational facilities.

Planned especially for Walden II by two young architects who were among the community's founding members, the central building has a pragmatic and simple interior design. A main passageway—called The Walk—connects the different wings and tiers. One section of this corridor climbs to a separate area reserved for the children's quarters; it is known as Jacob's Ladder. The Walk serves as a functional link between levels and as an informal meeting area. In fact, the narrator compares it in this respect to the deck of an ocean liner. It is also an aesthetically pleasing passageway, the ladder section being lined by flower beds and artwork. Branching off of The Walk are common rooms, dining halls, meeting rooms, art studios, and corridors leading to residents' rooms. These regions are also decorated with art and sculpture, which can be borrowed from a community collection.

While it is never made explicit, it seems that most social interaction is reserved for the public areas along The Walk and The Walk itself. Members' personal rooms are much more a realm of peace, quiet, and privacy. Each member has his own room—even husband and wife have separate quarters—and a member's room is literally his castle. One can furnish one's room as one likes. In marked contrast to the general neatness of the public domain, an individual residence may be kept in whatever state of disarray its occupant can tolerate. Many Walden members derive satisfaction from participating in the construction of their own chambers. New members and second-generation members often choose to work at the building of the residence wing that will soon house them.[7]

The architectural design of the main building controls population densities within individual functional areas. Walden II's largest auditorium holds a maximum of 200 persons (one fifth of the membership), and most other public rooms are a good deal smaller. This restriction on the number of people who can participate in any activity at the same time reflects the community's deliberate opposition to crowds. Large social groupings are deemed ineffective and undesirable modes of providing the excitement and interaction required only by those who lead bored and barren lives. Walden II's members find interpersonal contact in small groups to be more pleasant and more compatible with the diversity of interests in the community.

Aside from the issue of population, other aspects of behavioral engineering involving architecture are functionally specific to particular buildings or building sectors. Some of these are discussed below, in particular, the school rooms and the dining hall. One instance of the practical use of design to affect behavior concerns Walden II's agricultural workers. Workers who were involved with farm animals acquired unpleasant odors that interfered with their social relationships once they returned from their jobs. The community thus constructed a three-section shower house in which farmers could deposit work clothes in the first room, shower in the second, and put on clean clothes in the third. The innovation proved successful. Walden II's founder, Frazier, describes it, with a touch of irony, as a "real achievement in social engineering." [8] Yet it is also ironic that so few practical examples of the modification of behavior through manipulation of the physical environment appear in a behaviorist utopia.

THE HUMAN AGGREGATE

Walden II is the brainchild of a single individual, T. E. Frazier, a young Ph.D. in psychology, who apparently developed his ideas concerning behavior modification and its implications for the creation of utopia while in graduate school. Since its early days, Walden II has been continually growing. Ideologically, the community is committed to growth. This does not mean that Walden II, or the other settlements in the movement, are always willing to accept new members. A variety of factors affects the number of openings available. The community maintains that it can assimilate only a limited number of newcomers without endangering its own stability. The rate at which new Waldens can be begun is dependent upon the availability of managers skilled in the science of behavior and other functional requisites for successful community life. Once a new settlement is established, increased numbers of new members can be accepted. Walden II carefully regulates the amount and nature of available information about itself to keep the flow of applicants within satisfactory limits. If the community were depicted as flawless, the quantity of potential recruits would become unmanageable. Walden II's psychologist closely observes the impact of newcomers. He can increase or decrease the rate of admissions depending upon his empirical analysis of the community's absorptive capacity.[9]

To join Walden II formally, a would-be member agrees to abide by the Walden code, the community's rule book. He also agrees to work according to the community's schedules and to forego any personal claim to the products he produces with his labor. Should he leave, he is entitled to take with him only those objects that he already owned before joining the community. For its part, Walden II guarantees to the newcomer all the rights and privileges of the other members.

Once an individual joins Walden II, he enters a society that is almost completely without status distinctions. To be sure, there is differentiation in the community. Adult members are divided into the occupational categories of planners, managers, scientists, and workers. There are areas of specialization within these broad groupings. Also, in private life, members focus their interests and energies on different fields. However, none of these distinctions is permitted to have any meaning in terms of one's status in the community. All occupations are considered of equal value. Any titles that might imply higher status are eliminated; for example, the community's doctors are addressed as "Mister." The sexes are treated equally. It is considered offensive to mention the amount of time one has lived in the community, much less to use such a factor as a basis for prestige. Finally, even individual acts, unrelated to subgroup membership, are not allowed to result in status distinctions. Walden II simply refuses to have heroes. It does not recognize with special favor any contribution made to it by one of its members. It defines any work done by one member as a service for another as an act accomplished by the community as a whole.[10]

Whatever the problems in the early days of the community, present-day members of Walden II possess a plethora of skills, which are distributed among the populace according to individual interests and capacities. Skinner observed that the community's members have as great a range of mental and physical abilities as that found in the rest of the United States. In terms of specific skills, Walden II's members are able to manage agricultural and small-scale industrial projects without outside assistance. They provide the community with food, clothing, education, medical and dental care, and so on. Furthermore, the community encourages the development of skills that are not of a direct economically productive nature, for example, skills in leisure pursuits, the creative arts, and the sciences. In fact, because Walden II offers its members full freedom of expression and ample time to think and to work creatively, it claims to be able to maintain the highest traditions of Western culture.[11]

In light of the community's ability to shape motives and emotions, it is hardly surprising that members of Walden II should exhibit a distinct personality structure as well as a common ethical perspective. The normal daily mannerisms of the members differ so much from those common elsewhere that a visitor is immediately struck by their uniqueness. As the novel's narrator observes, upon encountering an informal discussion among Walden residents:

> The scene before me was simple enough. These were delightful people. Their conversation had a measure and cadence more often found in well-wrought fiction than in fact. They were pleasant and well-mannered, yet perfectly candid; they were lively, but not boisterous; affectionate, but not effusive. But they were of another world, and I could not even be sure they were speaking a language I knew.[12]

This observation indicates that Walden II's members have not become robotlike, performing the behavioral equivalent of salivation on cue. On the contrary, it is only the general direction of their personality development that has been modified. Walden II's members do have emotions and feelings, but those emotions that would lead to unhappiness in the community have been weakened, while others that are compatible with community life have been strengthened. Thus, Walden II's members are relatively free of ambition, jealousy, and envy. They do not smoke or drink, for they no longer suffer the anxieties that produce such behavior. Their emotional repertoire emphasizes energy, affection, and tolerance. They have the requisite desires to find life in their community satisfying.

ORGANIZATIONAL STRUCTURE AND FUNCTIONING

Government

Walden II is not a sovereign state. It is a community with limited powers of self-government existing within a larger and more powerful political entity, the United States. Thus, before explaining Walden's governmental structure, it is necessary to consider the relationship between the community and the outside society that can dominate it. In general, members of Walden II dislike and distrust all social forms inferior to their own, a category that, from their point of view, includes all past and present efforts at human political organization. These systems are rejected because they permit one group of men to exert power over others through force and coercion. This criticism extends to the American government. However, because they recognize the community's vulnerability to the power of either state or federal political institutions, Walden's members accept the obligations of citizenship as a matter of expediency.

Government in Walden II is constitutional, although the constitution itself, apparently formulated by the community's founders, is never fully described. Walden's government is small and highly specialized. It includes two types of officials: planners and managers. Planners sit on a board composed of six members, usually three males and three females. Their term of office is limited to a maximum of 10 years, and the terms are staggered so that the entire board is never changed at once. As their name implies, planners are charged with ensuring the success of the community as a whole. They initiate general policy, review the performance of the managers, and carry out some judicial functions. Planners are appointed officials. When one of them retires, the board chooses a replacement from a list of candidates nominated by the managers.

Managers are specialists placed in control of the numerous economic and social sectors of the community. Their purviews include such areas as food, health, play, arts, dentistry, supply, nursery school, and advanced education. The achievement of managerial status takes place through a lengthy process of gradual advancement in some field of expertise. The procedure resembles civil service: a member works through several intermediate steps, acquiring experience and demonstrating competence, before being promoted to the highest positions.

As administrative officers in charge of a functional sector, managers have considerable power. They are entitled to requisition labor and to supervise the operations of workers in their domain. Enormous authority is sometimes delegated to managers as a prerogative necessary to the completion of their task. For example, the manager of health is empowered to regulate the members' diets, supervise sanitation, require that members receive medical examinations, and quarantine the entire community from the outside world. In addition, the managers and planners have the authority to amend the Walden constitution. A unanimous vote of the latter together with a two-thirds majority of the former (without any participation by the membership) is sufficient to institute such changes.

Political life at Walden II ceases once one moves beyond the work of the government functionaries. Popular participation in decision making is virtually nonexistent. The community's members do not elect representatives, debate issues, or support policy alternatives. However, a member can protest against the initiation or continuation of a rule or policy he dislikes. Such complaints may be taken to the managers and, if rejected, be appealed to the board of planners. But a member may not seek to mobilize support for his position by discussing the issue with other members.[13]

Skinner's rationale for this overtly undemocratic political structure rests on the assumption that a science of behavior makes possible a science of government. Such a science permits the experimental determination of what programs will provide the greatest satisfaction for the individual and success for the community. Like all sciences, however, the science of government is best left to the scientists, that is, to experts in the field. Untrained citizens simply lack the requisite skills. They may know what they want, but they are not capable of determining how their wants may be satisfied collectively. Furthermore, this lack of political competence is not a source of distress to the ignorant. To Skinner, most people simply desire a happy daily life and a secure future. With these goals met, as they are in Walden II, the populace is more than willing to relinquish the burdensome tasks of government to professionals.

The governmental practices of Walden II flow logically from this foundation. Political leaders should be selected on the basis of merit (ability in the science of government), and the best evaluators of such competence are the managers, who have years of experience behind them. Political issues are really technical problems. Careful study of each member reveals whether there are any open or latent protests, and, as Frazier comments (carrying the technical analogy still further):

> these protests are taken as seriously as the pilot of an airplane takes a sputtering engine. We don't need laws and a police force to compel a pilot to pay attention to a defective engine. Nor do we need laws to compel our Dairy Manager to pay attention to an epidemic among his cows. Similarly, our Behavioral and Cultural Managers need not be compelled to consider grievances. A grievance is a wheel to be oiled, or a broken pipe line to be repaired.[14]

In evaluating the actual performance of Walden II's government, one may well wonder whether in fact it would operate despotically, serving the interests of the rulers rather than of the ruled. However, a number of factors substantiate the nonoppressive character of Walden II's government. Positions of authority are allocated according to merit; there are no hereditary titles or vested interests. When a member does find himself in the role of planner or manager, he may wonder if the game is worth the candle. The work of an official is difficult. Moreover, planners and managers must spend one fourth of their work time at physical labor. There is no additional pay or other material benefit for taking on governmental responsibility. Officials do not receive special status or distinction; in fact, most members do not even know the names of all the planners.

As a further obstacle to personal elitism and possible tyranny, Walden II imposes a set of norms designed to make the rise of a charismatic leader impossible. People at Walden II never express gratitude for a service performed by another member as part of his job; such services are considered to be performed by the community with the individual acting as its agent. Loyalty is thus always general, never personal. Also, the practice of government is concealed from the membership, so that no one may know which specific official has developed a program that benefits him. It is considered bad taste for a member to reveal his contributions to the group. These measures make it almost impossible to distinguish a particular leader to whom one might render increased allegiance and, parenthetically, to whom one might complain.[15]

Assuming that Walden II is not at present despotic, what is the likelihood that this absence of oppression can be sustained? Lord Acton's warning that power corrupts can be translated into the behaviorist hypothesis that the environment produced by the exercise of power elicits increasingly ruthless and immoral responses from those who experience it. Is such a prospect possible for Walden II? Skinner does not think so. He relies primarily on the nature of positive reinforcement itself as a check on repression. Walden II's leaders have no police, no army, and no guns or bombs. Their only power is the ability to reinforce behavior. Thus, in terms of physical force, the members always outnumber the officials, and in any situation in which government policies failed to deliver satisfaction, they could literally "throw the rascals out."

We have several reservations about the persuasiveness of these arguments. For one, an organized minority is quite capable of dominating a substantially larger unorganized majority of equal armament or, in Walden II's case, lack of armament. Walden II's populace is politically unorganized. The lack of political experiences and attitudes of the membership, combined with the regulation prohibiting discussion critical of the existing code, makes the possibility of their future mobilization into an organized force very unlikely.

There is a still greater problem in Skinner's analysis, however, one that derives from the implications of reinforcement theory. The leaders of Walden II can alter conditions to increase the happiness (positive reinforcement) of the membership. They also have the capacity to define those desires the satisfaction of which will result in happiness.

The implications of this power are less benign than Skinner suggested. Members' happiness can be a genuine check on the policies of the leadership only if the basis of that happiness is independent of those leaders. But Walden's officials have a dual power: they can both change the environment to give people what they like and condition the people to like what they get. For example, if the officials should decide to extend the members' work assignments to generate an economic surplus for their own luxury, they could first condition the membership to accept, if not enjoy, an increased expenditure of effort at work. Thus, to imply that the major restraint on the power of the planners and managers is the members' subjective recognition of unhappiness and the tendency to protest that such a recognition induces is to argue that the members control that very force that is being relied upon to control them.

Economy

As a collective, Walden II owns and controls the means of production in the community. Its productive activities include agriculture, community services, and small industry. Specifically, Walden II raises sheep, dairy cows, poultry, and pigs. It builds its own houses, has its own wood and metal shops, and maintains its own laboratories. Furniture, textiles, and several other products are manufactured for "export" to bring in "foreign exchange" (U.S. currency). Walden II seeks to maintain satisfactory working conditions for its members. Efforts are consistently made, through mechanization and experimentation, to reduce the number of uninteresting or unpleasant jobs.

Walden II's members constitute the work force that produces its goods and earns its income. Jobs are allocated according to a labor-credit system. Each member, male or female, owes the community 1200 labor credits a year. The credits are "earned" through the performance of work. While the average rate of "pay" is one credit for an hour's work, the credit value for specific jobs varies considerably. Walden II recognizes that certain tasks are generally easier and more desirable than others. To truly equalize the work obligation of every member, the number of credits paid per hour for each job is adjusted according to the demand for that job. Thus, a pleasant job, such as working in the flower garden, would earn only 1 credit per hour, whereas working in the sewers pays 20 credits per hour.

By employing this system, Walden's members are free to choose whatever job they wish. The laws of supply and demand ensure that the available workers are distributed among the necessary assignments. If too many people wish to perform a certain task, its credit value will decline. Thus, those who perform the task will receive fewer credits and will have to carry out additional work to meet their obligations, and those who find the low credit value insufficient will decide to select some other job.

An interesting question posed by this system is how to respond to a worker who performs poorly at a job. The community will remove a worker (or a manager) from a position if his level of performance is inadequate. However, there are no additional sanctions for doing an unsatisfactory job. Poor performance is viewed as an illness for which the most likely cure is a transfer to a task more in line with the worker's aptitudes. In the unlikely event that a worker fails to meet the demands of every job to which he is assigned, the disease would be deemed acute, and he would be referred to one of the community's psychologists.[16]

The voluntary allocation of job assignments distributes the labor force in such a fashion as to maximize personal satisfaction rather than efficiency. A member may be the most competent in the community at a particular task, but he need not work at it if he prefers some other job at which he is much less skilled. Interestingly, despite Walden II's reliance on cultural conditioning, it does not condition its members to select the jobs at which they are most competent, nor for that matter are members conditioned to enjoy the most difficult jobs available.

As regards economic distribution, Walden II is solidly egalitarian. Every member has his food, clothing, and medical care provided by the community. There are no extra privileges or higher allocations for leaders or hard workers. While the level of economic well-being produced by the distribution system is highly dependent upon the resources the community has available, it is also affected by the organization of the distribution process itself. Walden II seeks to combine a high standard of living with low per capita consumption. Practically, this involves two distribution strategies. First, the community accepts the communal ownership of goods and the centralized provision of services. For example, Walden II collectively owns and operates a fleet of trucks and autos, which is far smaller than would be necessary if each family possessed a private vehicle. Similarly, there is a central radio network rather than 300 or 400 separate sets. Second, the community's values discourage excess or conspicuous consumption, while its isolation keeps out many of the inducements to consume that originate in the outside world.

The overwhelming implication in the novel is that the normal functioning of Walden II satisfies all of its members' wants. In one case, an elderly woman is interviewed concerning her satisfaction with the community. She responds by telling the story of her meeting with the member whose job it is to seek out complaints about the community's operations. "Is there anything you'd like that you haven't got?" the worker asks. "Yes," the woman replies, "to tell you the truth there is . . . I've always wanted to look like Greta Garbo." Such a request is admitted to be beyond the present capabilities of Walden II, but the incident achieves its purpose of suggesting that genuine discontent is an extremely rare phenomenon.[17]

Family

Relationships between men and women in Walden II are monogamous, thus reflecting the community's normative disposition toward deep and sustained affection. Marriages take place early, usually when the couple are in their teens. There are no economic reasons to delay the union of a couple, and it is considered desirable to permit the full and immediate satisfaction of normal sexual impulses when they appear, thereby making adolescence as brief and painless as possible.

Selection of mates, while essentially a matter of personal preference, is an object of serious community concern. Walden II employs several measures to guarantee the compatibility of marriage partners. The cultural norms that the youth encounter in their education stress the development of affective relationships rather than a sportive or competitive attitude toward sexuality. Easy and frequent contact between members of the opposite sex is facilitated. Boys and girls see each other regularly during their education. If interaction is needed in the adult years, a social manager makes use of "ingenious devices" to encourage intimate, satisfying, personal contacts. Finally, Walden II has an "engagement" period, which is used for a rigorous examination of the couple's prospects. Immediately after engagement, a couple pays a visit to the community's manager of marriages. He compares their interests and school records, as well as their medical background. Should any significant difference in intellectual ability or psychological temperament be detected, the manager advises against the marriage. This recommendation causes a postponement in the couple's plans; usually, upon reconsideration, their intention to marry is abandoned.[18]

Upon marriage, a couple enters into a relationship markedly different from the normal family life in American culture. A communal economy has removed from the family any functions connected with earning a living or dispensing earned income. Since all household tasks have been communalized, and often mechanized, there is no family division of labor, for there are no family services for such labor to perform. Furthermore, since children are raised communally, the family has no obligation to accomplish the socialization of future generations. These factors contribute to two fundamental features of the Walden family. First, family relationships are initiated and maintained exclusively on the basis of affection. There are no economic or social reasons either to start or to continue a relationship in which love no longer exists. Second, relationships between men and women are fundamentally egalitarian. Both sexes have identical social obligations and privileges, identical labor-credit requirements, and identical status vis-à-vis the community. Only when women are actually pregnant are they less able to participate in community life than men, and Walden II's women generally complete their childbearing at a very early age.

Despite the best efforts at cultural engineering, some of Walden II's marriages fail. Since the couple has undergone the community's compatibility test while engaged, the most likely cause of a breakup is the intrusion of an outside disturbance, for example, an extramarital lover. Such affairs are relatively infrequent. They are not fully justifiable according to the community's values, as they always lead to hardship for the rejected mate. To the extent that they result from emotional needs for intimacy not fulfilled in marriage, the community seeks to eliminate their cause by strongly encouraging highly affectionate, but nonsexual, friendships between men and women. However, extramarital affairs do take place, and when they do, Walden II's response is to try and preserve the threatened marriage. Immediate counseling is offered with either a psychologist or some other disinterested third party. A divorce is granted once it becomes clear that nothing can be done.

Once divorce occurs, several aspects of Walden II life serve to mitigate its harmful effects. Gossip about personal relationships is forbidden. Other community members seek to assist all parties in making a prompt readjustment. The ready availability of alternative sources of affection and potential new mates helps to smooth over the crisis. Finally, Walden II members are aided by their own cultural conditioning. To a great extent, they do not develop, or at least they are easily able to endure, such feelings as jealousy and wounded pride.

Raising and educating children at Walden II is a communal enterprise. Contact between a child and his natural parents is deliberately kept to a minimum. Parents do visit and play with their children, but children are taught to see themselves as the sons and daughters of Walden

II rather than of two individuals. Community members consider every child at Walden II as their own. It is considered bad taste to show special attention to one's own child. Thus, if a parent takes his child on a picnic, he is expected to take several of the child's friends along as well. As a result of this norm, children receive as much favor and attention from other adults as they do from their parents.

Numerous arguments are advanced to defend the community's restrictions on parental influence over their children. For one, child rearing is considered a science that requires the talents of skilled practitioners. Needless to say, an untrained mother is hardly adequate for such a complex task. Mothers at Walden II apparently recognize this fact, for they are generally relieved that the community has accepted the difficult responsibility of child raising. Second, communal child-rearing prevents the young community member from becoming dependent on his parents or any other single individual. This is necessary preparation for adult life at Walden II, where people depend on the entire community rather than on specific individuals. Third, the child at Walden II has a greater variety of suitable adult models to emulate than the child raised in a nuclear family. There is no disproportionate contact with members of either sex, for both men and women accept jobs in child rearing. Moreover, every adult whom a child decides to imitate at Walden II is a happy, well-adjusted person. Finally, it is alleged that the child's acknowledged needs for affection and security are better met through communal rather than family arrangements. Instead of having only two individuals as sources of affection and guarantors of security, the Walden II child is loved and protected by a vast number of persons, all seriously concerned about his welfare.

Education

Walden II accepts the responsibility of totally planning human education. By employing the science of behavior, it seeks to shape the basic values, emotions, and motives of its children. Once these have been formed adequately, academic education presents no problem. The child will be self-propelled toward the proper objectives. Walden II's educators have fortuitously discovered that nature had done part of their job for them. Human infants, prior to conditioning, are already replete with desirable motives. They are already curious and eager to learn and to control their environment. Thus, the major task of the community's human engineers is to ensure that the best motives are not discouraged by negative environmental responses to the child's efforts.

Through their control of education, Walden II's cultural engineers replace natural and social selection as the mode of conditioning for the community's children. Instead, they employ an approach to human development both conscious and egalitarian. Rather than choosing those best suited to survive or succeed, they educate all of the community's children to thrive happily in their environment.

Of course, with the control of education comes an awesome responsibility: the cultural engineers are designing nothing less than the entire set of characteristics and behavior patterns of a new generation. They must make the difficult decisions as to which values and motives should be rewarded and which should not (see below). For now, it will suffice to note two general tendencies in the perspective of Walden II's educators. First, the community's planners select a model of human development for their children according to their expectations about the kind of environment the children will be living in as adults. It is therefore interesting that despite the utopian goals of Walden II, much of the children's training is directed toward enabling them to cope with disappointment, defeat, and unsatisfied wants. The training even involves causing the children unhappiness now to protect them against greater unhappiness later. This reveals that the design of Walden II is not predicated on the assumption that there is a structure of social institutions that can eliminate human unhappiness. On the contrary, the implication is that even life in utopia will have its unpleasant moments and that the only way to mitigate their effects is to prepare through conditioning those who must endure them. Second, Walden II's educational practices and goals are not fixed. In this area, as in others, the community maintains a consistently experimental approach, constantly bringing forth and testing new ideas and techniques.

With this background in mind, it is now possible to consider the specific structure of Walden II's educational system. When a baby is born in Walden II, it is first placed in the community's lower nursery. Here, the infants are kept in air-conditioned cubicles where temperature and humidity can be regulated to ensure comfort and health. Life in the cubicle is idyllic. All of the infant's needs are met. Physical and psychological obstacles are gradually introduced to begin the process of developing the child's capacities. For example, parents are permitted to play with the baby briefly or to take it out of doors as a means of building resistance to disease. Also, at about age six months, minor discouragements are presented in order to develop the child's perseverance. One mechanism for accomplishing this is the use of specially designed toys. A music box may play only after the baby has learned to pull a string. At some later point, it is adjusted to require two pulls, and then three, and so on.

Children from three to six undergo further ethical training. This is actually instruction in emotional development, for in behaviorist terms, virtues can be reduced to forms of self-control. One lesson, administered to children of three or four years, teaches the child to endure a delay of gratification with minimal unpleasantness. Each child is given a lollipop that has been dipped in powdered sugar so that evidence of a single lick can be detected. Instructors inform the child that he may eat the lollipop later in the day if he manages to refrain from tasting it before then. At this point, the children are encouraged to think about their behavior as they look at the lollipop. Their own hunger demonstrates to them the need for techniques of self-control. The instructor then hides the lollipops, advising the children to notice whether they now experience an increase in happiness or a reduction in tension. To drive the lesson home, a distracting activity, such as an intriguing game, may be arranged. According to Walden II's educators, the lesson is easily learned. In subsequent tests, the children immediately conceal the lollipops in their lockers to make the waiting period less unpleasant. Subsequent lessons teach the children techniques of psychological concealment, ways to avoid thinking about lollipops. As part of this instruction, the children wear the lollipops around their necks, making psychological control a necessity since physical concealment is impossible.

Another ethical exercise instructs the children in mastering feelings of envy. After a long walk, the children return home, tired and hungry. Bowls of hot soup are waiting for them, but first they must count off, heads or tails, and await the toss of a coin. That half who called the side of the coin that lands up may immediately begin their meal; the remainder must stand and watch and learn to control their feelings of resentment.

Punishment is not considered an acceptable educational method. If a child fails to learn at the same pace as his fellows, he is required to repeat a lesson, but he is never subject to negative reinforcement. Despite the fact that Walden II's educational norms prohibit punishment, it is nonetheless true that many of its training methods are unpleasant for the child. The community's leaders defend such practices by arguing that increased satisfaction and self-control in adult life more than compensate for the tribulations of learning. What Walden II's children gain as a result of their education, Frazier explains:

> is escape from the petty emotions which eat the heart out of the unprepared. They get the satisfaction of pleasant and profitable social relations on a scale almost undreamed of in the world at large. They get immeasurably increased efficiency, because they can stick to a job without suffering the aches and pains which soon beset most of us. They get new horizons, for they are spared the emotions characteristic of frustration and failure.[21]

While their ethical training is going on, the children continue to move forward in the educational process. They gradually come to depend less on adults and more on their peers and on their own self-control. To facilitate this process, the children's quarters and schedules are arranged so that the young are able to focus on and emulate those who are slightly older. This permits them to acquire much of the next age level's behavior and motivation patterns without adult intervention.

The children pursue academic and vocational training while they are learning to control their own life-style. Numerous schoollike facilities—workshops, laboratories, libraries, reading rooms, and gymnasiums—are provided for their use. Visitors are quick to notice the "noninstitutional" character of these facilities, an atmosphere that blends well with the virtual absence of set or structured educational programs. Behavioral training has maintained and reinforced the children's natural curiosity. Thus, all that is necessary is to provide the children with techniques of learning and let them loose to go their own way. Considering this attitude, it is not surprising that Walden II has done away with standard grades and exams. The children learn at their own pace according to their own interests.

Without setting up formal restrictions, the community does seek to affect the educational preferences of its youth. Certain subjects are esteemed more than others. Music and art are strongly encouraged. Instruction is available on almost every musical instrument, and there are usually co-artists to work with, as well as eager and appreciative audiences to watch and listen. The study of history is denigrated, apparently because the community feels that the past is fundamentally unknowable (objective sources do not exist) and because it wishes to focus on the understanding and manipulation of current forces. Also, applied rather than theoretical science is acclaimed as better able to meet the community's needs. Finally, as an effort to direct students' attention to community problems, Walden II employs ongoing work projects as training sites.[22]

There is no upper limit to education at Walden II. The full-time instruction of young people generally concludes with the equivalent of an undergraduate program. However, those who wish professional training have only to announce that intention, and they receive special preparatory courses and are sent off to an appropriate institution at community expense. The expense is considered to be an investment that will be repaid by the future services of the student. There is apparently no doubt that the youth will choose to return to the community once his training has been completed. For those who do not pursue professional goals, ongoing educational materials are always available, and continuous self-education receives cultural approval. Furthermore, it is a formal community rule that every member must explain how to perform his job to any other member who is interested. The scope of educational opportunity available to a member is thus the totality of knowledge shared by the membership.[23]

A BEHAVIOR SETTING: THE DINING HALL

Walden II contains several dining halls. They are all small, holding about a dozen tables of various sizes. Each has its own distinctive architecture and atmosphere. One hall in which diners may enjoy a leisurely repast is pine-paneled in Early American decor. Another hall is white-walled, for those in a hurry seeking a fast, efficient meal. Still other halls are designed as an English inn, or a Swedish dining room, or in modern style. This diversity of appearance has a behaviorist purpose. It is intended to enable the community's children to feel comfortable in some of the housing interiors they may encounter outside of Walden II.

At the center of the dining halls is a common serving room that operates cafeteria style. Members pick up elliptical trays, take napkins from boxes with their names marked on them, and make a selection from the day's menu. The trays on which food is carried and eaten are another example of Walden II's efficiency-oriented cultural engineering. They may be conveniently arranged around a table without cluttering. They are transparent, thereby enabling dishwashers to inspect both sides with a single motion to determine if they are thoroughly clean. While this may appear trivial, the value of such devices is related to the members' concern for the welfare of their fellow workers. Frazier pointedly asks one of the community's guests:

> "would you mind turning one of these trays over from side to side one thousand times? Perhaps you will concede the result. Either you would work quickly and finish with painfully cramped muscles, or else slowly and be bored. Either would be objectionable. Yet some one of us would be compelled to do just that three times a day if our trays were opaque. And it would be *some one of us,* remember, not an 'inferior' person, hired at low wages. Our consciences are clearer than that!" [24]

As regards food quality, the organization of Walden II ensures that it meets the highest standards. Unlike the staff of commercial establishments who seek to prepare inexpensive but profit-making meals, Walden's cooks have no objective other than serving food that will be eaten and enjoyed. It would make no sense to offer less than optimal quality, for the materials saved would only be presented to the same members at a different time and in a different form.

Although members are free to eat at any dining hall they choose, the total capacity of all the rooms is only 200 persons, one fifth of the population. Overcrowding is avoided through the encouragement of staggered living schedules. Any adult can dine at any time, within certain limits, choosing any companions he desires. No regimentation is employed. If one time period does become overcrowded, a shift in preferences is achieved by the simple placing of a notice on the bulletin board indicating the hours at which less crowded facilities are available. For some fortuitous and unexplained reason, the preference for less crowded conditions is always stronger than whatever motivation accounted for the widespread selection of the crowded dining period in the first place. Hence, a mere bulletin is sufficient to redistribute diners temporarily.[25]

SOCIAL CLIMATE

Personal Ideals and Value System

Being a utopian community, Walden II is involved in the practice of creating a new type of person with new motives, new capacities, and new values. Essentially, Walden II's ideal person is capable of achieving personal happiness without interfering with the happiness of others. To accomplish this dual objective, he must acquire a set of ethical values, or in behaviorist parlance, develop certain techniques of self-control. First, Walden members learn to accept social equality. They are satisfied with having as much as but no more than others. This attitude extends to status and power as well as material goods. Walden II members are noncompetitive. They do not wish to participate in any activity in which one person's success is based upon another's failure.

Despite their efforts to achieve equality, the community realizes that certain people may have pleasures in life that others find unavailable. Even if given equal opportunities, some people create great art while others are unable to do so. Some people find that the person they love readily returns their affection, while others are less fortunate. To counteract these situations, Walden II's members are trained to withstand those instances of inequality that cannot be avoided. They have conquered feelings of jealousy, can control their pride, and are willing to accept their limitations. Interest-

ingly, the power that is concentrated in the hands of the community's managers is not considered to be an example of inequality. To most Walden II
members, such authority is not a scarce resource unfairly distributed but
rather an unpleasant burden that they are delighted to pass off to those who
desire it.

While members are free to select whatever occupational and recreational activities they prefer, the community advocates the full development
of creativity in the arts and sciences. To induce interest in these areas, Walden II offers instruction, a collegial atmosphere, sufficient time, and appreciative audiences. Thus, the ideal member is a man or woman of creative
energy, rather than a languorous and sleepy loafer relishing a short workday
and a lack of responsibility.[26]

Why has Walden II selected this model of human development? Why
did the founders feel that these particular values satisfy the double objectives of personal happiness and communal peace? Walden II's answer relies
on science, specifically the science of behavior. Thus, Frazier, claiming the
problem to be "simple enough," phrases it as follows, "What is the best
behavior for the individual as far as the group is concerned? And how can
the individual be induced to behave in that way?"

Walden's founders approached the first question by working out a
moral system that would later be subject to experimental modification.
Then they faced the dilemma of how to get the membership to live up to
it. Despite their belief in the power of science, Frazier and his assistant
began this effort by methodically analyzing a wealth of nonscientific evidence. They examined historical works of morals and ethics—Plato, Aristotle, Confucius, the New Testament, and so on—to discover all known
methods of controlling human behavior through techniques of self-control.
By the term *technique of self-control,* they refer to a moral precept such as
"Love your enemy." Once the techniques had been collected, it remained
necessary only to devise a means of transmitting them. The answer to this
problem was found in operant reinforcement and behavioral conditioning.[27]

Since behavioral control in Walden II is claimed to be a science, its
practice is always open to experimental modification. In other words, the
community has an experimental code of ethics: one set of values can be replaced if a better set is discovered. Has Walden II actually developed a coherent science of ethics? Can science actually provide direction to human
destiny? Even if the science of behavior was developed as fully as Skinner
envisioned in Walden II, it would still be of limited use in questions of
morals. The reasons for this limit relate to the nature of ethical questions
and to the requirements of the experimental method.

A scientific experiment involves the manipulation of independent variables to determine their effect on a dependent variable. In the case of Walden II's experiments, the independent variables are combinations of structures and rules in the community and motives and desires of the membership; the dependent variable is the happiness of the membership. Thus, an experiment involves changing the independent variables to produce a change in the dependent variable, to wit, more happiness.

At this point, Walden II's system of experimental ethics has just made what is probably its most important decision without the benefit of science or experiment. Employing happiness as the objective of the experiment equates happiness with ethical value. This position can be defended only on philosophical and not on scientific grounds. Science can explain only what is; it cannot advise what should be. Scientific experiments may indicate that one event causes another, but they cannot impute ethical value either to the causal or to the resultant event. Or, in strictly logical terms, one cannot derive from "is" statements—the only kind that experiments can produce—an "ought" statement. Thus, Walden II's ethics in fact begin with a philosophical premise: the objective of the good life is happiness. Walden II's system of ethics has not replaced philosophy with science; it has simply based its science on superficial philosophy.

The above argument reveals only one of the problems in Walden II's system of ethics; there are numerous others. Assuming happiness is our objective, how are we to measure happiness? Furthermore, how are we to aggregate subjective measures of happiness? Suppose the community considers a prospective innovation that makes most people happier but a few people less happy. Then the community must cope with the problem of making comparative judgments. It must determine whether the total increase in happiness produced by a new measure is greater than the amount of unhappiness that it causes. Nowhere in his novel did Skinner indicate that he had a solution to this dilemma.

Beyond the question of measuring happiness is another problem in Walden II's ethical system. Can the result of an experiment in ethics give the planners sufficient information to design the future structure and conditioning patterns of the community? Suppose the community's planners increase the number of hours in the workday. They could evaluate the results by questioning the membership as to whether or not they were happier. But if the members reported unhappiness, the planners could change the impact of their experiment simply by conditioning the membership to find increased work more satisfying, or perhaps by conditioning them to desire consumer goods that could be earned only through longer workdays.

Assuming that the conditioning is successful, the experiment now indicates that the innovation will produce happiness.

The above analysis indicates that the planners have too much power over their variables to benefit from experimentation. If a planner can modify both social structure and human motives, hopes, and dreams, then his problem is changed from isolating the one or two models that may prove utopian to selecting which of the innumerable utopian possibilities he should adopt. The planner must employ some criteria for making a choice among these alternatives if the future of the community is not to depend on a few leaders' arbitrary whims.

Personal Relationships

Cohesion. Relationships between individual members of Walden II and the community as a whole are highly cohesive. Interestingly, this bond is maintained despite the fact that there are almost no activities in which the entire community participates and the fact that the community refuses to use propaganda to inculcate loyalty to it. The only practice at Walden II that is communitywide and somewhat propagandistic is the Sunday meeting. At these sessions, philosophical or religious works are presented, and a brief "lesson," concerned with some aspect of community ethics, is discussed. The objective of these activities is to inspire group loyalty.

Walden II's social organization manages to combine a structural division into subgroups with an absence of subgroup self-consciousness or subgroup self-interest. This is most noticeable in the occupational sphere. Although the community has distinct vocational sectors, those who work in different areas identify themselves with the entire community rather than with their colleagues on the job. One factor that explains this situation is the equality in income, status, and privilege that accompanies every job. Indeed, part of the rationale for requiring all workers (including planners and managers) to perform physical labor is to eliminate status differences among work groups. Another explanation for the lack of occupational subgroup identity is the fact that Walden II's mode of job placement permits such flexibility in assignment that individuals rarely work with the same people at the same job over any extended time period.

Since Walden II lacks self-conscious subgroups, the only significant relationships members can develop, outside their connection with the community as a whole, are between one individual and another. Such ties are promoted by a pattern of social life that avoids situations that might lead to antagonistic contacts between persons. Members of Walden II do not compete at their jobs or in recreational activities. Interpersonal comparisons rarely take place, rivalry is discouraged, and children are taught to accept their limitations. Little or no satisfaction can be gained by an attack on anyone else.[28]

While social contact occurs readily at Walden II, one may wonder about the depth of interpersonal associations, especially considering the community's role as a provider of goods and services. The community as a whole meets its members' needs, and specific individuals play only limited roles in such processes. In fact, it is difficult to see how anyone at Walden II can actually do very much for anyone else. One cannot nurse a friend who is sick or help someone through hard times or give advice on personal problems; all of these services are provided by the community's professionals.

However, there is one way in which one person can be important to another at Walden II—that is through the giving and receiving of love. Love is one aspect of life that is largely excluded from the science of behavior and left to the individual (except that the manager of marriages must agree to a proposed marital union). It is also one of the few areas in which an individual must face the consequences of his competence as a practitioner. At Walden II, "you get and keep the affections you deserve." Or perhaps it might be said, one loves or loses depending upon one's ability to reinforce positively one's possible lovers.[29]

Support. Walden II is a totally supportive community. It meets the needs of its members for food, clothing, and shelter; educates their children; provides medical, dental, and psychological services when needed; and offers ample recreational facilities. These benefits are guaranteed to members even if illness or advancing age impairs their ability to earn labor credits. The community seeks to make all necessary jobs as satisfying as possible, thereby ensuring that the price of economic security is not unreasonably high.

Walden II makes every effort to encourage and facilitate friendships, social contact, and the expression of one's creative abilities. The entire membership serves as a source of emotional support and assistance during times of personal difficulty. If any of the community's services are deemed inadequate, Walden II solicits complaints and grievances so that the managers may attempt to make improvements.

Of course, the ability of Walden II to provide this extensive system of security is dependent upon its economic and political viability. Walden II cannot guarantee its members a high standard of living unless it produces sufficient goods and services itself or earns enough to purchase them elsewhere. Furthermore, the physical security of community members is in part dependent on Walden II's political status vis-à-vis the United States government.

Spontaneity. A cursory examination of life in Walden II seems to reveal a remarkably unregimented society. People choose their own jobs; they set their own hours. They interact with whomever they choose, pursue whatever hobby interests them, consult any book in the library. There are some restrictions on one's freedom of action. Everyone must obey the Walden code, the community's moral guidelines. One must follow the orders of the manager at work, although if his dictates are not to one's liking, one can always work somewhere else the following day. Members have no personal income and their consumption choices are limited to whatever variety is contained in the goods purchased or produced by the community. Still, these are hardly stifling restrictions, and if measured on a continuum which rated societies from spontaneity to regimentation, Walden II would appear to be solidly in the spontaneous section of the spectrum.

Unfortunately, a simple analysis of Walden II is misleading. For the appearance of spontaneity conceals the reality of prior psychological conditioning. Members of Walden II are trained to act and to feel in prescribed ways. Can such conditioning be reconciled with any degree of spontaneity? To answer this question, the concept of spontaneity must be more rigorously defined. Spontaneity may refer to the exercise of free will, the making of an unconditioned, undetermined choice by a human mind. Or it may refer to behavior that is conditioned by some aspect of the environment but that is unpredictable because mankind cannot understand the complexity of the stimulus–response pattern. This behavior would be spontaneous in the sense that it is unplanned or out of human control. Finally, spontaneity may refer to the subjective feeling of freedom. The individual does not recognize the forces that impel him to act as he does; he thinks he is doing exactly what he wants to, even though he may have been conditioned to have certain patterns of desires.

Walden II rejects the first definition of spontaneity, the exercise of free will. The community's position is that such a state is impossible. "I deny that freedom exists at all," states Frazier. "I must deny it or my program would be absurd. You can't have a science about a subject matter which hops capriciously about." [30] Frazier recognizes that his denial of free will is an assumption, not an experimentally substantiated fact. He argues that the success of the science of behavior at Walden II indicates that his assumption is a highly plausible one.

To some extent however, spontaneous behavior does take place in Walden II. For example, those aspects of the physical and social environment not under human control are still conditioning people, but in a manner that is unplanned and probably not understood. One reason the community permits this kind of behavioral control by accidental forces is that the planners do not yet understand how to condition all aspects of human action. Frazier admits, "I didn't say that behavior is always predictable, any more than the weather is always predictable. There are often too many factors to be taken into account. We can't measure them all accurately, and we couldn't perform the mathematical operations needed to make a prediction if we had the measurements." [31] The community also allows the rule of accident because it has no need to control every single act of every member. For example, it makes no difference whether a given member chooses as his hobby playing the saxophone or the guitar, or painting with oils or with watercolors. Since each of these activities may be satisfying to the individual and harmless to the community, nothing is lost if random factors are allowed to determine the selection.

To a great extent, however, Walden II has the capacity to condition the behavior of its members. It also has the inclination to do so since its goal is a perfect society, and over the long run, random conditioning is as likely to produce misery as happiness. As has already been noted, behavior at Walden II is controlled through operant conditioning, a method that precludes either of the first two types of spontaneity but that is still compatible with the third. Because Walden II never employs punishment or coercion, its members do not feel forced to perform acts against their will. On the contrary, they experience the feeling of free action and of free choice, the feeling that they are selecting behavior that maximizes their satisfaction. Walden's planners acknowledge and endorse this form of spontaneity, claiming its prevalence as one of the community's great achievements. As Frazier explains:

> We can achieve a sort of control under which the controlled, though they are following a code much more scrupulously than was ever the case under the old system, nevertheless *feel free*. They are doing what they want to do, not what they are forced to do. That's the source of the tremendous power of positive reinforcement—there's no restraint and no revolt. By a careful cultural design, we control not the final behavior, but the *inclination* to behave—the motives, the desires, the wishes.
>
> The curious thing is that in that case *the question of freedom never arises.*
>
> . . . this is the freest place on earth. And it is free precisely because we make no use of force or the threat of force. Every bit of our research, from the

nursery through the psychological management of our adult membership is directed toward that end—to exploit every alternative to forcible control. By skillful planning, by a wise choice of techniques we *increase* the feeling of freedom.[32] (Italics added)

System Maintenance and System Change

Walden II sees itself as the single best hope for the future of humanity. As such, it is determined to survive. For the most part, the community expects threats to its existence to have an external rather than an internal genesis. Happiness is the great guarantee of internal harmony. As long as the science of behavior fully meets everyone's needs, there is no difficulty in assuring the cooperation of members. The outside world, however, with its instability, greed, and fear, poses more serious dangers for the community.

Walden II's posture toward the world beyond its boundaries is based on *realpolitik*. Where morality works, it will be employed. But when fidelity to conscience would jeopardize the community's security, expedience must be tolerated. Walden II employs a variety of tactics to protect itself. It demands sufficient work from its members to meet its needs for "foreign exchange," and it moves toward self-sufficiency as a long-term goal. It accepts the obligations local and national governments impose upon it—taxes and conscription—because it realizes that it lacks the power to resist.[33]

Clarity. Walden II maintains a formal list of community rules, referred to as the Walden Code. Several of its provisions have already been mentioned, such as the prohibition against gossip and the ban on discussing the community with outsiders. Since Walden II relies on voluntary compliance with these regulations, it must ensure that the membership is provided with accurate information concerning the precepts they must follow.

In their typically professional manner, the community's managers devise special techniques to keep the members aware of the rules. In simple cases, posting a notice in an appropriate place may prove sufficient. More serious and complex statutes are likely to be the subject of discussion in a weekly meeting. On such occasions, the objective of the regulation is noted and its application in practice described.

One regulation that required "drastic measures" for its proclamation and implementation reveals the specific techniques that the managers use to disseminate the community code. The rule in question defines as a socially acceptable act the open expression of boredom during conversations that members find boring. It was introduced as a new element in social interaction with the following measures. First, the rule was explained at a weekly meeting. This was accomplished with much joking rather than solemnity, as the managers consider a humorous atmosphere helpful in carrying out a significant change in custom. Each member was requested to immediately begin following the rule at least once a day. Also, small cards were placed on the dining room tables reading, "Have you been bored today? If not, why not?" When someone suggested that the cards themselves were boring, they were immediately removed to demonstrate the value of the rule. As an extra effort, one member wrote a play (for which he received labor credit) that dealt with issues of boredom. Through such procedures the rule was kept in members' awareness until it became commonplace and customary.[34]

Social Control. Enforcement of the Walden Code is based on the community's theory of the nature of man. According to the science of behavior, men are neither naturally good nor naturally evil; they are, however, malleable. Thus, they can be made to live a satisfying group life—in freedom and in peace—provided their physical and social environment is so constructed that everyone's needs are satisfied and everyone wants to obey the necessary regulations. Following this view, Walden II employs only one mode of law enforcement, operant conditioning. By creating a situation in which individuals are positively reinforced for obeying the rules, the community induces voluntary compliance with its precepts.

Since Walden II's conditioning processes are not yet foolproof, members may on occasion break a rule. These violations are generally minor. Indeed, from the perspective of United States law, Walden II has no crime at all; its police record is clean. Still, the community must respond to the infractions of its code that do occur. Walden II's policy is to view rule violations as symptomatic of psychopathology. Those who break regulations are never punished or forced into unwilling compliance, but instead they are sent to the community psychologists for treatment. Since most mental or emotional disorders are discovered at a relatively early stage, therapy is usually successful.

Of course, there is a possibility that treatment will not be effective, that a member will continue to violate the code. In seeking to discover the community's response to such a situation, one visitor in the novel queries how Walden II would deal with a member who adamantly refused to fulfill his work obligation. No specific strategy is presented. Instead, Frazier first observes that there is only a remote probability of that degree of rebellion's actually taking place. Then he simply avoids the issue by commenting, "We should deal with it somehow. I don't know. You might as well ask what we should do if leprosy broke out. We'd think of something. We aren't helpless." [35] One should recognize, however, that if the premises of Walden II's organization are valid and if the managers continue to increase their competence in the science of behavior, then rule violation will become an obsolete social phenomenon.

Innovation. At Walden II, innovation, based on scientific experimentation, is a common occurrence. The community delights in each new successful technique or invention. To spur on the search for new and creative innovations, all habits, customs, and techniques are deemed fair game for Walden researchers. Criticism is encouraged as a means of identifying areas in need of improvement. Even the community's ethics are not protected from critical examination and modification. Moral principles are tested experimentally and adopted if they prove superior to the values they are to replace. Then the new ethics themselves become targets for further innovation. [36]

One limit on innovation at Walden II is the refusal to employ propaganda. This reduces to the decision not to tamper with the variables in an experiment once it has already begun. Suppose Walden II adopted the rule that all members, on meeting a fellow member for the first time that day, must recite the Walden Code in its entirety. An experimental test of the rule would seek to determine if it increased the members' happiness. Of course, Walden II has the technical capacity to prejudice the results of its experiment by employing behavioral techniques (propaganda) to encourage its members to enjoy reciting the code. However, it refrains from doing so, thereby ensuring the validity of its investigation. As Frazier points out, "Happiness is one of our indicators, and we couldn't evaluate an experimental culture if the indicator is loaded with propaganda. . . . Walden II must be *naturally* satisfying." [37] In response to this argument, a candid observer might point out that since Walden II has already previously conditioned its members, it makes no sense whatever to speak of natural satisfaction. In fact, from the perspective of the community's indicator of happiness (a member's subjective response), the happiness produced through propaganda is no less valid than that produced through other behavioral influences.

At this point, it is necessary to resume the line of argument begun in the section on personal ideals and value system. Previously, we considered the problems Walden II would encounter in experimentally developing new moral values. This line of argument can now be extended to the experimental testing of all innovations. What we must discern is the nature of the critieria Walden II uses to evaluate the worth of an innovation. From our previous analysis, we recognize that happiness itself is an inadequate criterion. There are simply too many combinations of values, motives, and structural patterns that would satisfy it. Which of these should the community adopt? Moreover, what would happen if every member reported satisfaction? Would all innovation cease? Some further criteria are necessary.

Careful reading of the novel reveals that these criteria do exist. Although they must be picked out of several speeches by the community's founder, they can be combined into a coherent outlook. When such a procedure is applied to Frazier's speeches, the following pattern emerges. One of Walden II's objectives is to develop the intellectual and scientific capacities of the community. In part, this is a desire to use Walden II as a giant laboratory that can bring to full fruition the science of behavior. But there is a broader purpose here, for Frazier seeks the eventual development of "the most alert and active group intelligence yet to appear on the face of the earth." [38]

Logically, we are tempted to consider this a subgoal. Once human happiness has been achieved, what is to be accomplished by one's continually expanding his scientific capabilities? Two pragmatic reasons for such development are suggested. First, there is the question of self-defense. Frazier observes, accurately enough, that throughout history cultures that remained static were eventually overthrown by more aggressive adversaries. Unless scientific and cultural progress assures Walden II of a competitive edge, "less efficient cultures will somehow come out on top." Second, at least in the near future, human technological abilities will be increasing while man's capacity to control his own power seems unable to make similar advances. A science of behavior is thus needed to oversee the effects of the other sciences. Since *Walden II* was completed in 1948, shortly after the dawn of the atomic age, one can well commiserate with Skinner on this issue.

However, our long-term question still remains. Once Walden II's security is ensured, once technology has been brought under control by a science of behavior, is there anything to account for Walden II's continual dynamism? Here, we come to the final values of Walden II. Apparently, for Frazier, the struggle has no objective because it is the objective. Human destiny requires dynamism; a successful utopia in equilibrium would be unacceptable. The science of behavior has opened Frazier's eyes to virtually unlimited possibilities from human endeavor. Even if he cannot demonstrate any good to be achieved at the height of scientific progress, the climb itself is sufficient justification. In what is probably the most succinct statement of the ultimate purpose of Walden II, Frazier exclaims, "We want never to be free of that feverish urge to push forward which is the saving grace of mankind." [39] The trail that began with the scientific method has concluded with the Protestant Ethic.

TWIN OAKS: AN EXPERIMENTAL WALDEN II

Walden II enjoyed only limited attention in the first decade after its publication. Then, becoming merged with the rising utopian aspirations of the 1960s, it blossomed in popularity. Some devotees became so enchanted with Skinner's model that they determined to put it into practice. In the past dozen years, several Walden-type settlements have been established. Of these, the most well known, and the one most likely to survive, is the Twin Oaks community located in Louisa, Virginia, about 100 miles southwest of Washington, D.C.[40]

Twin Oaks was founded in June of 1967 on a 123-acre farm by 8 determined communitarians. Since then, the commune has grown slowly: there were 15 members in 1969, 45 in 1971, and about 50 in 1975. Most of the residents have been young, white, and middle-class, with some notable middle-aged exceptions. As in many of the intentional communities of the 1960s, turnover has been considerable. In the first years of its existence, turnover was estimated to be 70%, and the average stay at the commune was only three months. Only 2 of the original 8 members still lived at the community four years after its formation.[41]

The structure at Twin Oaks closely resembles the design of institutions in Walden II. The Virginia communitarians allocate work according to a labor-credit system that equalizes the burden of various jobs by altering the time to be spent performing them in accordance with members' preferences for the activity. General leadership is in the hands of three appointed planners; specific functional domains—such as animals, auto maintenance, construction, the library, and recreation—are controlled by managers. A community code includes numerous provisions lifted directly from Skinner's novel. For example, Rule 2 states, "All members are required to explain their work to any other member who desires to learn it." [42] Still, one is struck much more by the differences rather than the similarities between Twin Oaks and Walden II. These differences highlight flaws in the Walden II model that cast doubt upon its usefulness as a basis for a functioning society.

To begin with, Skinner never seriously analyzed how his utopia might function in the face of the inevitable challenges posed by real social and physical environments. Thus, Walden II seems to find prosperity effortlessly, but Twin Oaks has always had to fight for its economic life. Even today, the settlement is not self-sufficient and must send several of its members to work at distasteful outside jobs in neighboring cities. Similarly, in Walden II, agriculture responded easily to technical management, and nature yielded before science. Twin Oaks, however, has found it otherwise. After several disastrous experiments, the community virtually abandoned any hope of supporting itself through farming. In addition, rural topography proved so devastating for the settlement's vehicles that a book by one of Twin Oaks' founders includes an entire chapter on the problems of "wheels" and the repair thereof.[43]

Secondly, the first-generation settlers of Walden II seem to have avoided entirely any serious interpersonal, social, or political conflicts among themselves. Twin Oaks was not so fortunate. True, Twin Oaks could borrow the labor-credit system directly from the pages of the utopian novel. But it still had to deal with nonfictional members who manipulated others into doing their work for them or cheated on their labor reports. One wonders how Frazier would have responded if a member who owned the land on which the community had been established threatened to terminate the lease unless he was made a planner. Similarly, despite its reliance on planners and managers, Twin Oaks must deal with political disputes. A major issue that has divided the community is whether revenues should be allocated for improving the standard of living of the present membership or for expanding the size of the settlement.[44]

Finally, it is noteworthy that the amount of serious behavioral conditioning at Twin Oaks is rather limited. Members have attempted a few minor efforts at conditioning on a group level. For example, cigarette smoking was negatively reinforced by the removal of the community's only supply of tobacco into less and less accessible areas. Also, some individuals practice self-conditioning by graphing their behavior patterns and then programming changes through schedules of reinforcement. However, these measures do not even begin to approach the degree of conditioning envisioned in Walden II, and the failure of Twin Oaks to employ more substantial behaviorist projects indicates the difficulty of applying reinforcement techniques to the daily affairs of an ongoing community.[45]

In conclusion, Twin Oaks can stand proudly as one of the few communes of the 1960s that has demonstrated a capacity to endure. Membership turnover has declined; in fact, there is a waiting list of applicants for admission. Many of the settlement's economic and interpersonal dilemmas are being resolved, and the prospects for the community's continuing existence appear excellent. However, Twin Oaks is certainly not a working model of Walden II.[46] Moreover, as yet, it shows no signs of developing into the progenitor of a new golden age.

REFERENCES AND NOTES

1. In addition to *Walden II,* Skinner's most well-known works include: *Behavior of organisms.* New York: Appleton-Century, 1938; *Science and human behavior.* New York: Macmillan, 1953; and *Beyond freedom and dignity.* New York: Macmillan, 1971.

2. For brief discussions of the principles of behaviorist psychology, see the following articles in the *International encyclopedia of the social sciences,* Vol. 9 (New York: Macmillan and The Free Press, 1968): L. Casler, Instrumental learning, pp. 130–135; S. S. Pliskoff and C. B. Ferster, Reinforcement, pp. 135–143; and R. Solomon, Avoidance learning, pp. 148–153.

3. B. F. Skinner. *Walden II.* New York: Macmillan, 1948, p. 89.

4. Ibid., p. 256.

5. Ibid., p. 90.

6. Ibid., pp. 21, 23.

7. Ibid., pp. 40–41, 68, 246–247.

8. Ibid., p. 79. See also: pp. 41–45, 228–229.

9. Ibid., pp. 7–12, 25–26, 78–79, 225–226, 228–229.

10. Ibid., pp. 55–56, 133, 235.

11. Ibid., pp. 88–94, 126–127, 160.

12. Ibid., p. 28.

13. Ibid., pp. 54–55, 164, 189, 269–270.

14. Ibid., p. 269. See also: pp. 266–270.

15. Ibid., pp. 54, 195–196, 232–235, 237, 263–264, 288–289.

16. Ibid., pp. 51–54, 57, 76–82, 172–173.

17. Ibid., pp. 34–36, 51, 53, 61, 63–66, 219, 233.

18. Ibid., pp. 129–136, 160–161.

19. Ibid., pp. 96, 99, 140–148.

20. Ibid., pp. 113–115, 123–124.

21. Ibid., pp. 112. See also: pp. 95–99, 107–113, 124.

22. Ibid., pp. 90–91, 117–120, 237–239.

23. Ibid., pp. 120, 122, 163.

24. Ibid., p. 48.

25. Ibid., pp. 44–50, 68–69.

26. Ibid., pp. 57 88–91, 127, 237.

27. Ibid., pp. 105–107.

28. Ibid., pp. 90, 102–103, 127, 169–172.

29. Ibid., pp. 140, 147, 163–164, 247, 300.
30. Ibid., p. 257.
31. Ibid., p. 259.
32. Ibid., pp. 262–263.
33. Ibid., pp. 163, 196–202.
34. Ibid., pp. 164–165.
35. Ibid., pp. 164, 173–174, 269.
36. Ibid., pp. 29–30, 174–175.
37. Ibid., pp. 205–210.
38. Ibid., p. 209. See: pp. 291–292.
39. Ibid., p. 290.
40. For further information on organized efforts to create a Walden II model in practice, see: Bouvard, M. *The intentional community movement.* Port Washington, N.Y: Kennikat, 1975, pp. 152–153; Kanter, R. *Commitment and community,* Cambridge, Mass.: Harvard University Press, 1972, p. 166.
41. Kanter, op. cit., pp. 19–20; Bouvard, op. cit., pp. 162–165.
42. The entire Twin Oaks behavior code is reprinted in Bouvard, op. cit., pp. 187–188. See also: Houriet, R. *Getting back together.* New York: Coward, McCann & Geoghegan, 1971, pp. 293–295; Bouvard, op. cit., pp. 174–179; Kanter, op. cit., pp. 23–25, 26–27.
43. Houriet, op. cit., pp. 308–309; Kanter, op. cit., pp. 19–20. Bouvard, op. cit., pp. 170–174. The problem of vehicles is described in: Kinkade, K. *A Walden Two experiment.* New York: William Morrow, 1973, pp. 71–81. See also: pp. 61–81.
44. An account of the difficulties presented by undesirable traits among early members can be found in: Kinkade, op. cit., pp. 44–49, 235–239. On political disputes at Twin Oaks, see: Bouvard, op. cit., pp. 176–177; Kinkade, op. cit., pp. 226–228.
45. Houriet, op. cit., pp. 315–317; Bouvard, op. cit., pp. 167–168; Kinkade, op. cit., pp. 261–265; French, D., and French, E. *Working communally.* New York: Russell Sage Foundation, 1975, pp. 164–165.
46. Kanter, op. cit., p. 31; Houriet, op. cit., pp. 309–310; Bouvard, op. cit., pp. 154–155, 163, 181–183; Kinkade, op. cit., pp. 56–67.

PART III: A SYNTHESIS OF ENVIRONMENTAL AND UTOPIAN PERSPECTIVES

CHAPTER 7

An Environmental Perspective
on Utopia

INTRODUCTION

At this point, it may be useful to recapitulate briefly what has been presented thus far. We have discussed two modes of thought—environmental theory and utopian speculation—in light of their historical development, the issues they focus on, and the problems they encounter. We have critically examined four utopias, providing a detailed data base for subsequent analysis. We now wish to direct each mode of thought toward the other. In this chapter, we consider how environmental thought can inform the utopian imagination, how it can contribute to the utopian project, and how it can assist in resolving, or at least clarifying, the problems that have arisen within utopian thinking, particularly the problems suggested by antiutopians.

Our discussion is in two sections. The first section—the theoretical relationship—denotes the manner in which distinct methods and patterns of historical development have resulted in broad differences between environmental and utopian perspectives.

The second section focuses on the implications of environmental thought for the construction of utopias in six substantive areas: the selection of local environment, the complexity, the innovation and change, the planning of the social environment, the balance, and the scale.

THE THEORETICAL RELATIONSHIP

In general, utopists do not base their systems on environmental theory, nor do they elaborate on the ecological requirements and parameters of their future societies. Although nature often intrudes into utopia for aesthetic reasons utopian theorists largely ignore the issues environmental theorists focus on. Utopists do not make an empirical analysis of the ongoing interaction of people and their actual environment and then project their findings into the future. Although utopists claim that their "laws" follow "the order of nature," in fact, they are quite arbitrary. "Instead of trying to discover the laws of nature," Berneri noted, utopian writers "preferred to invent them, or found them in the 'archives of ancient prudence.' " [1]

Moreover, utopias rarely present "natural" or "primitive" social structures as an acceptable human ideal. Even those utopists who describe a society in or close to "the state of nature" are usually seeking to convey a veiled criticism of corrupt "modern" institutions rather than endorsing a return to tribal culture. Utopias tend to remove man from nature, and they often employ the environment to support artificial human institutions. Aldous Huxley quickly added electricity, as well as drugs and medication, to his tropical island utopia. And Zamiatin, like many antiutopians who carry utopian logic to an absurd or horrific conclusion, extended the tendency to wall off nature to a future in which a great Green Wall separates an entirely fabricated civilization from everything natural. Expressing that logic, Zamiatin's character exclaims:

> "Man ceased to be a wild animal the day he built the first wall; man ceased to
> be a wild man only on the day when the Green Wall was completed, when by
> this wall we isolated our machine-like, perfect world from the irrational, ugly
> world of trees, birds and beasts." [2]

An acknowledgment of these dual tendencies—the failure to employ ecological analysis and the construction of social systems removed from natural surroundings—simply raises a new question. Are these trends endemic to utopian thinking? Do they indicate that utopian speculation cannot incorporate ecological theory or that it cannot envision a satisfying future for man closer to nature? The answer to these questions requires an understanding of the reasons why utopian thought has developed in this fashion.

Utopian theory and scientific theory approach issues concerning the environment from different methodological perspectives. Basically, utopists are not inductive theorists. They do not discern "laws" of a given era and extrapolate them to a new society. The essence of their endeavor is the conviction that social, political, technological, and even natural laws can be broken—somehow, at sometime. Utopian thought is basically deductive. Utopists declare certain ethical and social principles and then deduce the details of a society that conforms to these principles. Thus, in two of our utopias, Oneida and the kibbutzim, ideology served as the guiding framework upon which everything else was based. Even Walden II was developed as an effort to deduce a model of social organization from the potential of underlying principles (albeit scientific principles).

Does this mean that utopias cannot accommodate ecological findings? Decidedly not. Regardless of the source of a utopist's basic premises, he or she may still employ the methods of scientific analysis in the process of deducing an ongoing social system. For example, assume that a utopist believes that all those dwelling in utopia should receive adequate food from communal storehouses. Science plays no role in legitimizing this goal. But environmental theory can guide the construction of social institutions that might satisfy it. The environmental scientist might stipulate minimal capabilities in the technology and expertise of food production as prerequisites for such a goal. He might point out that without population control, this particular utopia may eventually be offering equal access to empty storehouses.

Similarly, if it was ideology that directed the Zionist pioneers to establish settlements near malarial swamps, it was the scientist who directed that they exterminate the mosquitoes (or drain their breeding grounds) in order to survive. Thus, the utopist is perfectly capable of bringing the fruits of environmental research to bear in his vision. He must always do so, however, with a skeptical eye, remembering that environmental science is as much a social and historical product as economics or ethics. Even within its realm, today's impossibilities may become tomorrow's realities.

In considering the utopists' preference for removing man from "natural" environments, we face a different issue. The utopists' attitude on this point is basically a product of history, tradition, values, and social theory. Lewis Mumford, in an intriguing essay, "Utopia, the City, and the Machine," considers the extent to which the first utopian visions (Plato's), which are still emulated (H. G. Wells), had their roots in the historical first cities of the Near East and in the historical first "machines," which were in fact "labor machines," organized masses of conscripted workers working with mechanical precision. These two forms, the city and the machine, so increased the limits of human power that they captivated the imagination of those thinkers disposed to consider the human prospect. As

Mumford noted, "Through the greater part of history, it was the image of the city that lingered in the human imagination as the closest approach to paradise that one might hope for on earth." [3]

If this were the sole basis for the predominance of the urban form in utopia, one might classify the problem as relatively minor. In fact, this "archetypal" image of the city includes many of those aspects of utopia most criticized by antiutopians: hierarchy, rigidity, and coercion. There is ample reason to dispense with it. But the crux of the problem is not loyalty to the city; it is the value of its alternative. What precisely would constitute a more "natural" environment? For that matter, on what basis can any environment be termed more natural than any other? The apparent criterion is the degree of human interference with natural processes—the more natural region being that least interfered with. Yet if men are to live in a natural environment, they are almost certain to affect it, thereby rendering it no longer natural. Indeed, the purely natural utopia would be one of self-imposed environmental determinism, in which the human inhabitants yielded without resistance to every environmental impact, a highly implausible notion.

To a utopian, such a prospect constitutes blasphemy. It violates his basic objective, the design by men of their own destiny. For that reason, the natural utopia is a contradiction in terms. Further, from a pragmatic point of view, the entire earth has been modified by man and is consequently unnatural. The only path forward is to seek a superior "unnatural" environment. Does this point of view reject all elements of a return to nature? Is it an endorsement of a concrete future? Again, the answer is in the negative. The logic that Zamiatin carried to its extreme can be halted short of the Green Wall. The formation of an environment on human terms does not demand the elimination of all spontaneous natural interaction. On the contrary, such an objective would have disastrous consequences. Rather, the utopian environment must be one of ecological balance, a goal that, as we shall see, utopists are adept at developing.

SUBSTANTIVE ISSUES

Selection of Local Environment

Utopias are not ethereal. One of their advantages is that they are an attempt at the realization of abstract forms in a "living" context. Hence, a utopia must have a location, a place. The region selected for a utopia is often fictitious, an unknown land beyond the sea. Our objective in this section is to inquire whether utopists include, in the location of their utopias, elements necessary for the foundation of their ideal society anywhere in the real world. Thus, we ask whether utopian writers recognize that locating their society demands more than map coordinates. A utopia must be located in a real environment, an area with a specific climate, soil, animal and plant life, topography, and water resources: a functioning ecosystem. Is the utopian environment described adequately? Can it support the social structure set in its midst? In general, our utopias demonstrated only minimal consideration of the ecological characteristics of their physical environment, although Oneida and the kibbutzim quickly expanded their ecological knowledge in order to survive.

Oneida's Perfectionists directed little attention to the environmental characteristics of their community site; it was simply an available location for a movement in scattered disarray after the Putney disaster. The New York valley fortuitously provided ample water and fertile soil. Yet, despite their best efforts, the settlers proved incapable of developing an agricultural base sufficient to support their community. They were thus forced to modify their original intentions in order to establish a viable economy. As a result of the large amounts of capital they acquired, the inventiveness of their membership, and the substantial resource of water power on their property, the Perfectionists escaped financial disaster and transformed themselves into successful industrial entrepreneurs. But the very modifications that enabled them to adjust their economy to their environment had effects detrimental to their ideology. Oneida's industries led to the hiring of a separate, nonmember class of employees as well as to the technical education of community youth at outside universities. These factors were instrumental in dissolving the communal and religious ties that bound the Perfectionists together.

The Zionist pioneers who established the first kibbutzim were deeply concerned with the location of their settlements. However, this concern was based more on ideology than on ecology. They selected Palestine as their goal because of its historical significance as a Jewish homeland, and they migrated there despite the environmental obstacles. However, ecosystems have little respect for human tradition. Once the settlers actually began to establish their communities, they had to adjust their values to the necessities of a different landscape.

Some of the pioneers' principles proved functional in the new environment. A communal, socialist economy survived where autonomous households would have failed. The admiration for physical labor proved compatible with a land that required all to work as hard as they could. On the other hand, the wish to create liberated, unstructured, spontaneous societies found an unfavorable climate. Survival in Palestine necessitated organization and discipline. Certain areas could not be settled without environmental modification. And so the kibbutzim restructured the environment, draining swamps and establishing irrigation networks. They employed technology to increase their ability to prosper in the environment. Buildings were designed to withstand the weather; machinery was brought to the fields to intensify agricultural production.

These technological innovations had unintended effects on ideology and social structure. Increasing occupational specialization introduced rigidities into the allocation of communal labor. The importance of technical expertise challenged the status of those who performed physical labor. Finally, despite experimentation and innovation, many kibbutzim found that agriculture could not fully support the consumption demands of their members. Like Oneida, they were forced to industrialize, and like Oneida, they employed outside workers in their factories, thereby tolerating a breach of one of their most significant beliefs. However, unlike Oneida, kibbutz ideology and social organization proved flexible enough to tolerate these changes and yet continue in existence.

One might have expected *Walden II*, written by an environmentally conscious behavioral scientist, to reflect an increased concern for ecological factors in the selection of a site. Just the contrary is the case. Skinner's treatment of the environment is the most cursory of all. There is no detailed analysis of local geographic variables that might aid or hamper the development of a community. Walden II-type communities can apparently exist without danger that ecological factors will force fundamental modification of their structure. In pursuing the techniques that he believes will eliminate sociological obstacles to human perfection, Skinner tended to disregard organic and ecological factors. He apparently assumes that the scientific method will permit the control of nature, as it permits the control of men.

Normally, in the case of a utopian novel, one is limited to a critical dispute with the author's logic. However, with Walden II, additional evidence is available. Skinner's novel encouraged some individuals to develop Walden II communities of their own. As discussed above (Chapter 6), one such group has published an account of its first years. They found the environment to be much more of a problem than they had been led to expect. After substantial travail, they had to abandon any hope of supporting the community through agriculture. Modern technology proved to be less capable of dominating nature in reality than in fantasy. The creators of the experimental Walden II have managed to keep their community in operation by adjusting to local conditions, but environmental factors have had a much more pervasive effect on them than *Walden II* would have led them to expect.[4]

Factors related to the advantages of specific locations did receive consideration in the planning of Columbia. Economic and social aspects of the location, important to the marketability of the homes in the project, proved to be the primary focus of attention. Rouse sought an area close to employment opportunities for the breadwinners of Columbia's future families. Similarly, Columbia needed to be contiguous to a highway system to provide access to services and institutions not available in the new town itself.

Although the builders of Columbia adapted their plans to the topographical characteristics of the Maryland countryside, they failed to conceive of the New Town site as a functioning, interconnected, and dynamic ecosystem. Since the area where Columbia now stands was fertile farmland, Rouse had an unusual opportunity to build a community that could be ecologically integrated with its surroundings. Columbia might have been a major consumer of local agricultural production. In turn, the wastes of the New Town could have been processed and returned to the soil, completing the ecological cycle. An experiment of this magnitude, however, was beyond the ambitions of the planners or, for that matter, of public attitudes at the time. Rouse designed Columbia to acquire necessary resources through its economic interactions with institutions that managed distant ecosystems.

There was little expectation that local environmental factors would exert major influence on the anticipated life-styles of Columbia's residents. This confidence resulted from two factors. First, the widespread assumption in advanced industrial societies is that sufficient technological sophistication is available to deal with all but the most unusual environmental conditions. Second, Columbia traded its dependence on aspects of its own local environment for a dependence on organizations in the surrounding macroenvironment. When Columbia first came into being, a reliance of this type could be accepted much more sanguinely than today. Should these outside organizations fail or falter, Columbians would have to change their community radically to utilize local ecological conditions adequately.

This analysis indicates that none of our utopian communities were based on a rigorous understanding of the particular environments in which they were located. As a consequence, they either had to depend on other social organizations as mediators between utopia and the environment (Columbia), or they had to modify their structures (Oneida and the kibbutz), or they could be expected to have to carry out such modifications. When technology was employed to meet environmental limits, unforeseen social consequences resulted. When the community chose to rely on outside sources of environmental control, it left itself vulnerable to the actions of institutions that had no necessary commitment to the preservation of its values or structures.

These findings make evident the fact that utopia cannot be sensibly conceived of except in a real environment. Each of the environments we have considered offered ample scope for utopian possibilities. The utopias in our case studies failed to comprehend the parameters within which their social visions had to function. Therefore, they had to restructure unworkable models or be prepared to develop new structures, efforts that are considerably more problematic than the production of an original design based on sound ecological and social analysis.

One additional point must be noted. The discussion of local environments is particularly relevant to the utopias described above because they were expected to exist in a single, small area (Walden II is a possible exception). However, modern utopists have tended to replace the dream of social perfection on some lost island with that of a worldwide structure in the distant future (time replaces space as the means of assuring sufficient distance between a utopia and present circumstances). In a world utopia, local conditions are still of significance. Any utopian macrostructure will have to be sufficiently flexible to endure in varying environments. However, new problems of scale arise in the consideration of a planet-sized society. These are of sufficient scope to require separate discussion.

Complexity

The utopist seeks to bring order and stability to the chaos of life. Patterns of behavior are prescribed and regulated; uniformity supplants diversity. To some extent, this tendency may be a logical (but still resistible) concomitant of the utopian intellectual enterprise. The utopian writer seeks to organize the structure of an entire, ongoing society. He must categorize and simplify if he is to present a cogent statement rather than floundering in an endless mass of detail.

There is another root for the utopist's preference for simplification: the idealist element in utopian thought. The utopist often accepts the notion of social perfection, the possibility of an unimprovable society, the end point of human progress. This objective is fulfilled by the depiction of an image of life in perfect congruity with those principles that the utopian writer values most highly. Thus, the utopist pursues a singular goal. Why accept the possibility of a plurality of forms when it is possible to conceive of the ultimate form itself. The utopia cannot lower its standards: all buildings, institutions, and people must be perfect and hence identical.

In our case studies, one can observe an effort to simplify social practices and to render them uniform, although the degree to which this occurred varied among the different societies. Skinner's vision of scientific structure and conditioned personalities stresses a fundamental homogeneity, even while accepting a certain degree of diversity. The experimental utopias proved less rigid, since they faced the immeasurable complexity of living people and institutions. Still, for all their theoretical opposition to "legality," Oneida's Perfectionists admitted little variation in major life activities. The kibbutz, a generally flexible model, imposed limits on occupations, dwellings, consumption, and acceptable values. Although Columbia sought social heterogeneity by attempting to assure access to different ethnic and socioeconomic groups, the majority of Columbians seem to reflect prevailing patterns of suburban conformity.

To some extent, the concern for uniformity extends to the utopist's attitude toward the physical environment. Walden II's environment has a well-trimmed, managed appearance, implying that regulation is as common here as within the human dwelling areas. In addition, Skinner alluded to the use of conditioning techniques in wildlife management when sheets are tied to an electrified fence and then, after the appropriate response has been learned, strung by themselves to control the movement of the community's sheep.

Columbia replaced a complex, functioning rural ecosystem with a much more homogenous and dependent urban configuration. As is common in advanced industrial societies, however, even greatly simplified regional environments can maintain stability as specialized elements in broader and more intricate social and ecological systems. An analysis of the kibbutzim leaves no doubt that their early settlers utterly reshaped the environment they found on first reaching Palestine. However, the barren and fruitless nature of these regions was such that human organization increased their complexity. The kibbutz, then, a utopia in an abused and vacant wilderness, is an exception to the usual pattern.

The general tendencies in utopias to achieve uniformity in social structures and to simplify the natural environment comes as no surprise to antiutopians. They reject both trends—for aesthetic reasons—and for political ones. The critics argue that uniformity must be enforced, with a decline in variety that is proportional to the increase in repression. In opposition to the utopian prospect, the antiutopians place their faith in the intrinsic heterogeneity and unpredictability of the natural and instinctual impulses of man. When we examine the ecologist's perspective on these issues, it appears the antiutopians have found an ally, albeit one who avoids their preference for the literary and the melodramatic.

The ecologist's preference for environmental diversity stems from the prospect that diversity provides extended possibilities for feedback systems. These can reduce oscillations in natural cycles, thereby increasing ecosystem stability. The relevant hypothesis concerns the relation between the diversity of species in an ecosystem and the stability of its population, to wit, the greater the variety the greater the stability. A model of interactions between predator and prey populations illustrates the concept. Consider two ecosystems, A and B. A is a simple system, with only one predator species and one prey species. B is complex, with the same species as A plus several other predator and prey species. Suppose an external factor (the weather and its effect on local plant life) reduces the population of the prey species found in A. The predator species in A is in a hopeless situation; it can find no other source of food and its population will decline. In B, however, such an event is less destabilizing. The predator species can seek other prey. There may be some decline in population, but it will be minimized.[5]

Simple ecosystems are also susceptible to "invasion" by new species that find little competition in their ecosystem. For example, Bates observed, "Animals and plants, accidentally or intentionally brought into simple island communities by man, often undergo catastrophic population explosions. Hawaii has seen many examples of this. The efforts at cure have involved attempts to restore a steady state by increasing the complexity of the system through the introduction of parasites and predators of the invading aliens." [6]

Ecological study of the relationship between diversity and stability is a relatively recent focus of analysis. Hypothesis and findings are tentative. It is not certain whether diversity is always correlated with stability, nor can one confidently assert that increasing environmental diversity will necessarily increase environmental stability. However, there is general agreement on the contention that when man enters an ecosystem and drastically reduces its diversity, he also markedly increases its vulnerability to catastrophe.

An example of this phenomenon is the notorious openness of cultivated crops to outbreaks of agricultural pests. Farmers generally plant dense clusters of single species. Since the life cycles of herbivorous insects and other pests are specialized to a single host plant, such organisms thrive on homogeneity. But predator species tend to require greater environmental variety; hence, their numbers decrease, allowing the pests to multiply without predator control.[7]

These environmental considerations suggest that man limit his proclivity to oversimplify the ecosystems on which he is dependent. But what of his social structure? Does environmental theory support the maintenance of variety in cities as well as in forests? Of course, one can suggest the power of cultural consistency. A society that values diversity in nature (even for functional reasons) may have difficulty legitimating the absence of diversity in other aspects of life. Natural variation would constitute an ongoing contradiction and temptation.

Are other aspects of society susceptible to collapse if oversimplified? What about one-industry economies? How can they respond to a change in demand or in sources of raw materials? Or consider transportation. One society might rely on a collection of planes, trains, buses, autos, bicycles, and horse-drawn carriages. Another might develop the utopian vehicle of the future, superior to all the others. Which of the two is more likely to find itself in the unenviable situation of having all motion cease? [8]

Thus, the utopian project stands vulnerable to the combined criticism of antiutopians and ecologists in terms of its tendency to oversimplify and render homogeneous both the physical and the social environment. How can utopists respond to this critique? What is demanded is that utopias encourage environmental and social diversity. What changes in the activity of producing utopias might facilitate such an outcome? The tendency toward uniformity has its roots in the particular manner of utopian creation: the solitary intellectual engaged in developing an idealist and abstract design. This process can be modified.

First, the defects of an idealist perspective can be avoided if the utopia is viewed in terms of history. Utopias should be constructed with the recognition that they portray a future envisioned by people with a historically limited outlook. Instead of the utopia's being defined as the best of all possible worlds, it would become the best possible world as seen from the necessarily limited perspective of the present. A component of each utopia should be the understanding that it would eventually be supplanted by subsequent utopias. Each utopian society needs to incorporate sufficient variety and flexibility to permit the growth of its successor. At the environmental level, for example, this requirement might result in a utopia's maintaining the existence of plant and animal species that play no role in their own society but that could prove necessary as an organic basis for a subsequent utopia.

Second, the limits on diversity related to the unrestricted insight of a single individual could be avoided by the collectivizing of the utopian project. More than mere collaboration, such a mode could bring together a group of futurists with diverse backgrounds and views. If they accepted the notion that elements of the society that they envisioned must be agreed to by a majority, then it is hard to conceive of an end product that would not guarantee substantial variety.

Finally, there is the problem of how to merge deductions from principles and abstract categories with the complexity of living systems, without detriment to the latter. The best solution is to provide means by which the abstract framework can be informed and shaped by a substantial diversity of people. The artist or scholar is not alone in his concern for a more perfect society. That interest is shared by many political, economic, and social organizations, groups that are indispensable if elements of any utopia are ever to be realized. These groups are deeply concerned with the specific details of meeting the complex, interconnected needs of the myriad of individuals who make up any society, utopian or otherwise.

There is no surer way to prevent utopian planning from glossing over some unshapely detail than to give the people whose interests and desires comprise that detail a voice in the utopian project. Of course, such a course is likely to result in argument and dispute. Different groups will prefer different models. Some details and some interests will have to be sacrificed. But the utopian projects with the greatest appeal, and hence the greatest chance for genuine impact, will be those that accommodate the most details and that satisfy the greatest number of aspirations. In so doing, they will develop the variety and complexity our argument has led us to recognize that they require.

Innovation and Change

One of the most insistent criticisms of utopias is that they cannot change. Utopia, often located out of history and beyond time, seems to claim to have conquered both. It is static, motionless; it cannot develop because it is unimprovable. Indeed, perfection is as incompatible with innovation as it is with diversity. There is no basis for even minimal alterations. The antiutopians fear the use of totalitarian state power to ensure societal stability (i.e., lack of change). Echoing such a perspective, Mumford reflected:

> From the first, a kind of mechanical rigidity afflicts all utopias. On the most generous interpretation, this is due to the tendency of the mind, or at least of language, noted by Bergson, to fix and geometrize all forms of motion and organic change, to arrest life in order to understand it, to kill the organism in

order to control it, to combat that ceaseless process of self-transformation which lies at the very origin of species.

All ideal models have this same life-arresting, if not life-denying, property: hence nothing could be more fatal to human society than to achieve its ideals.[9]

An attempt to bring the environmental perspective to bear on this issue leads to complex and ambiguous findings. On the one hand, nature is dynamic. Through the processes of mutation and natural selection, organic species change through time, adapting themselves to their environment. Ecosystems also develop through time. In this process, known as ecological succession, the organisms in an ecosystem change their environment, thereby creating conditions favorable to their replacement by other species. Ricklefs offered the following example of a stage in succession:

Horseweed is extremely resistant to dessication and it rapidly colonizes bare fields, but its presence in fields moderates the environment by shading the soil, thereby reducing evaporation and increasing the humidity of the air near the surface. Desiccation becomes a less important factor in the environment, allowing desiccation-sensitive species to invade the community and eventually to compete more successfully than Horseweed.[10]

Over hundreds of years, and many such stages, simple grassland ecosystems can develop into complex forests.

On the other hand, ecological systems also have strong tendencies toward stability. As noted above, ecosystems are homeostatic: they have feedback mechanisms to restore equilibrium after a disturbance. Therefore, ecological succession may result in a final climax community that is "self-perpetuating and in equilibrium with the physical habitat." In such cases, a large, diverse, and interdependent structure has sufficient homeostatic capability to prevent further development.

Still, a climax community is stable only as long as the physical environment is stable. Environmental stability is unlikely over the long run. Extreme variation in weather, fires, geological changes, and so on can disrupt ecosystems and require new stages of succession to restore stability. Developments in neighboring ecosystems and ongoing evolutionary variation are additional destabilizing agents. Hence, an environmental perspective tells us that nature is always potentially dynamic and unstable and that human institutions must retain the flexibility and capacity for change that environmental perturbations may require.[11]

However, there is another equally significant element in the environmental concern with change. Modifications in the ongoing processes of an ecosystem—whether natural or man-made—will result in a homeostatic response as the system attempts to restore stability. The manner in which this occurs may significantly limit the number and type of modifications that are actually in the best interests of mankind.

First of all, a disruption of sufficient magnitude can overwhelm the homeostatic capabilities of an ecosystem. For example, consider, as does ecologist Barry Commoner, the fresh-water ecological cycle: fish—organic waste—bacteria of decay—inorganic products—algae—fish. If human beings dump enough of their wastes into a body of fresh water, an enormous increase in the algae population may result, with catastrophic consequences for the stability of the system. As Commoner explained:

> If the nutrient level of the water becomes so high as to stimulate the rapid growth of algae, the dense algal population cannot be long sustained because of the intrinsic limitations of photosynthetic efficience. As the thickness of the algal layer in the water increases, the light required for photosynthesis that can reach the lower parts of the algal layer becomes sharply diminished, so that any strong overgrowth of algae very quickly dies back, releasing organic debris. The organic matter level may then become so great that its decay totally depletes the oxygen content of the water. The bacteria of decay then die off, for they must have oxygen to survive. The entire aquatic cycle collapses.[12]

Hence, any society that may wish to rely on that aquatic ecosystem must ensure that changes in and around it do not move beyond the maximum threshold of its feedback mechanisms.

Second, even if innovations do not overwhelm an ecosystem, they may have secondary consequences that reach far beyond their immediate environmental impact. Ecosystems are interconnected functioning systems. What happens in one part has effects on other parts, and those effects have their own subsequent effects.[13] Thus, a farmer who uses pesticides to kill insects attacking his crop discovers that he is killing birds that acted as a natural mechanism for controlling other agricultural pests. People who dump mercury into the sea as a chemical waste find it returning to land in fish caught for their own consumption.

Third, if men seek to replace natural mechanisms of balance and to introduce their own pattern into an ecosystem (as in long-term agriculture), then they must stand ready to continue to interfere in that system to enforce stability (for example, with pesticides). Moreover, managed stability may require "subsidies" of resources (fertilizers) and energy from other ecosystems, which may eventually become depleted. This is especially true where the human goal is to maximize the productivity of a region, such as increasing crop yield per acre.

Finally, should men fail in their endeavor to maintain an artificial system, they can expect little or no help from natural restorative processes.[14] For example, one consequence of the modern "green revolution" is the widespread use of a few strains of high-yield crops. But if some blight capable of destroying these strains appears, and if man cannot defend his crops, then the elimination of low-yield strains may have so reduced the genetic variety of these plant species that new resistant strains cannot be developed. The man-managed system lacks the adaptive strength of the natural one. Men, therefore, may have to pay the price of their ambition: a major decline in their food supply.

These arguments demonstrate that the environmental perspective on change is not one-sided. Man must retain the capacity to change. However, he must also make certain that the specific changes, and the rate of change, do not damage those aspects of the environment upon which he depends or lead to subsequent costs or consequences with which he is unprepared to cope. Whether as a response to environmental variation or as a result of his own social and cultural dynamics, man's innovations must be oriented toward the return to, or maintenance of, ecological stability and balance. This point is of sufficient importance that we devote a separate section to it following our discussion of the issue of stasis versus innovation. Oneida demonstrated a model somewhat different from that expected by the antiutopians. The Perfectionist political structure was in effect an authoritarian one-man rule. Yet, the community maintained an intense commitment to improvement and technical innovation. Economic and social institutions were subject to modification, depending upon the financial situation of the settlement and the developing perspective of John Humphrey Noyes.

Considering the Perfectionists' first efforts at farming and their subsequent adoption of industry, it is apparent that they also introduced changes into the relatively primitive ecosystem they inhabited. Their attitudes toward pollution or ecological balance were no more advanced than those of other 19th-century entrepreneurs. Thus, the impact of their innovations was hardly likely to result in balanced environmental change.

Nevertheless, it was not the ecological consequences of Oneida's innovations that caused the community's undoing. In the midst of a largely rural nation, industrial-based ecological disturbance would take many years to reach levels capable of disrupting human society. There was ample room to push environmental consequences out of sight and out of mind. But the social effects of economic and technical change could not be so easily banished. In particular, the mixture of Oneida's essentially static theology and its dynamic economy and technology proved to be a highly unstable combination.

First, with Noyes's increasing age, the community inevitably faced a problem of succession, indeed a problem of succession of generations, since most of the central members were contemporaries of their leader. Lacking the orthodox faith of their parents, the young community members were both unsuitable as leaders and unwilling to accept continual second-class status in relation to their "spiritual" superiors. The bond of common belief disintegrated just when it was needed most.

Moreover, Oneida's economic structure no longer reinforced a commitment to group living. In its efforts to adjust to the demands of an industrialized market economy, the community had transformed itself from a society of comrades working together to a colony of managers who supervised their employees during the day and returned to their "communist" home at night. Hence, the mutual dependence of work in a common endeavor had been replaced by the more passive and autonomous relationship of common ownership. When religious leadership collapsed, there was no longer a rationale for superimposing a communitarian social structure over a capitalist economic base. A joint stock company could operate as profitably as a utopia, and Oneida became just another business in a competitive economic system.

Walden II also stands as a social model controlled by a small central elite but strongly committed to innovation. In this case, both the mode of government and the role of innovation are legitimated by a belief in the scientific method. The problem in Walden II is not that innovation will violate the community's values but rather that experimentation has been charged with devising the community's values, a task for which science is utterly unsuited. The experimental method may be used to reach a goal already set. But science alone cannot select objectives for humanity: it cannot design a utopia. Over the long run, Walden II is Bacon's House of Salomon run amok, furiously providing answers without any means of ascertaining the value and meaning of questions. Walden II will apparently innovate continuously without ever reaching or even defining a goal. Stasis will have been conquered only to be replaced by perpetual and purposeless motion.

Skinner does not elaborate as to how the environment will fare in the face of Walden II's ongoing innovations. However, Walden II's leader makes use of phrases such as "the conquest of nature" and "the triumph over nature." When such attitudes are a basic part of a system that may proceed to develop without moral restraint, the prospects for ecological stability are dubious.

Although the early settlers of the kibbutzim had strong principles, they usually lacked a firm commitment to any precise institutional form through which those principles might be realized. Thus, their ideology permitted some flexibility. Once in Palestine, they found that the rugged environment required a willingness to innovate in order to meet community needs and maintain high levels of production. The economic necessity of competing in national and international markets, as well as the impact on members' desires of consumption levels elsewhere in the state, increased the pressures for economic efficiency.

In addition, a new generation began to appear. Lacking the revolutionary experiences of their predecessors, these young men and women brought a new perspective to kibbutz life. They advanced new desires for expanded family life and for greater occupational variety. To all of these pressures, the kibbutzim responded with innovations: mechanized agriculture, a more rigid division of labor, and industrialization. Structural changes could and did conflict with kibbutz values. However, the settlements adopted a pragmatic attitude to these conflicts. They accepted modifications in their ideology rather than face an all-or-nothing confrontation between morality and change. They also resolved contradictions in kibbutz social structure by creatively employing innovations such as using industry to provide wider job opportunities for kibbutz youth as well as to increase income.

Kibbutz settlers had little alternative as to whether or not they would introduce change into local ecosystems. In many cases, the natural environment could hardly support human life. However, the difficult conditions ensured that the settlers undertook innovation with caution. Many kibbutzim have essentially developed and managed new ecosystems. Through drainage, terracing, special modes of plowing, and irrigation projects, they have restructured the environment to carry out highly intensive cultivation. What the long-run prospects of such systems are, including their dependence on energy reserves available elsewhere, remains to be seen.[15]

The planners of Columbia sought to design a community conducive to "human growth" and development. Although Rouse never specifically defined the direction of growth he envisioned, his practices make the outline of his objective quite evident. Columbia maintains the basic institutions of middle-class American life: nuclear family, work roles, laws, political structure, and educational system. Culturally, it reflects middle-class norms. Thus, it seems logical that Columbia residents were expected to be constrained by these structures and values. Their life styles do demonstrate a basically stable family life, the pursuit of economic success, and a strong tendency toward socially acceptable and law-abiding behavior.

In light of these objectives, the amount of innovation Columbia was designed to promote seems rather limited. The community was constructed to meet the requirements of an established and stable pattern of life. Only in relatively marginal areas—culture, recreation, and some social services—were modifications expected. In order to facilitate change in these areas, however, Rouse established the citywide Columbia Association and ensured that it would have funds adequate to its task.

If Columbia was not planned to promote basic change, how will it respond to unanticipated pressures for innovation? As regards modification of social practices, the issue remains ambiguous. When the youth culture and the women's movement introduced unexpected demands, Columbia adjusted its services to meet the new needs. Thus far, however, the challenges to middle-class life styles have been minimal. If they become more radical—perhaps the creation of urban communes in Columbian neighborhoods—the response might be more rigid.

Columbia's ability to respond to pressures for environmental change appears minimal. Once construction was completed, the community's physical plant offered few options for reorganization without staggering capital costs. Similarly, the community's major modes of interaction with the environment are already set. In fact, most of these are out of Columbia's direct control, being in the province of outside agencies: the country, public utilities, and the like. If large-scale environmental impacts, such as resource shortages or side effects from pollution, were to occur, Columbia would be no less vulnerable than any other unplanned city in an industrial society.

From the above evidence, it appears that the antiutopians were correct in their opposition to a static utopia. As a result of either external challenge (environmental or social) or internal dynamics, all of these utopias did change, or can be expected to change, in order to survive. However, both environmental theory and the experience of the utopian communities that attempted innovation indicate the destabilizing potential of social, technical, and ecological modifications.

The implications for a utopia are twofold. First, utopian models must have the capacity for continual development. To a large extent, this objective can be satisfied by the procedures suggested above to increase diversity. For example, eliminating the idealist component in a utopia removes one logical obstacle to the idea of an improvable (and changeable) utopia. Linking utopias to social movements ensures that the groups of individuals who create and experience one utopian model, and who in consequence develop changed needs and new ideas, will participate in the task of utopianizing once again.

Second, changes in a utopia, like the initial construction of a utopia itself, must be based on holistic planning. We refer here to a consideration of both the ecological and the social impacts of new proposals. Failure to plan holistically produces the possibility that the unintended consequences of one change will lead to equally unintended, and undesirable, new changes. Finally, men will have lost control of their own social structure. At that point, the utopia ceases to exist.

Planning of the Social Environment

The foregoing considerations indicate the necessity of careful planning of the social environment. Ecological balance may be achieved by many different types of communities. How is a modern utopist to decide which of the alternatives to follow? We believe that certain concepts developed in social environmental research can help to inform the construction of utopias. Specifically, the concept of "intersystems congruence" can inform utopists about how to construct the layout of cities and the plans of buildings. The human-relations perspective on organizational functioning can inform utopists about the organizational practices they might institute. Conclusions regarding the effects of different social climates can help the utopist develop an optimal social environment. A broad range of findings and concepts regarding the social environment have been comprehensively reviewed elsewhere.[16] We give brief illustrations from three of the five relevant areas here.

Architectural Variables: Physical Space and Building Design. A useful model in the exploration of the effect of the man-made physical environment on human behavior is the intersystems-congruence approach (see Chapter 2). Environments are viewed not as determining behavior in themselves but as setting broad limits on the phenomena that can occur in a given setting. Within these limits an environment may make some phenomena "either easier or more difficult to maintain so that all else equal these phenomena will tend to be found successfully maintaining themselves more in some types of settings than in others."[17] The physical environment provides a setting in which phenomena in other systems are more or less likely to occur.

For example, the effect of distance on social interaction and the formation of friendships has been studied extensively. The findings are unusually consistent and point to two main factors related to architecture and site plan. The first is the physical distance between doorways. As distance increases beyond two or three home entrances, the number of friends mutually chosen is extremely small and probably depends on contact in a community organization or some other social, nonarchitectural influence. The second major factor is the relative orientation of doorways or "fronts" of houses. The more indirect the orientation of two doorways, the less interaction is likely to occur. Close physical and functional distance is congruent with the formation of friendships and incongruent with social isolation.[18]

Another important area of architectural design is the arrangement of spaces within the interiors of buildings. Such spaces may be determined by the placement of walls or partitions to divide up large rooms, the arrangement of furniture inside a room, and the overall architectural design of the building itself. For example, friendship choices are affected by interior building design. Men living in open-cubicle barracks (no interior obstructions other than furniture) were correctly able to identify the occupants of more bunk locations than men assigned to closed-cubicle barracks. However, men in closed-cubicle barracks were more likely to choose men from within their own cubicle for free-time interaction. These men were also more likely to name men within their own cubicle as buddies. Restriction of sensory contact (e.g., visual and auditory) thus is associated with less social interaction with persons physically located farther away.[19]

A closed-cubicle design may enhance the development of small cohesive within-cubicle friendship groups and build up the morale and personal security of group members. However, closed cubicles may also result in more social isolates, as some people will not be compatible with the other people in their particular cubicle. Personal animosities resulting from crowded living conditions may be less easy to handle within the small closed cubicles. A clear understanding of a community's goals is necessary to a choice between the two living-area designs.

In a broader sense, building designs can be categorized as cohesive or isolating. A cohesive building encourages interaction and, hopefully, cohesion through its compact layout and the provision of central areas in which people can gather in large groups. An isolating building discourages large-group interactions and cohesion because of its extended layout, lengthy corridors, and many alternative routes for getting from one place to another. Architectural design can also facilitate residents' concern for a building's care and protection. For example, limiting the number of people who share common space may create a clear picture of who are to be its users and instill a feeling of responsibility for its defense.[20]

Physical environments can have an even wider impact by affecting the life styles and the values of the people who live in them. East London slum residents with widespread social networks based on their extended families and nearby neighbors were offered single-family detached housing in an outlying suburban area. The higher cost of the housing, plus commuting costs, made frequent visiting with those who remained behind in the slums impossible. Extended families were often broken up by the rehousing program. The new suburban setting encouraged people to try to "keep up with the Jones's," thereby emphasizing the importance of money and jobs. Putting a high value on "things," people became more "object-oriented" and less "people-oriented." This change was coupled with an emphasis on future time and planning ahead. Life was not as spontaneous as it had been in the old neighborhood.[21]

The behavior of people is affected by the man-made physical environments that they occupy. Studies in real-life and laboratory settings have demonstrated how environments encourage behavior with which they are congruent. Based on this understanding, the next task is to develop ways in which designers and architects can work with the people who will use their creations, so that the results will be congruent with the users' goals.

Designers can involve prospective users in the planning process. Architects should inquire about the needs of all those who are affected by their designs. James Holt, in examining who constitutes the user population of a new school, has concluded that it includes the entire community: both those who are directly involved, such as teachers, students, and administrators, and members of the community-at-large who pay taxes for the building and send their children there to learn. Holt advocated the formation of charrettes, or intensive group-planning efforts, to involve a wide range of people in the planning process. Community members encompassing the entire spectrum of users, together with professional educators, architects, engineers, planners, psychologists, business representatives, and local public officials, brainstorm for a concentrated time period to develop a clear conception of their design needs and solutions. Where the charrette technique has been used to plan facilities, the result has not been limited to innovative designs. There has also been reduction in the distance between people and their institutions and the creation of a more involved and cohesive community environment.[22]

Sommer has pointed out that users' input should not end with the process of designing a structure. He has called for the institutionalization of an evaluation of buildings, after they have been constructed, through the efforts of environmental consultants and the creation of a data bank for user information. Just as doctors and dentists see their patients periodically for checkups, so should architects and designers check on their creations to see if they are "healthy." Users would receive instructions on how their environments were intended to be used as well as supply their own feedback on how well the environment is serving their needs.[23] The physical environment that we create affects our behavior. By recognizing this relationship and closely examining both our objectives and the ways in which our designs function, we can create environments that are more congruent with our goals.

Organizational Structure and Functioning. Organizations can be conceptualized as environments that influence the behaviors and attitudes of the people who participate in them. There are four models of organizational functioning (scientific management, human relations, structuralist, and open system) that highlight variables that should be considered by managers and employees in understanding organizational environments. These perspectives suggest dimensions that should be useful in the analysis of environments and in the planning, facilitating, and evaluating of change.[24]

For example, scientific management grew out of the classical theory of organizations, which emphasized the sharp division of labor and the vertical chain of command depicted on an organizational chart. The division of labor entails breaking down each job into its simplest components, thus enabling individual workers as well as production systems to operate at maximum efficiency. Workers are assumed to be motivated primarily by material rewards. To ensure maximum productivity, incentives are manipulated so as to correspond closely to workers' output. Communication takes place vertically through a pyramidlike hierarchy in which each supervisor is responsible for his or her subordinates.

This classical organizational model and its derivative, scientific management, have been challenged by the discovery of informal social networks in industry. These social groupings play a central role in controlling productivity and communication. In reality, the formal chain of command depicted on an organizational chart is often bypassed and even avoided. The discovery of informal social networks added a human dimension to organize theory and led to a new approach called *human relations.*

The crux of human relations theory is as follows: (1) Social norms rather than physical capacity determine the level of productivity. (2) Social sanctions (i.e., co-worker respect) rather than economic incentives determine productivity. (3) Individual behavior is determined by the group rather than by an individual or by his or her supervisor. In short, informal communication and the informal social environment are more directly related to workers' productivity than are formal communication networks, physical conditions of workers, or exact monetary incentives.

General models of organizational functioning may help social planners to develop efficient organizational systems and/or to pinpoint problems in these systems when they occur. One model suggests that organizational factors determine the role positions and background characteristics of the people who enter an organization. This model indicates that role positions, members' background characteristics, and organizational factors all contribute to creating a social climate or atmosphere in which daily activities are carried out. The climate may be supportive of or antithetical to satisfaction and productivity (indicators of organizational impact). Finally, the impact itself may influence organizational factors. Productivity might generate growth, create new positions, and so on. The organization, the people who comprise it, and the climate in which they function are also affected by external circumstances, such as economic, social, and political conditions.

This overall model is useful in the analysis of environmental impact. Intermediate factors "condition" or mediate organizational impacts and the results of attempts at change. Thus, for example, in understanding the potential impact of an organizational factor such as work-group size, one must take into account the role concomitants of the people involved (blue-collar versus white-collar), average background and personality characteristics (educational level, degree of self-esteem), and the social climate of the work group. Related to this is the fact that it may be easier to change one of the intermediate factors (e.g., social climate) to effect a particular organizational impact (e.g., satisfaction or absenteeism) than it is to change an organizational factor (e.g., size).

Research from work organizations suggests that structural factors such as size, shape, and automation have an impact on employees and that some of these effects are negative. By understanding the mediators involved, specifically role position, average background and personality characteristics, and social climate, environmental planners can devise strategies to overcome the negative effects. For example, one can organize large work groups into several somewhat smaller groups, thereby making additional leadership roles available to employees. This would probably increase employees' identification and satisfaction with the work group and the organization.[25]

Richard Tanner Johnson's recent work indicates that these considerations may have practical implications for predicting the impact of different governmental structures. He studied the way in which recent presidents organized the White House staff and suggested that Presidents Nixon and Eisenhower needed structure and order, a strong chief of staff, and advisers in specialist roles. This created bureaucratic machinery that screened conflict. The problem with this system is that it gets the facts but fails to consider the attached emotions, for example, people's reactions. Thus, this kind of system may respond inappropriately to the public mood.

Franklin Delano Roosevelt apparently liked conflict and had no structure at all. Johnson suggested that this is a system that is conducive to generating new ideas. The teamwork approach used by John Kennedy lies in between these extremes. The problem is that a closed system of mutual support may occur, and advisers may feel so good about being on a team that they do not ask hard questions of each other. Thus, decisions that look drastically incorrect in retrospect can be unanimously approved. Johnson suggested that every President who has used the formal bureaucratic approach has had problems with scandals and that the system Richard Nixon used "set him up" for the Watergate disaster. Regardless of whether or not Johnson's analysis is accurate, it provides a fascinating example of how utopists might use information about organizational structure and impact in formulating practical policies.[26]

Social Climate. The social-climate perspective can sensitize people to what to look for in constructing social environments. The three types of dimensions (relationship dimensions, personal-development dimensions, and system-maintenance and system-change dimensions) provide a useful way of understanding the confusing complexity of social settings. These dimensions may help individuals select a wide range of environments in which to participate in their everyday lives. In addition, those responsible for constructing the environments of others can do so with a better awareness of the personal traits that alternative environments foster.

Furthermore, we do know something about the impacts of social environments. Although the empirical work in this area has focused mainly on environments such as high schools, colleges, and various types of work groups, the conclusions are probably applicable to small communities such as utopian societies.

Emphasis on relationship dimensions (e.g., cohesion, involvement, support, and expressiveness) facilitates patient growth in individual and group psychotherapy and mediates personality change in psychiatric treatment programs. But the overall results in psychiatric settings suggest that satisfaction and morale are related to relationship dimensions, whereas "objective" progress may need a somewhat more complex, carefully constructed, and demanding type of social milieu.

Students express greater satisfaction in classrooms characterized by high student involvement, by a personal student–teacher relationship, by innovative teaching methods, and by clarity of rules for classroom behavior.

But classrooms in which students feel that much material is learned are somewhat different from "satisfying" classrooms. The classrooms in which students report a great deal of content learning combine an affective concern with students as people (relationship dimensions) with an emphasis on students' working hard for academic rewards (competition) within a coherent, organized context (order and organization and rule clarity).

What do these and other studies tell us about the impacts of social environments? People are more satisfied and tend to perform better when the relationship areas are emphasized. They are also less likely to drop out, be absent, and report that they are sick. People also tend to do better in environments that emphasize competition and difficulty. Patients do better in treatment programs that emphasize autonomy and practical orientation. Students learn more in universities that emphasize independent study, high standards, criticism, and breadth of interests.

The clearest conclusion to date is that satisfying human relationships facilitate personal growth and development in all social environments. An emphasis on relationship dimensions is necessary, but it is *not* sufficient. Objective behavioral and performance effects seem to depend on a combination of warm and supportive relationships, an emphasis on specific directions of personal growth, and a reasonably clear, orderly, and well-structured milieu. These environments have a high expectation of and demand for performances. However, too much emphasis on competition and work pressure may have harmful physiological effects (e.g., heart attacks or peptic ulcers) and engender what we call the "diseases of civilization." Overly rigid control may inhibit curiosity and spontaneity.[27]

What types of environments utopists should construct is an open question. But the above findings at least clarify some of the issues involved. People who attempt to change community settings have an awesome responsibility. Since all the evidence is not yet in (and in all probability will never be in), the value judgments involved in efforts to construct new community settings must be openly faced.

At the minimum, plans for optimal societies should use information relevant to each of our five categories of environmental dimensions. Each method gives a somewhat different perspective on a community, and the use of all five should furnish relatively accurate and complete community descriptions. The major ways of conceptualizing environments can provide useful guidelines for developing more specific and detailed plans for communities and thus can help planners construct new environments. The presentation of information about social environments to their prospective members can reduce discrepant perceptions and expectations and enhance successful adaptation to the new environment. This type of information can thus be useful not only to planners of optimal societies but also to individuals who are deciding whether or not to join a new society.

Ecological Balance

To most antiutopians, fearful over the rise of state power and disturbed by trends toward centralized economic and social planning, the real problem with utopia is that it might actually achieve its goal of a static, orderly, homogeneous society. The antiutopian does not concern himself with the management of change. Change is valued for its own sake. One exception to this attitude is an antiutopian suspicion as to man's capability to control science and technology. This is a theme with deep roots in myth and legend. It is noted in rudimentary form in the fable of the sorcerer's apprentice or in Mary Shelley's *Frankenstein.* A more sophisticated literary treatment is found in *R.U.R.* (Rossum's Universal Robots), a drama by the Czech playwright Karel Capek that, in 1922, predicted that man would lose his power to command humanoid machines.[28] However, more often than not, the threat of rampant technology has been the subject of science fiction rather than formal antiutopias. The latter continue to be most disturbed by the thought that technology will work only too well, especially in the hands of a totalitarian government.

Modern ecological theorists have a different perspective. Confronting the wild dynamism of 20th-century societies, they wonder not how change can be preserved but rather how it can be restrained. In particular, the ecological theorist seeks to bring the rate of population growth, the expansion of industry, and the depletion of vital resources under deliberate human control. His concern is that change be kept in balance with a stable global ecosystem.

We will evaluate the manner in which our utopias cope with the question of balanced change in relation to several substantive issues: population control, efficient use of resources, control of industry and technology, and values compatible with ecological balance.

Population Control. Oneida's Perfectionists consistently recognized the desirability of population control, both as a means of keeping the community's numbers in line with the available resources and as a way of liberating the community's women. With the advent of the stirpiculture experiment, Oneida relaxed its determination to limit population. However, this was also a period in which Oneida's economic fortunes were rising, allowing the Perfectionists to support additional members without undue strain.[29] As regards both male continence and stirpiculture, the community, rather than the individual, retained the right to decide whether additional children were wanted. Moreover, the community made such choices with an intense awareness of the need to maintain a balance between population and economic resources.

Walden II's position on birth control is ambivalent. In practice, women are encouraged to have several children. However, the community's leadership is well aware of the Malthusian threat of overpopulation. The explanation of the apparent contradiction lies in Walden II's desire to resolve the population problem by expanding that culture (its own) that recognizes the need for birth control. Presumably, once the aggregate population of all Walden IIs has reached a level sufficient to guarantee the security, and probably the hegemony, of their social model, they will promptly begin to restrain population growth. Skinner does not discuss the implications for the global environment if other non-Walden-II cultures adopt similar programs of population expansion (a baby race as opposed to an arms race).

Kibbutz attitudes toward optimal population size have changed over time. In the early years, childbearing was discouraged by the necessity of struggling against environmental and political obstacles, as well as by acute economic hardships. In the 1940s, the kibbutz reproduction rate was below the level of replacement. However, improved economic and social conditions have resulted in a marked increase in the members' desire to have children.

Whether the kibbutzim will continue to tolerate a high birth rate is unclear. The community does not formally set limits to family size; rather, kibbutz norms indicate to members what is broadly acceptable. These norms are still in flux. On the one hand, kibbutz members are aware of their finite economic resources; too great an expansion in population may result in a decline in the standard of living. Some members are also aware of the potential disruptive effect of large families on communal participation and loyalty. Yet, the kibbutzim are also part of a movement and part of a nation. As in Walden II, members recognize that children can aid the community in ensuring its future security against competitive cultures. Which position will prove dominant remains unsettled.[30]

Columbia does not have a legal or statutory position on family size. As in all other communities in the United States, the size of a Columbian family is reserved to the discretion of husband and wife. However, since Columbia is an affluent community in a society that has already passed through "the demographic transition," population growth would be expected to hover around the replacement level. In addition, Columbia's social-service facilities are well suited to provide assistance in family planning.

Use of Resources. Oneida developed a substantial respect for efficiency, particularly in its early years, when economic resources were scarce. The fact that Oneida successfully marketed most of its output, combined with the fact that the community's norms prohibited misleading advertising and sale of inferior merchandise, suggests that the Perfectionists operated an efficient enterprise. In addition, the communal life-style of the membership reduced the resources and manpower necessary to meet their needs. The Perfectionists avoided luxuries, preferring a simpler and less materialistic life.

The Perfectionists generally made good use of their personnel as well. Everyone engaged in productive labor. Oneida used the enthusiasm generated by solidarity and communal effort to increase efficiency in low-priority work tasks. The community's "bees" proved an effective means of organization, which improved performance and increased personal satisfaction as well.

Walden II values efficiency so long as it is consistent with the well-being and happiness of its members. The actual processes of agricultural and industrial production are never thoroughly described. However, existence of a healthy, enthusiastic work force, and the willingness to experiment and devise innovative procedures in all activities, should be sufficient to provide a surplus of productivity. The coordinated use of collective resources in Walden II's communal economy avoids the duplication of equipment common in private ownership. Walden II's norms also discourage luxury and conspicuous consumption.

Chronically short of labor and resources, and in the midst of an alien and difficult environment, the early kibbutz settlers had no choice but to operate their economic sector as efficiently as possible. Kibbutzim offered the most spartan of living standards, especially in their first decades. Distribution priorities favored capital construction; personal consumption was relegated to secondary status. Resources that were designated for consumption were distributed on a communal basis. Central facilities for food preparation, clothing maintenance, and child care freed the greatest number of workers for labor in the fields. Recent increases in the standard of living elsewhere in Israel have encouraged demands among kibbutz members for a larger amount of personal consumption. These desires have been met to some extent, although consumption levels are still kept in check both by the ideological heritage of the past and by the economic necessity of keeping community expenditures in balance with production.

From the first, all kibbutz members were required to work. It was originally hoped that voluntary choice could be the primary basis of job allocation. Experience, coupled with increased mechanization of kibbutz agriculture, has indicated that a high degree of efficiency requires managerial and technical specialization. Occupational desires must therefore be restrained by criteria of competency. Nonetheless, the kibbutzim strive to maintain as close a merger between personal desires and productive requirements as possible, sometimes by expanding the scope of the kibbutz economy to provide greater occupational opportunity.

Relatively little information is available concerning the use of resources in the productive sectors—the industries and shops—of Columbia. Presumably, those that exist outside the monopolistic sectors of the American economy must be able to compete with alternative suppliers of their goods or services. As consumers, however, Columbians are as wasteful as their compatriots. Columbia's relative affluence permits its residents to squander resources on conspicuous consumption. The community was not designed to use resources efficiently, at least from an environmental point of view. The single-family homes that predominate in Columbia are notoriously wasteful of materials and energy. Similarly, Columbia encouraged the use of electric dryers instead of solar heat, as if the former energy source was as inexhaustible as the latter. Arising in a period before the first shortages shattered the complacency of the industrial world, Columbia is like an overweight aristocrat who may have to adjust to leaner times.

Control of Industry and Technology. Oneida stands as an example of a utopian community that attempted to ride the back of the tiger of technology and industrialization and, in the manner of the fable, was devoured instead. The original plan and theology of the Perfectionists did not provide for either industrial or technological developments. However, pressures to maintain financial solvency in a highly competitive economy forced the community to abandon its original vision of agricultural self-sufficiency and to attempt other more profitable enterprises. Once they began industrial manufacturing, the Perfectionists expanded their operations and increased their income. But the machines that served their economy required more workers and skills than the original membership had available. Hence, outsiders had to be hired and the community's youth sent away for further training. These developments proved incompatible with the community's social and religious ideology. Since Perfectionist ideology lacked flexibility, it collapsed, carrying the entire communal effort along with it.

In Walden II, it is assumed that behavioral conditioning, combined with the labor-credit system, will produce a level of affluence sufficient to allow the community to restrain its economic activity without hardship. Technology, however, is a more ambiguous factor. If control of technology simply means the ability of a society to manage the social consequences of employing machines, then Walden II would face little difficulty. Experimental testing in Walden's laboratories would indicate the implications of each innovation; only those compatible with community structure and norms need be adopted.

But what if technology is understood in a broader sense, not as an aggregate of mechanical devices but as a mode of logic that produces these devices? In that case, control of technology means the management of scientific development, particularly of applied scientific development. The dilemma here is that, according to this definition, Walden II itself is a single, massive technological project. What is there in Walden II, the scientific experiment, to control its own methodology? The answer, as we have already argued, is: nothing at all. Science in Walden II has become both end and means. Instead of controlling science and technology, Walden II ensures their domination over all aspects of society.

Although the kibbutzim began as agricultural settlements with limited capital equipment, the combined pressure of a harsh physical environment and a competitive outside economy encouraged intensive mechanized methods of cultivation. Continuing demands for new sources of income has led to continual increases in kibbutz industrialization.

The communal settlements tried to reduce the strain on their values and social structure brought on by these innovations. They were fairly successful in transferring the principles of managerial rotation and worker participation in decision making from the agricultural fields to industry. The kibbutzim also used growing industrialization as an opportunity to deal with other social problems, such as the need for greater occupational variety for youth, women, and the aged. However, the spread of industry required major violations of kibbutz norms, most significantly, the large-scale hiring of nonmember employees, a practice that had previously been vigorously resisted. Because kibbutz ideology consisted of a collection of principles rather than a systematic theology, as in the Oneida colony, the abandonment of one or two values did not initiate a collapse of the community's entire moral order. Although unable to avoid the disturbing effects of industry, the kibbutzim have proved sufficiently flexible to accommodate modifications of their structures and beliefs.

New Values. If a society is to be capable of balanced change, it must have principles as well as institutions compatible with that objective. The culture that prizes material wealth as its highest value, for example, is less likely to restrain economic growth than one that advocates simplicity or asceticism. Modern ecologists have already recognized the need to redefine the purposes of human life so that they are consistent with a state of balance with nature. Our final concern in this section is whether the values of our utopias provide suitable models for such a reorientation.

The values of the Oneida Community were generally compatible with ecological balance. Perfectionism defined an individual's primary goals as self-improvement and faith in God, neither of which requires an unusual interference with nature. Oneida was also solidly noncompetitive and egalitarian. Problems arose, however, in regard to the relationship between the community's norms and its economic activities. Community industries, through their impact on Oneida's social structure and the outlook of its youth, eventually subverted the roots of Perfectionist ethics.

Individual values at Walden II are designed to ensure stability within the community. The objective of each member is to maximize his own happiness without decreasing the satisfaction of others. Member satisfaction is more highly valued than economic growth. However, Walden II's principles of harmony do not extend to the environment. Competition with, or triumph over, nature is a legitimate activity. Walden II appears determined to bring natural phenomena under control, much as it brings human behavior under control. And since Walden II's passion for scientific development knows no bounds, its struggle with the environment likewise seems an endless conflict.

Kibbutz ideology has had mixed implications for the community's interaction with its environment. Early settlers came to Palestine with a mission to transform the local environment to support communal colonies. Once that transformation had been effected, kibbutz values boded well for a balanced management of the ecosystems that had been created. The kibbutz member preferred solidarity to competition; he was proud of his society's egalitarian structure. Moreover, satisfaction was initially sought through the dynamics of communal life rather than through the acquisition of wealth.

The postrevolutionary period of kibbutz development has included a change in the values of the first settlers. Of primary importance is the fact that new desires for material consumption have appeared. These demands reflect the rise of a new generation without revolutionary experience, as well as a decline in communal activity in favor of family life. Many kibbutzim have had to adopt increasingly intensive agricultural methods and to construct industrial plants to satisfy these new consumption demands. Both activities suggest an emphasis on economic growth that is likely to involve depletion of environmental resources and further interference with the balance of local ecosystems.

Reflecting the practices of the culture that surrounds them, Columbians do not demonstrate a commitment to principles that would assure the maintenance of environmental balance. The New Town itself embodies the values of material affluence and growth, albeit planned affluence and growth. Value changes more conducive to ecological stability—such as opposition to consumerism and demands for the recycling of wastes—have not penetrated the community to any significant degree. Norms at Columbia are not fixed and residents may be affected by national programs urging environmental reform. An effort to implement environmental values at Columbia, however, would involve sacrifice and lower living-standards for the populace, two consequences likely to engender opposition to the ecological point of view.

Conclusions. We can now evaluate the performance of our utopias according to the criterion of ecological balance. As regards population control, three of the models grant to society—through either normative or political means—the authority to regulate the level of population and population density. Columbia allows family size to be a matter of personal preference. The adverse ecological implications of this policy are mitigated by the fact that Columbia exists in a socioeconomic system in which those preferences are likely to approach zero population growth.

Many aspects of our four social frameworks are conducive to an efficient use of resources. Full employment permits effective deployment of the totality of a community's human capacities. Communal institutions avoid waste and duplication. Social control of the economy directs that production allocated for internal use be channeled to meet significant community needs. In terms of consumption, three of the utopias avoided luxury and waste, although the kibbutzim are being affected by consumption patterns in other sectors of their state. Columbia, on the other hand, reveals a life style based on affluence and high levels of personal consumption.

With the exception of Walden II, each of the communities sought to keep industry and technology under social and moral control. They had mixed degrees of success in this endeavor. Oneida and the kibbutz found that environmental factors and the rigors of economic competition demanded that they industrialize. In these cases, industry and technology produced unintended impacts, eventually causing either community collapse or the modification of utopian values. Similarly, the New Town at Columbia sacrificed some of its limited plans for environmental preservation at the altar of profit for the developer.

Communal utopian values are generally compatible with ecological balance. Although specific details vary, these societies tend to be egalitarian and noncompetitive. Personal goals are ethical, aesthetic, and humanistic rather than materialistic. Individualism is constrained by a high concern for social commitment and social welfare. However, there are notable exceptions. Walden II's social objective is furious and unlimited scientific progress. The kibbutzim are placing greater value on material consumption. But none of these models is as ill suited to environmental stability as Columbia, an attempt to utopianize the resource-hungry, high-consumption, growth-oriented, middle-class American life-style. Columbia's residents would have to alter their values and practices significantly before they could exist in balance with their environment.

Excluding Columbia, our utopias are basically compatible with ecological balance, provided that they can successfully confront two disequilibrating factors. The first of these is technology and industry. Utopists must learn from the experience of Oneida and the kibbutzim. Intensive planning of the rates and types of technological and industrial development is necessary both to avoid ecological disturbance and to prevent a disruption of those social forces and values capable of restraining further development.

But if such planning is to be successful, it must cope with the pressures that result in rapid industrial expansion, particularly the competitive requirements of the external economy and the higher consumption demands influenced by external models. These pressures result from forces outside the utopian model rather than from internal dynamics. A nonutopian external environment is the second disequilibrating factor. It can best be considered by inclusion in the discussion of our next issue, the issue of scale.

Scale

A cornerstone of ecological thinking is the idea of the interaction and interdependence among elements of ecosystems. This holds true both for small, local systems (a pond) and for macrosystems (the earth). In other words, changes that you cause in your ecosystem may affect other local systems, changes in other systems may affect you, and changes that disrupt the entire planetary ecosystem, like the proverbial spit into the wind, may be blown right back in your face. More concretely, a community that has eliminated water pollution is vulnerable if it exists downstream from another community that dumps its garbage into the water. A society that emits enough carbon dioxide to alter the composition of the earth's atmosphere may find the planetary ecosystem responding with weather changes that ruin its harvests.

Since our case studies involve small local communities, the environmental perspective noted above raises several questions that they must confront. Are these societies vulnerable to ecological or social disturbance from other ecosystems or cultures? Do they in turn have characteristics that cause disturbances elsewhere? Could these models be expanded to provide a global, utopian social order?

As members of a small community that had enough problems ensuring its own survival, the Perfectionists never seriously considered the social or environmental implications of extending their model to a world scale. Had they done so, they would have encountered serious obstacles. For one, Oneida's stability centered on the memberships' loyalty to a single individual. Even a modest increase in the number and size of Perfectionist settlements would have placed unsupportable strains on Noyes's personal and informal methods of maintaining control. Second, Oneida demanded the deep religious dedication of its members. Individuals capable of such convictions proved difficult to locate, even in that relatively more religious era. Widespread expansion of the Oneida model would require the development of a potent program of mass conversion. Otherwise, Oneida could never grow to be more than it was: the haven of a small, select group of zealots.

With only a few settlements in existence, the Walden II movement recognizes its political vulnerability to other modes of social organization. Walden II, at least, takes seriously the problem of self-defense. The community carefully regulates the information it makes available about itself to outsiders. Also, it employs its limited political resources (i.e., votes) to maximize community influence. However, the true solution to Walden II's comparative weakness is growth. By encouraging population growth, starting new colonies as rapidly as possible, and continually innovating to improve living conditions, Walden II settlements can increase their power and thus their security.

With Walden II, Skinner introduced a model that he apparently believes has the potential of a world utopia. Unfortunately, he offered little information as to how such a macrostructure would differ from a simple aggregate of innumerable Walden IIs. He did not discuss the environmental or social problems that must be met in a move from community to planetary scale. How will Walden II deal with pollution? How will it distribute energy resources? Is a blanket faith in science sufficient? What are the implications of Walden II's predilection for endless scientific dynamism applied to a global environment? Skinner seems to see nature as material upon which man can exercise and improve his creative powers. He thereby condemns his future planners to an eternity of frustration, constantly struggling to avoid the catastrophic environmental consequences of their own attempts to manipulate the earth's ecology.

The kibbutzim are vulnerable to outside forces. Much as does the rest of the state (perhaps more so in border areas), kibbutz settlements must confront hostile foreign neighbors and the possibility of military attack. The socialist communities must compete economically with other producers in both the national and the world markets. Competitive pressures have contributed to the mechanization and industrialization of the settlements and to the social consequences thereof. Partly as a response to the challenge of the attraction of living patterns elsewhere, the kibbutzim have begun to tolerate higher birth rates among their own populace, thus providing a core of kibbutz-trained and -educated youth to ensure the continuance of the settlements.

Although others have admired the kibbutz social form and suggested its applicability to other areas, the kibbutzim have never attempted to establish themselves outside of Palestine. To the extent that the kibbutz is intimately connected to the Zionist project—composed of members of a single ethnic group, committed to a single geographic region, embodying the values of the *halutz*—it can exist only as a local and restricted utopian venture. However, if one abstracts the kibbutz from its historical context and considers its structural elements alone, then it would seem to have definite potential.

As democratic socialist communities, the settlements have shown themselves to be flexible and capable of tolerating diversity. They are a stable social form without any internal dynamic requiring material growth; much of the expansion in their economy and population has resulted from external pressures. In addition, the kibbutzim are oriented toward the management of ecosystems under conditions of scarcity. But, of course, the kibbutzim have never had to manage a national economy or environment. much less a global one. Whether they could cope with the organizational requirements of that task remains to be demonstrated.

Rouse and the planners who designed Columbia envisioned a community of a specific and limited size. They had no intention of creating a dynamic social form that might move beyond the boundaries of Howard County. However, since the New Town has been advanced as a model of community planning, the practicality of spreading it to other regions must be critically analyzed.

To begin with, the New Town does not approach self-sufficiency. It is economically, politically, and ecologically dependent on external forces. It is thus vulnerable to changes in those sectors that control resources or institutions essential to the maintenance of its well-being. For example, Columbia depends on resources delivered to it through transportation nets organized and operated by others. Most of its residents derive their income from outside employment. These facts indicate that a New Town's survival depends on its integration into an existing social order. A dependence of this type is an obstacle to any development that despite internal benefits, serves to structurally separate the New Town community from the rest of society.

More serious questions concerning the suitability of the New Town as a utopian model arise when one considers the impact of Columbia on other regions. The New Town is an elite sector integrated into the larger society of which it is a part. Economically, Columbia represents the top of an organizational pyramid: its residents occupy professional and managerial roles in external institutions, and they enjoy levels of income concomitant with those positions. But the top of a pyramid depends upon its base. For members of the Columbia community to maintain their real income level, status, and world view, non-Columbia-type communities in which individuals have lower incomes and lesser status must exist.

In its ecological impact on other regions, Columbia is similarly elitist. Other communities produce the fuel for Columbia's cars, the timber for its homes, and the food for its families. It is in these areas, external to Columbia, that most of the ecological disruption connected with mining, logging, large-scale industry, and agriculture takes place. Any impact on Columbia is indirect and secondary. In order to perform these functions that Columbia requires, external ecosystems are prevented from achieving the kind of balance between residential and commercial zones that Columbia offers. Thus, the New Town requires an ecological and economic base upon which its utopian aspirations are founded. Yet, regions that serve as that base may find that their relationship to Columbia-type communities blocks their prospects for developing a utopian form of their own. In short, one cannot speak of the New Town as a global utopian model; its very existence depends upon the continuing existence of nonutopian structures.

This analysis of the way in which our utopias interact with external social and environmental forces, and of their programs and prospects as models for a global system, reveals several ground rules for any utopia. First, the environmental necessity of stability and balance clearly implies that utopia must be worldwide or at least part of a world order. Competition with other economic groups or social orders has consistently been a prime cause of excessive material or population growth. The most stable societies become defenseless; the most dynamic ones are environmentally disequilibrating. Only a utopia based on a world order can enjoy enough security to enable it to limit and manage its growth.

Second, any utopia must provide sufficient diversity, must be sufficiently open, to be attractive to a worldwide variety of peoples and cultures. But no single model should be structured so as to prevent the utopian development of another area. If the quest for utopia is not to be based on war, then a new social order must win the voluntary support of the masses of humanity. No restrictive or homogeneous cultural form or highly stratified model is likely to garner allegiance on a broad, multinational scale. North American utopians must accept the needs, idiosyncracies, and values of their Asian comrades, and vice versa, or utopia will collapse for both.

Finally, a future utopia must be enormously flexible. Interaction between the various cultural modes provided for above will result in incessant creativity, criticism, and social change. Each facet of utopia will serve as a challenge and as an inspiration to each other facet. Utopians will be adrift amid a sea of alternatives. In such a context, rigid institutions cannot survive. They will surely crumble as new generations discover flourishing possibilities elsewhere. A feasible utopian social structure must be capable of absorbing new influences, of modifying itself, and, finally, of presiding over its own transformation into a successor model.

REFERENCES AND NOTES

1. Berneri, M. L. *Journey through utopia*. Boston: Beacon, 1950, p. 4.
2. Zamiatin, E. *We*. New York: Dutton, 1924, p. 112.
3. Mumford, L. Utopia, the city, and the machine. In F. Manuel (Ed.), *Utopias and utopian thought*. Boston: Houghton Mifflin, 1966, p. 18.
4. See Kinkade, K. *A Walden Two experiment*. New York: William Morrow, 1973.
5. Odum, E. *Fundamentals of ecology*. Philadelphia: Saunders, 1971, pp. 148–154, 255–256; Ricklefs, R. *Ecology*. Newton, Mass.: Chiron Press, 1973, p. 766.
6. Bates, M. The human ecosystem. In G. Love and R. Love (Eds.), *Ecological crisis*. New York: Harcourt Brace Jovanovich, 1970, p. 42.
7. Odum, op. cit., pp. 267–268; Ricklefs, op. cit., pp. 771–775.
8. Bates, op. cit., pp. 43–44.
9. Mumford, op. cit., p. 7.
10. Ricklefs, op. cit., pp. 751–756 (quote on p. 754). See also: Odum, op. cit., pp. 251–264.

11. Ricklefs, op. cit., pp. 756–757; Odum, op. cit., pp. 264–267.
12. Commoner, B. *The closing circle.* New York: Bantam Books, 1971, p. 32.
13. Ibid., pp. 29–37.
14. Odum, op. cit., pp. 267–270.
15. Orni, E., and Efrat, E. *Geography of Israel.* Jerusalem: Israel Program for Scientific Translations, 1966, pp. 277–308.
16. Moos, R. *The human context.* New York: Wiley, 1976.
17. Michelson, W. *Man and his urban environment: A sociological approach.* Redding, Mass.: Addison-Wesley, 1970, p. 25.
18. See, for example: Festinger, L., Schachter, S., and Back, K. *Social pressures in informal groups.* New York: Harper, 1950; Gans, H. *The Levittowners: Ways of life and politics in a new suburban community.* New York: Pantheon Books, 1967; Athanasiou, R., and Yoshioka, G. The spatial character of friendship formation. *Environment and Behavior, 5:*43–65, 1973.
19. Blake, R., Rhead, C., Wedge, B., and Mouton, J. Housing architecture and social interaction. *Sociometry, 19:*133–139, 1956; Heilweil, M. The influence of dormitory architecture on resident behavior. *Environment and Behavior, 5:*377–412, 1973.
20. Newman, O. *Defensible space.* New York: Macmillan, 1973.
21. Young, M., and Willmott, P. *Family and kinship in East London.* New York: Free Press, 1957.
22. Holt, J. Involving the users in school planning. *School Review, 82:*706–730, 1974.
23. Sommer, R. *Design awareness.* San Francisco: Rinehart Press, 1972.
24. Bromet, E., and Moos, R. The impact of organizational structure and change. In R. Moos, *The human context.* New York: Wiley, 1976, Ch. 8.
25. See, for example: *Work in America* (Report of a Special Task Force to the Secretary of Health, Education and Welfare). Cambridge, Mass.: MIT Press, 1972.
26. Johnson, R. *Managing the White House: An intimate study of the presidency.* New York: Harper and Row, 1974.
27. For a review of relevant studies, see: Moos, R. Social climate: The "personality" of the environment. In *The human context,* op. cit., 1976, Ch. 10; Kiritz, S., and Moos, R. Physiological effects of social environments. *Psychosomatic Medicine, 36:*96–114, 1974.
28. Capek, K. *R.U.R.* New York: Doubleday, Page & Co., 1923.
29. Carden, M. L. *Oneida: Utopian community to modern corporation.* Baltimore: Johns Hopkins University Press, 1969, pp. 51, 63.
30. Talmon, Y. *Family and community in the kibbutz.* Cambridge, Mass.: Harvard University Press, 1972, pp. 51–73.

CHAPTER 8

A Utopian Perspective
on the Environment

THE THEORETICAL RELATIONSHIP

Broadly speaking, the weakness of environmental theory is its failure to comprehend man. This flaw dooms "laws" and "generalizations" to perpetual revision as they struggle to keep pace with human events. Since his appearance on the planet, man has persisted in revolutionizing himself and his world. Moving from hunter and gatherer, to farmer, to master of artifact and technique, man has refused to accept a static niche in the order of things. He has experimented with myriad forms of social organization: families, tribes, nations, empires. He is an unstable object of analysis. He defies the orderly processes of intellect as they struggle to define his character.

As a science, environmental theory's standard of understanding is the ability to generate causal hypotheses, the validity of which can be demonstrated through their predictive power. Even if one accepts this standard, environmental thinking has proved inadequate when confronted with human behavior. This should not be surprising. The methods of environmental science are oriented toward the comprehension of physical variables—chemical, biological, geographical—and of the responses of organisms regularly related to these variables. They are ill-suited to the analysis of cultural phenomena, to an understanding of political conflict, or to a comprehension of the power of a dream. A brief review of the modes of environmental thought discussed in Chapter 1 illustrates this inability to provide a complete or reliable explanation of human action.

Once geographers had moved beyond astrological or mystical approaches to the study of man and his environment, they attempted to develop a scientific theory that could account for relationships within this area. Their first effort at explanation produced *determinism*. Determinism implied that human responses to geographical variables could be understood in the same manner as the interaction of purely physical factors. There was no difference between calculating the effect of climate on soil erosion and discerning its impact on human character. Assuming the validity of this approach, geographers proceeded to suggest precise, causal hypotheses linking environmental variables to social, political, and economic behavior. However, empirical data generally failed to confirm the determinist hypotheses. Similar environmental conditions often resulted in divergent cultural patterns. Likewise, human societies often underwent major structural changes even though local geography remained stable. Despite its apparent formal rigor, determinism proved little other than its own lack of reliability.

To avoid the defects of determinism, geographers considered a new perspective: possibilism. *Possibilism* freed the theorist from the burden of introducing specific, causal hypotheses. He was thus less likely to fall into error. However, possibilists were also unable to explain very much about human behavior. The number of possible environmental options is extensive. If man is to judge the value of these possibilities, then an understanding of human responses to the environment is dependent on an understanding of human judgment. Societies do not necessarily select possibilities that maximize their wealth or growth, or even their likelihood of survival. How could a possibilist predict which criterion a specific society would give priority? In short, possibilism transferred the questions of human behavior to students of economics, psychology, and political science, leaving to itself only the task of determining whether suggested projects were in fact possibilities.

Probabilism brought theorists back to the problem of predicting the likelihood of a response. By a detailed analysis of the components of human decision-making—including psychological, cultural, and political factors—the probabilist hopes to ascertain patterns in the way a society interacts with nature. He can then evaluate future possibilities in terms of that pattern and can logically suggest the most probable alternative. The difficulty with this perspective is that the accuracy of the probabilities is dependent on continuity in the decision-making pattern. If a major cultural shift occurs, such as a decline in the desire to maintain traditions or a rise in the appetite for material consumption, then wholly unexpected decisions will result. A change in the political decision-making structure also requires a reexamination of the probabilities. In short, a probabilist analysis retains validity only so long as men are the prisoners of their past. History's lesson is that such bonds are always eventually broken.

Pragmatism is even more vulnerable to this line of criticism. Lacking a theory of decison making—or, for that matter, a theory of man–nature interaction—pragmatist findings are based solely on the assumption that things will stay basically as they are. There are often long-standing patterns in human behavior. Thus, for some period of time, the pragmatist may accurately predict what men will do in relation to their environment. However, it is also a virtual certainty that at some point (which the analyst cannot anticipate) these predictions will be utterly wrong.

Neodeterminism, especially as elaborated on by Meggers, is actually a misnomer. Unlike formal determinism, this position does not offer a causal theory of human behavior. On the contrary, it is a theory of limits, seeking to define those natural bounds that can restrict man's endeavors without suggesting what in fact those endeavors will be. Thus, if agricultural potential sets an upper limit to what civilizations can achieve, it also sets a barrier to what neodeterminism can explain. Within that limit, man's relationship to his environment is neither determined nor understood.

As the science of ecology has developed, scholars have been able to understand more fully the environment upon which man depends. Ecology requires a holistic perspective, encompassing the organic and inorganic elements of ecosystems. It covers a variety of levels of analysis—from physical and chemical processes to animal and human behavior. Most important, it recognizes the dynamic interaction of these elements and processes in an ongoing, homeostatic network. Nevertheless, man's role as an agent of change presents problems that ecological theory has great difficulty in resolving.

Ecological analysis has achieved its highest level of theoretical sophistication through the use of the ecosystem concept. In terms of human behavior, however, the ecosystem does not provide a causal model. Man clearly must live within some ecosystem. He must interact with his environment in order to survive. But the form of that interaction is not dictated solely by the ecosystem; rather, it varies with different human institutions, desires, and technical capabilities. In fact, man's interaction with an environment may change its structure, thereby offering additional scope to new types of social and cultural organization. Lest men become arrogant with this degree of autonomy, ecologists warn us that the environment may give men enough rope to collectively hang themselves. Human societies are capable of modifying their environment sufficiently to destroy its ability to sustain their own existence.

Even without a causal model, ecological theorists do make projections concerning the future of man. A classic example is the Club of Rome's world-scale computer simulation of environmental trends. Projects of this nature are not predictions of what necessarily will happen. They are extrapolations of the ecological consequences, *assuming* human action continues in current patterns. This assumption is almost certainly invalid. At some point, limits will be reached that make the continuation of contemporary practices quite unlikely. For example, projecting an exponential increase in human population might lead to the prediction that people will eventually be literally standing on each other's shoulders. That extrapolation simply suggests that at some point the birth rate will drop, probably drastically.

Ecologists can evaluate the likely consequences of given practices in relation to the environment. On the basis of such evaluations, they can argue that some practices must eventually be modified. What they cannot say is what the modification will be nor precisely when it will occur. They cannot predict whether men will foresee their peril and engage in constructive action or whether environmentally destructive behavior will be carried onward to the last moment and then ended, abruptly and catastrophically.

Some scholars have suggested specific alternative modes of social action as substitutes for current practices incompatible with environmental stability. They have proposed a steady-state economy, a world order, and new values. However, these designs are not explanations of what will occur; they are statements of what could occur. Furthermore, although they satisfy criteria developed out of ecological analysis, the suggested programs themselves cannot be derived exclusively from an understanding of, or a concern for, ecosystems. When they indicate how necessary social functions are to take place within the parameters of environmental stability, they reflect a stance in regard to sociological and political theory. When proposals are weighed on the basis of moral principles, they reveal the value orientation of which they are a product. In other words, these suggested measures constitute much more than an extrapolation of ecological trends; they are the first steps in the development of an environmentally sound utopia.

That those who seek to devise a response to the environmental crisis have moved in the direction of utopian speculation is not surprising. For utopian thought stands ready to offer solutions in the very area in which environmental analysis has encountered its greatest difficulty: the dynamics of human action in relation to nature. Unlike theorists who seek to explain what will occur if the world continues in the customary manner, utopists begin their project by speculating about what might happen if some fundamental transformation were to occur. What are the alternatives, they ask, that lie beyond the status quo, even beyond any extrapolation or reform of the status quo? What possibilities are opened up by the prospect of qualitative social change?

By so phrasing their inquiry, utopists enter areas inaccessible to environmental science. They attempt to explore actively a future that has broken with past trends, a future that cannot be predictably plotted. This is a unique type of exploration, for utopists create what they "discover." Of course, utopists make no effort to depict comprehensively every potential significantly distinct from the present. Rather, they make deliberate value choices. Then, using these values as a foundation, they attempt to portray the structure of an alternative society in its entirety. Utopists feel free to construct new cities, design new institutions, and arrange new customs. They may offer radically new ways of meeting age-old human needs. They may even argue that a transformed social environment will transform human needs.

In performing these acts of social creation, utopists initially move beyond the limits of science. They embrace the imagination and focus on the openness of the future rather than on the constraints of the present. But this divorce between science and imagination can never be total. The utopist's imagination must be tempered by reason. He cannot suggest that everything is possible, that all boundaries can be crossed, that every obstacle can be overcome. Utopia cannot be pure fantasy. The utopist recognizes that the province of science must be encountered even within his perfect society. The utopian city must exist on earth. Utopian man must eat, sleep, and procreate, and he must have the material requisites for those activities. The world transformed is still the world, a finite place, a realm of physical and social environmental limits. Utopia can challenge science, but it cannot banish it.

Utopian thought can contribute to the understanding and the design of man's future relationship to the environment. However, utopists' perspectives on the environment, if they are to have any value, must be based to some extent on the findings of environmental and social scientists. These groups must inform utopists about the environmental parameters that every future society must confront. They must make utopists aware of the structure and the dynamics of existing human groups and institutions, or it is out of this living material that any future society must be developed. With these restrictions in mind, we believe that utopists have their special role to play.

We have touched on the outlines of the utopian perspective on environmental thought. Many of our arguments require more detailed discussion. Thus, several substantive aspects of this broad issue—including the problems of ethical choice, human motivation, qualitative transformation, holistic planning, and political impact—are the focus of extended analysis in the following sections.

SUBSTANTIVE ISSUES

Ethical Choice

Utopia liberates the future from the narrow minds of the present. Rejecting determinism, it insists that the outline of tomorrow has not already been plotted on graphs and computer printouts, to be passively awaited by a sterile humanity. On the contrary, utopia reveals itself as an alternative to the expected, and in so doing, it raises the prospect of other alternatives. Moreover, where alternatives exist, passivity becomes an impossible strategy. Inaction no longer represents the necessary consequence of fate, but rather the abandonment of judgment. At the least, utopia demands this much of man, that he evaluate his options and make his choice.

But if future alternatives are to be selected, what are the criteria upon which the selection will be based? Here, scientific and technical analysis can play a significant role. Utopia must be constructed out of finite quantities of physical materials and arise out of specific human institutions; science can help indicate the future availability of these resources and the structural characteristics of current social forms. Equally important, it can suggest the extent to which these resources and structures are malleable. As has already been noted, only certain patterns of man–environment interaction are capable of ongoing stability. Environmental science must play a role in identifying these patterns. However, utopian thought demonstrates that technical analysis by itself cannot provide sufficient criteria for men to choose the most promising alternative.

It is not enough for technical analysis to prove that an innovation will probably work. Present institutions work; they function; life goes on. At the core of utopian creation is the belief that a different form of society can not only work but work better. Such a claim—that utopia will be superior to contemporary society—leads to an immediate question: Better in what terms? Suppose utopia offers equality instead of competition, tranquillity instead of excitement, aesthetics instead of materialism? Why are these changes an improvement? The answer is that utopian innovations are better in terms of some ethical system, of some set of values. To understand a utopia means that one understands the principles it is attempting to realize. To commit oneself to a utopia includes a dedication to the values upon which it is based. Thus, in addition to technical decisions, the construction of a plan for utopia requires normative decisions. In Polak's words, utopia "assigns to the *human conscience* the task of choosing among various possibilities for society" [1] (italics added).

F
"THE
IMAGE OF
THE
FUTURE"

The normative element intrinsic to the selection of a utopia has implications for the decision-making process necessary to carry out such a selection. Who is competent to make a serious moral decision? How can moral agreement on a societal scale be achieved? Choices among values are not the exclusive prerogative of technicians or experts, be they natural scientists, social scientists, or philosophers. There is no persuasive rationale for allowing any one group a priority in making normative decisions. Similarly, it is difficult to find an acceptable reason for excluding any group from such a process. The ability to make moral choices has long been considered the mark of a sane and mature human being. Thus, the normative component of selecting a utopia must be open to everyone.

Even if we agree that nearly everyone is entitled to participate in decision making, how are the choices actually to be made? The very size of our decision-making body suggests that disputes will almost certainly occur. How can a unity of ethical direction be achieved? This problem is not unique to the selection of a utopia. Every human society struggles with the dilemma of reaching a moral consensus out of the disparate values of its members. Such agreement is created in the political arena. It is through the processes of political discourse, conflict, and compromise that social values receive authoritative status. A utopia, as a normative proposal for an entire society, is necessarily political, and it is only through political means that a utopia can be realized. Some of the complex issues involved in the determining of how political procedures can cope with the problems of moving toward a utopia are confronted in a subsequent section on political impact.

An examination of our case studies illustrates the extent to which the adoption of new values constitutes a rationale for the utopian effort. However, moral justification does not provide a blank check for social and environmental reconstruction. Utopia cannot wholly substitute normative decision making for scientific analysis. That which men believe ought to be done must be moderated by an understanding of the physical and social environment, of the limits of the materials and methods to be used, and of the limits of the people and social units involved. In practice, the attempt to live according to new ethical patterns is a formidable undertaking. Moreover, the ethical challenge to current institutions, out of which utopia is born, is a mode of human expression extremely difficult to control. Yesterday's heretics may have little time to enjoy the status of priests before they find some new dreamer's theses defiantly nailed to their door.

The Oneida Community arose as the social form of a new religion and a new ethical perspective. It was Perfectionist convictions that brought the members together and Perfectionist values that accounted for their economic, political, and social practices. Despite the fervor of their beliefs and the social devices they developed to ensure spiritual constancy (e.g., mutual criticism), the Oneida communitarians could not maintain their principles under prevailing historical conditions. Eventually, the gulf between norms and practices became too great: the values yielded, and the utopian experiment ended.

Those who emigrated to Palestine to begin the kibbutzim did so to further deep ethical goals: the formation of a new man in a new community and a new state. Life in the kibbutz signified an abrupt transition from the customs and norms of European culture. While seeking to form communities that embodied their values in social life, the settlers substantially modified their local environments. The land could be changed—but only at a price. Often the price included acceptance of levels of technical and managerial specialization imcompatible with fully democratic and egalitarian ideals. As at Oneida, values yielded.

In addition to environmental factors, the kibbutzim discovered a second threat to the continuity of their principles. A new generation appeared with new experiences and value orientations of its own. The sabras accepted most of the fundamental tenets of kibbutz ideology, but in some areas, including consumption levels, work expectations, and family cohesiveness, they pressed for modifications. Again, slowly and moderately, kibbutz norms shifted, this time to accommodate the new human aggregate.

Walden II is unique in that it institutionalizes a program of continual ethical change. Values are subject to scientific analysis and consequent improvement. However, happiness, the supposed objective of experimental development, is as open to scientific manipulation as are all other psychological states. Thus, as we have argued previously, science moves beyond ethical constraint. Instead of serving a social value, it becomes the ultimate value. Furthermore, since the same methodology used to determine policies toward the environment is used to establish values, there is little chance that practices in one of these areas will have immediate destabilizing effects in the other. Walden II is therefore virtually immune to internal criticism of its values until it reaches the point at which its scientific interference with the environment causes such a cataclysm that no amount of conditioning can convince the membership that they are still happy. Presumably, the membership will then have to adopt norms on some other nonscientific basis.

Of our four case studies, Columbia introduced the smallest shift in values from current societal norms. Rouse and his planners endorsed the continuance of basic American values: they never sought to challenge the fundamental institutions of American society. Columbians were expected to be individualistic and competitive and to abide by middle-class standards of propriety.

However, values at Columbia have differed marginally from average community norms and, perhaps more significantly, from average community adherence to norms. To begin with, Rouse sought to emphasize a special set of established American values—particularly the importance of neighborhood friendships, family cohesiveness, religious tolerance, and the aesthetic quality of living areas. Since he believed that these values were threatened by current modes of city planning (or the lack thereof), Rouse's development can be understood as a conservative effort to maintain basic norms against the organizational trends of contemporary life. Second, in a few critical areas, Rouse did seek to embody new normative perspectives in Columbia. This effort is especially noticeable in his support of racial tolerance through integrated housing, social control of architecture and building maintenance enforced through legal agreements, and citizen participation in community decision-making focused in the Columbia Association. Thus far, Columbia's residents have tended to endorse these attitudes.

Since Columbia's value orientations are so close to those in the rest of American society, it might be expected that the New Town would have little difficulty in maintaining its normative system. This presumption is supported by the fact that the New Town is deliberately structured so as to sustain these norms. Aesthetic building designs are required by legal convenant; social interaction is encouraged by the physical layout of homes and service facilities. Nevertheless, two major factors indicate that Columbia's ideals may have limited historical longevity. First, as a private economic venture, Columbia must subordinate its other norms to a single primary value: profit. In those cases in which the developer's visions and principles have come in conflict with economic requirements, such as the greenbelt contemplated for the community's perimeter or the provision of low-income housing, principles have been sacrificed to assure a respectable bank balance. Such a fate may await some of Columbia's other normative preferences. Second, with the exception of a handful of structural influences, Columbia has no way of determining the values of future residents. There are no ideological requirements for entrance into the community, and the New Town is completely open to the introduction of ideas and principles developed in other regions. Cultural changes outside Columbia, combined with population mobility patterns throughout the United States, may result in an influx of residents holding values very different from those prevalent today.

Human Motivation

As we have already noted, the actions that men initiate today are in part a consequence of their understanding of, and expectations for, the future. Is there any reason to anticipate beneficial effects from this orientation? Kenneth Boulding raised the forensic question, "Why worry about posterity?" Why not "eat, drink, and be merry?" [2] History demonstrates that there have indeed been human groups willing to narrowly pursue their own welfare, all the while acknowledging the "deluge" that was sure to follow. Modern man could follow this example; it might be fun while it lasted.

Of course, it is not difficult to counter such a totally irresponsible attitude toward the future. For one, eating, drinking, and merrymaking are often the prerogatives of elite strata alone. Less-privileged classes lack the option to trade off subsequent decades for a glorious present. Working for a better future may in fact be their only opportunity to experience these satisfactions. Second, the deluge may arrive faster than it is anticipated, especially when people accept its future appearance and do nothing to avert it. In answer to his query above, Boulding observed, "there is a great deal of historical evidence to suggest that a society which loses its identity with posterity, and which loses its positive image of the future, loses also its capacity to deal with present problems, and soon falls apart." [3]

These arguments suggest that people must seriously undertake the task of creating the future if they are at least to maintain their own welfare. Another category of future-oriented acts remains to be explained, however. Why should we seek to construct a qualitatively superior world that we may never live to see? In particular, why should we do so if the effort requires extreme sacrifice and struggle? This is an unavoidable issue for anyone who seriously considers a response to the warnings of coming environmental degradation. Why, as Margaret Mead asks, should men "plant trees which take two lifetimes to mature" or "take thought to stop the forests from being depleted, the good soil from being washed to the sea, or the gene pool from being exposed to too much radiation?" [4] Why conserve resources and limit population if the primary beneficiaries of such acts will be born a century hence?

One answer, which people have often found meaningful, is that struggle and sacrifice under current conditions, without prospect of immediate reward, may be justified as a contribution to an extraordinary human project: the creation of a new society, a utopia. Utopia stands as a unique goal. The quest for utopia enables men to pursue objectives that are currently unattainable but that might become the birthright of all. It offers nothing less than the chance to define the human species of the future by helping to shape the conditions under which that species will live.

Even the form of utopia is conducive to its power as a motivating force. Its emphasis on the interaction of characters within the daily minutiae of utopian life permits the preutopian to experience imaginatively existence in a new social order. It is one thing to consider a social model in terms of abstractions—for example, Thomas More's Utopia as authoritarian and bountiful—and quite another to fancy oneself sitting at a Utopian table, smelling the incense, and awaiting service in accordance with one's age and status. Of course, the "experience" will be only a dream, but as Bertrand de Jouvenel explained:

> A dream: aye but that is a capital point; a dream, while less than reality, is much more than a blueprint. A blueprint does not give you the "feel" of things, as if they existed in fact: a dream does so. If you can endow your "philosophical city" with the semblance of reality, and cause your reader to see it, as if it were actually in operation, this is quite a different achievement from a mere explanation of the principles on which it should rest. This "causing to see" by means of a feigned description is obviously what More aimed at: it is also the essential feature of the utopian genre.[5]

An examination of our case studies reveals that in three cases, the long-term goal of building a utopia, a new society more perfect than that from which the builders came, served as a rationale for enduring the privations concomitant with that task. In the fourth case, Columbia, a vision of social improvement motivated the developer to take some economic risks that would otherwise have been unnecessary.

Oneida's attempt at utopia began with a handful of determined Perfectionist families in a few rustic cabins. With little more than their vision of a new religious community to sustain them, they constructed their central dwellings, increased their numbers, and established a viable economy. Similarly, the first kibbutz settlers, with limited experience and meager resources, struggled against a rugged, alien environment to establish both a new nation and a radically innovative and egalitarian form of society. Even Walden II, despite the speed at which it achieved success, had its lean, early years. Moreover, those members who joined as adults are not able to experience the full benefits of behavioral conditioning, a privilege available only to those born into the Walden children's quarters. Still, the adults go on to create the organization and structures that will enable future generations to live a fully utopian life.

The utopian task proved much less challenging for the creators of Columbia. Rouse and his planners did not commit their lives to the construction of their dream city; rather, they advanced a substantial amount of venture capital. Still, a less innovative community design might have been a more secure investment, and Rouse stood ready to attempt the less certain gamble in order to realize a more optimal social model.

Residents of Columbia can become part of the utopian project with relative ease. Membership in the New Town requires neither special motivation nor the capacity for long-term struggle. Moreover, once a family has moved to the New Town, they can immediately begin enjoying a lifestyle that must be deemed highly comfortable even when judged by current American standards. Thus, the experience of living in Columbia is not likely to generate feelings of meaningful accomplishment comparable to those that accompany participation in forms of utopian construction that require effort and sacrifice.

If one grants our thesis that the revolutionary construction of a utopian social order can motivate people to forsake whatever satisfaction they might have gained through participation in their present society and choose instead to attempt to transform it fundamentally, then another problem emerges. What is to motivate the inhabitants of utopia? What of the generations born into the perfect social system? Is their primary motivation to be the conservation of the achievements of their revolutionary forebears?

Literary utopians apparently believe this to be the case. For example, Thomas More devised a network of familial and religious institutions to ensure that each generation would be suitably indoctrinated into the values of the utopian system. Walden II is expected to change, but only through the processes devised by the original founders. Skinner had no expectation that fully conditioned generations would have any desire (or capability) to seek to modify the overall experimental framework of Walden II.

On the other hand, the experimental utopias find that social stasis, even utopian stasis, is difficult to maintain. The generation that actually constructs the new social order may feel justified in its conviction that it has established the foundations of a better society. But their children discover the utopia as an accomplished fact rather than an object of struggle. The worth of the new institutions has a lesser sanctity. Moreover, the experience of life in a utopia may direct the creative energies of a second generation toward desires for change unforeseen by their parents. If, as in the Oneida colony, these desires are incompatible with the fundamental principles of the revolutionary generation, then the utopia is probably doomed. However, the experience of the kibbutzim is that moderate change, change in degree, can be tolerated. Columbia is also capable of accommodating some changes in recreational forms and in cultural and social services that may be desired by a younger generation or by incoming residents. Although such modifications are marginal to the central organization and values of the community, their cumulative impact could result in substantial variation from the precise forms conceived of by the society's founders. Most importantly, the achievement of innovation through intermediate stages may permit reform without forcing a destructive intergenerational cleavage.

As long as people are capable of developing conceptions of a better future, human societies—utopias included—will produce within their own membership motivation for social change. This does not mean that change will necessarily occur. The success of those bearing the banners of social transformation depends on many specific factors, including the structural stability of the society and the processes available for resolving political conflict. The implication of this ongoing process is that a utopia must anticipate and plan for institutional reorganization and provide a structure through which cumulative change can occur. If a society's organization and values exhibit sufficient flexibility, then innovation may proceed without causing excessive turmoil. More rigid systems, on the other hand, will face political crises if moderate pressures for change are denied and forced to build in intensity. In such cases, the entire system may be rejected and the process of utopian creation begun anew.

Qualitative Transformation

A Utopia arises out of a profound dissatisfaction with the present. Its roots are the conviction that the limit of human achievement has not yet been reached, that there exists a potential for social progress still unrealized. In addition, a utopia opposes the future that is expected to arise automatically out of the present. It rejects the dynamics as well as the structure of the existing order. The first premise of utopian speculation is that the future may be a challenge to the present rather than a mere extension of it. And the utopist strives to provide that challenge with content. He raises the prospect of a major qualitative transformation of the existing social order.

However, a utopia is not the only alternative to the status quo. Indeed, opposition to utopianism often arises from those who want some change but question the utopian mode of change. Instead of an abrupt transition to a fundamentally new society, they suggest the use of gradual reforms to ameliorate the inadequacies of current conditions. Their notion is to maintain those societal forms that are of value and to introduce measured changes to rectify the rest. On what basis can the utopist claim that his program and method are preferable to those of the reformer?

To begin with, utopists seek qualitative change because they question the performance of central institutions in their own society. The concept of centrality is crucial here. All institutional sectors of a society are not of equal significance in their impact on the framework of social life. Certain economic and political structures dominate the pattern in which other forms of activity take place. If the utopist is opposed to the design of these central sectors, then simple reforms will not suffice. A person who condemns slavery will not be satisfied by promises that slaves will have a shorter work week or will not be beaten. And once a central institution changes, there will be significant reverberations in other secondary and dependent sectors. Thus, the abolition of slavery would probably result in the abandonment of a plantation economy and the subsequent revision of an aristocratic culture based on that economy.

Second, the utopist prefers qualitative change because it permits the reorientation of numerous institutions and sectors so that they come into balance with one another. Proponents of moderate change attempt to deal with social transformation on a piecemeal basis, directing their attention toward one problem area at a time. Societies, however, are integrated entities wherein modifications of one sector have consequences for others. Alterations in one institution necessitate corresponding adjustments in the interrelated areas. If such adjustments do not occur, a measure that successfully accomplishes its immediate objective may set off dynamics that foster future instability.

Consider an environmental reformer who wishes to do something about air pollution in a capitalist economy much like our own. He suggests a modification of the society's mode of transportation: the addition of anti-smog devices on automobiles. Assume that the reform is technologically sound; cars equipped with the devices actually run cleaner. However, in certain social sectors, there are less beneficial consequences. Because of the expense of the additional apparatus, new cars cost more. Therefore, people buy fewer new cars. Since alternative means of transportation have not been provided, people repair and continue to use their old cars—which are major pollutors. Even worse, the drop in car sales leads to large-scale unemployment in the auto industry. Because the antipollution reform is not part of an overall program of economic transition to ecological balance, alternative job opportunities are not available. Assuming our reformer is humane, he will wish to alleviate the hardship he has wrought. But now he is no longer dealing with a tangential social issue but with a very central question: the allocation of resources in the economy. Whatever he accomplishes in this area will almost certainly have serious impact on several secondary sectors. At this point, our reformer may wish that he had advocated a complete program in the first place. Needless to say, with such an admission the utopist can only agree.

There is another reason for the utopist's advocacy of qualitative change. A reformer does not challenge the established values of a society (or the values of its elites), just as he does not reject central institutions. In fact, reform is often demanded in the name of these values, as a means of preventing their corruption or decay. The utopist stands for a new ethics. He criticizes the very criteria through which conservative and reformer alike evaluate society. Indeed, even when the utopist and the reformer agree on some general issue, such as the desire to preserve environmental stability, their reliance on different standards is likely to result in different priorities of policy implementation. An environmental reformer may seek to reduce ecological disturbances to permit the orderly development of his society's economic institutions. He may consider specific proposals in terms of the society's prevailing value orientation, for example, the maintenance of a satisfactory rate of economic growth. A utopist, however, can set ecological balance as a primary social principle and then design economic structures and levels of activity compatible with its requirements.

Finally, utopists suggest that radical social change always involves political conflict with those in power, who are beneficiaries of the status quo. Reformers, assuming that they are of independent mind and interest, do enter such conflicts. However, as moderates, they do not challenge the structural basis of the distribution of power in society. As a result of this restraint, the potential of their programs is reduced. Reformers must face the full political force of vested interests opposed to change. To achieve progress against such formidable resistance, they must inevitably rely on the cooperation and support of some of those in established positions of power with whose viewpoint they disagree. Equally inevitably, they must compromise their objectives as the price of a limited victory.

Furthermore, even when substantial gains are achieved, reformers have difficulty influencing the distribution of the costs of their programs. Those who possess political and/or economic resources may use them to pass the expense of effecting change on to those least able to defend themselves. Thus, the cost of adding antipollution equipment to a factory may be passed on to consumers in the form of higher prices. Similarly, the highest social cost of a change in the direction and rate of economic growth may fall on the workers least capable of finding new forms of employment.

Utopians who wish to see the realization of their vision must also confront the bastions of a society's elite strata. However, the utopist is much more capable than the reformer of developing new sources of political power. Because of the breadth of his speculation, the utopist is able to suggest alternatives to groups denied access to society's central institutions. For those whose hopes are blocked by established political and economic patterns, for whom the transcendence of these structures is in fact the primary basis of hope, the prospect of qualitative change may prove the most meaningful option. If these groups can be mobilized, then the utopian venture may enter the history of action as well as the history of ideas.

As the above arguments reveal, a utopia represents a special kind of alternative to the present. It seeks to create a discontinuity in human experience, a break with existing structures. Instead of striving to stave off the end of an established society, it struggles to define the direction of a new era. A utopia justifies the extent of this transition by insisting that only through a project of this scope can the contradictions of the old order be resolved and qualitative advancement in social development be achieved. Three of our case studies demonstrate the way in which utopian ventures attempt to fundamentally remove themselves from the society out of which they arise. One case, more reformist in approach, is hampered by some of the obstacles to reform noted above. All of the cases, however, reveal the willingness to apply creativity to devise innovative approaches to solve problems against which traditional methods have proved ineffective.

In the kibbutzim, Zionist pioneers sought to construct a social form bearing little resemblance to that static, traditionbound villages from which they had come. Instead of separate families of traders and craftsmen, they created closely knit communities in which each contributed according to his ability and received according to his needs. Long-established traditions of homage to the patriarch and the scholar were challenged by new values: the advocacy of sexual equality and physical labor. Although innovative in many areas, kibbutzim are often cited for their progress in combining productive efficiency and economic democracy.

In somewhat similar fashion, amid American industrialization and concomitant class conflict, the Oneida settlement struggled unsuccessfully to maintain a community of economic equals. Moreover, the Perfectionists replaced parliamentary democracy with theocratic despotism and rejected the nuclear family in favor of group marriage, collective child-rearing, and selective breeding practices.

Walden II is the young colt that will take over the mantle of civilization from the collapsing United States of the postwar period. Arising out of the hopeless chaos of an irrational society, it offers scientific order, a fully managed social organization employing the experimental method to reach greater heights of human achievement. Among its successful practices is a labor-credit system designed to equate the subjective burdens of all of the society's workers. This experimental structure will not only devise new institutions, it will also form new people to use them: entire generations fully educated according to the principles of behavioral conditioning and therefore perfectly molded to thrive in the Walden II environment.

Unlike the other case studies, Columbia does not attempt a qualitative break with the existing socioeconomic order. It directly challenges neither the basic institutions nor the basic values of American society. To be sure, the New Town does offer serious and often innovative responses to certain current social problems; however, its limited programs are more capable of mitigating the harmful effects of a social pattern than of eliminating its causes. For example, Columbia insists that some of its residences be reserved for members of minority groups, but the New Town is incapable of affecting the high levels of unemployment that constitute the most serious block to the economic welfare of minorities. Similarly, Columbia has constructed some low-income housing, but it can do little to reduce the proportion of people who must endure low incomes. Even in its encouragement of more secure and satisfying family relationships and friendships, Columbia is incapable of challenging those macrocultural trends and economic processes that have all but eliminated the extended family and tend to disrupt nuclear-family stability as well.

This is not to say that Columbia's model of life has nothing to offer. On the contrary, the New Town has produced significant improvements in the aesthetic quality of residential living and in the level of community participation in local affairs. Fundamentally, however, Columbia demonstrates the fact that a "planned" community that lacks utopian goals or a utopian political base cannot deal with crucial social and ecological issues any better than other communities.

Of course, any attempt to produce a major transformation in central societal institutions is a rare and serious event in human affairs. The effort requires great commitment and sacrifice. It involves significant risks. Political and social change cannot be programmed with certainty, and the consequences of error may be extraordinarily costly. As the antiutopians warn, the effort to create perfection may in fact result in its opposite. For this reason, among others, the mere appearance of a utopian proposition, however attractive, is unlikely to motivate large numbers of persons to actively seek its full realization.

However, if a society's central institutions face difficulties with which they are unable to cope, then change becomes unavoidable. If the central sectors are themselves the source of the dilemma, then the need for fundamental restructuring becomes even more acute. At such historical junctures, utopian ideas may receive more attention and support precisely because they offer alternative directions for change. According to the analyses of contemporary environmental scientists, current political and economic practices in the central sectors of both the developed and the underdeveloped world require substantial modification. Innovative ways of regulating growth and allocating resources on a global scale are needed. In such a context, the very radicalism of utopia, its willingness to contemplate a qualitative restructuring of the entire social order, enhances its value as a relevant social model.

Holistic Social Planning

According to our previous arguments, modern environmental theory suggests that a major transformation is needed in the basic structures of human society. Environmental science can provide some understanding of the shape that transformation must take if it is to reduce the ecological disturbances that have made it necessary (see Chapter 7). We go on to argue here that ecological analysis indicates two general criteria that any model of a new society must satisfy. The first requires that the major structures of the society be planned and coordinated; they cannot be left to spontaneous individual decision-making. The second criterion demands that the model be holistic in perspective, encompassing as fully as possible the interaction between the physical and the social environment.

We have previously observed that current environmental theory views ecological factors as part of an interrelated system. Indeed, Barry Commoner argued that the statement, "Everything is connected to Everything else" can stand as the "First Law of Ecology." [6] This interconnectedness requires that the institutions of a new society be organized in terms of the structure and the dynamics of the total environment. Efforts to achieve optimal balance between forms of social organization and isolated parts of the environment are likely to fail precisely because no single aspect of an ecosystem in fact functions in isolation.

The design of a society whose institutions can prove compatible with environmental balance requires a fully holistic perspective. Holistic though they may be, ecologists do not possess such a perspective. Ecological methods provide explanations for physical phenomena. For example, they permit an understanding of the chemical paths through which pollutants travel in air and water and an evaluation of their environmental consequences. However, these same methods cannot be employed to measure the social costs of pollution; they are insufficient for an evaluation of alternative political measures to combat pollution. Such an analysis requires the assistance of those familiar with paradigms capable of explaining political and economic phenomena.

Consider a case in which farmers use nitrogen fertilizer to improve their crop yields. An ecologist may demonstrate that this fertilizer accounts for unwanted nitrate levels in the water supply. But his discipline provides little insight into how the amounts of fertilizer used could be reduced. Fertilizer could be banned or taxed. Farm prices could be adjusted so that farmers could earn satisfactory incomes by growing less. Different crops could be introduced into the area. The whole region could be transformed into a wilderness preserve. Each of these alternatives might resolve the nitrate problem. However, they would satisfy very different social interests and incorporate very different values. They would also have varying impacts on other aspects of society. Ecology provides no basis for making a choice among these alternatives other than noting any undesirable environmental effects they might have.

If ecologists lack the requisite holistic perspective, who does possess it? Can utopists bridge the gap between the various facets of the physical and the social environment? In fact, this is precisely what utopias attempt to do. Each utopia may be considered a holistic social plan that strives to organize the institutions of men and the dynamics of nature into a stable pattern. Even a cursory scan of our case studies reveals them to be plans for the future of humanity, or part of humanity, that are readily analyzed according to a broad set of geographical, economic, psychological, and other variables.

Of course, utopias do vary in the kind and degree of planning they employ. Oneida and the kibbutzim began with only basic values and a general outline of institutions. Skinner provided Walden II with a method of planning (scientific experiment) and a criterion for evaluating plans (the members' happiness). Columbia incorporates many of society's major institutions as "given" and attempts to plan ways of improving their performance. Still in each case, an observer can perceive an organized holistic structure, a comprehensible plan. Utopist critics of the status quo can never be accused of being mere prophets of doom. One may fault the utopist for the contents of his alternative but never for having failed to offer an alternative.

Utopists make a genuine effort to bridge the gaps between various facets of the physical and the social environment. However, the rigor of the holistic approach often leaves much to be desired. Utopists, for all their wisdom in understanding that the linkages between different institutional and physical structures are of paramount importance, often lack the expertise to understand the dynamics of these structures in developing a working pattern of relationships. The Oneida Perfectionists failed to anticipate the contradiction between their organization of production and their social relationships. Skinner, a psychologist, failed to perceive the sociological ambiguities in his procedures for cultural improvement through science. And Columbia's developers failed to foresee the economic and ecological consequences of Western affluence upon the world's environmental stability.

Can a modern utopia improve upon the quality of holistic planning evident in earlier social experiments? The answer to that question depends upon whether the new utopian effort can devise a more effective planning process. The designers of the social models presented in our case studies possessed no special planning method that enabled them to comprehend the full complexity of societal interactions. Essentially, they based their planning on the often eclectic and unsystematic understanding of social processes of a single writer or upon the combined expertise of the members of a small social movement. Today, a single perspective that encompasses physical and social phenomena still does not exist. But contemporary utopists can achieve a greater understanding of the totality of societal interactions by expanding the breadth and the openness of holistic planning perspectives. Instead of being the product of a secluded genius, or of a small and often culturally homogeneous group, utopia can arise as the creation of numerous men and women who pool their diverse knowledge and experience into a common outlook for a common project.

Lacking a single analytical method, a utopia then becomes method in action. Its holism derives from the merger of the minds, the values, and the wills of the participants in the planning process. To be sure, a utopia must be informed by the best specialized knowledge available, both from separate disciplines and from interdisciplinary theory. But science alone cannot provide for the fullness of the human future. Man must create his destiny out of the totality of his resources—aesthetic, intellectual, and political. These disparate modes of understanding, represented in the diverse capacities of individuals, can be integrated through collective discourse and practice. It is as a communal project, therefore, that utopia achieves a comprehensive outlook capable of holistic planning.

How can holistic social planning enable people to structure their institutions so as to maintain environmental stability? Environmental problems generally result from the combined acts of masses of human beings. Therefore, the action of a single individual will have virtually no effect on the overall performance of the ecosystem. Moreover, in the absence of organization, it is almost impossible for individuals to devise personal strategies that in concert with others, will have the desired macroecological effects. In this situation, an individual mindful of his own interests is likely to continue behavior harmful to the environment rather than to pursue a futile effort to effect improvement. This problem can be overcome through planning. Individuals can coordinate their decisions so that each personal act, as part of a planned whole, serves to further the overall social and environmental objective.

Consider the case mentioned above in which farmers use nitrogen fertilizer to improve their crop yields. Unfortunately, much of this nitrogen, in nitrate form, is drained into the water supply of a nearby city, constituting a public health hazard. Assume that the farmers are people of goodwill, who do not wish to be responsible for imposing environmental risks on their neighbors. How can they, as individuals, respond to this situation?

Each farmer finds himself essentially in the same position. He wants to use as much fertilizer as he can to maximize his income without adversely affecting the city's water. How much of a reduction in fertilizer usage will satisfy these two objectives? The farmer, as an individual actor, cannot answer that question. Nitrate levels are determined by the aggregate fertilizer usage of all farmers. The answer, therefore, is dependent on what the other farmers do. But, in the absence of coordination, no single farmer will know what reductions the others are willing to accept. A reduction in fertilizer usage by any single farmer acting alone will have virtually no beneficial effect on the nitrogen pollution problem. In addition, no one farmer has any assurance that others will act in such a fashion as to make his own reduction meaningful. Thus, the logical action for all farmers is to use just as much fertilizer as before. They will then at least maintain their income without risking a loss that may accomplish nothing.

A planned response might produce quite a different result. If the farmers meet together, they can determine how much of an aggregate reduction in fertilizer usage is necessary to return the nitrate content of the water supply to a safe level. They can then divide that amount by the total number of farmers or use any other mutually agreeable method of distributing the loss. This planning permits them to solve the nitrate problem with the smallest loss of income. And, as an added benefit, it allows them to share equitably a burden for which they are all equally responsible.

Planning can accomplish more than the coordination of individual decisions in the task of restoring environmental equilibrium. Planning can also change the social structures that establish the conditions on which individual decisions are based. The individual human decisions that contribute to the environmental crisis—decisions to have another child or to buy a second car—are made in specific historical contexts, contexts that can be radically changed. Men and women often decide to have large families so that they can rely on a child for support in their old age. Establishment of a viable system of social security might modify their social environment sufficiently to eliminate this consideration. People use automobiles in part because their homes are separated from the places in which they work and shop. A regional design that integrates these functions within a single area would reduce the need for personal transport. Economic growth is defended as a means of ensuring profit from enterprises and full employment for workers. But in a communitarian economic system, the former objective would become meaningless and the latter could be achieved without continual expansion. The organized change of societal structures may thus make the regulation of individual decisions unnecessary.

Assuming that planning accomplishes its objective of coordinating ecological requirements and social policy, does it also lead to other, less desirable effects? Advocates of utopian planning confront a vocal opposition. From the antiutopian perspective, an endorsement of planning suggests nightmarish images of a society in which every facet of life is regulated by an all-powerful and central bureaucracy. This charge must be evaluated. Does the requirement of holistic social planning necessarily lead to a regimented society?

To begin with, social planning does not bring constraint into an otherwise free world. Compulsion, the act of being forced to act in a manner other than one desires, is intrinsic to life in society. The structure of society and the aggregate acts of individuals within that structure constrain human behavior through the determination of a physical and social environment. The necessities of that environment can be self-enforcing. Planning is simply one mode of unavoidable social restraint, a mode characterized by being collective and deliberate.

For example, a hunting and gathering society must adjust its behavior to the supply of game. One way of accomplishing this is to allow each hunter to kill as much as he desires until the animal population is decimated. At this point, however, at least a part of the society faces an edict of nature: relocate or starve. On the other hand, the society could organize the constraint itself, by limiting the number of animals taken or by sending hunting parties to other areas. Although the form of the limit varies, the existence of the limit cannot be avoided. Consider a modern case. The motorist attempting to drive to the beach on a holiday weekend finds his neighbors in aggregate forcing him to spend hours on the road in stop-and-go traffic. Planning might have resulted in different days off for different industries or perhaps in restricted access to public facilities. In both cases, the individual's actions are restrained by the interference of others.

Planning is only one of many forms of compulsion that may result from human interaction in society. Planning, however, is unusual in that it can permit individuals to choose the way in which they will be constrained. A holiday motorist has only two options in an unplanned context. He drives in a traffic jam or he stays home. Planning offers a variety of alternative strategies—which might involve work schedules, modes of transport, availability of recreational areas, and so on. Any plan selected will involve constraint, but it may produce the greatest satisfaction possible under the circumstances. Where major ecological disturbances are involved, the constraints imposed by planning may prove to be much less costly to human welfare than the pressures resulting from unregulated behavior.

Even if an antiutopian acknowledges that planning is necessary in certain circumstances, he may still continue his critique. How can one be sure that planning will stop at this level? Planning must be viewed as a means rather than an end. The utopian objective is not the planning per se but the use of planning to achieve specific environmental and social objectives.

There is no logical reason to continue planning beyond the minimum amount necessary to reach those goals. Thus, the fact that it is necessary to regulate the use of the farmers' fertilizer does not require or imply that it is likewise necessary to regulate whom the farmer marries, when he wakes up in the morning, what he has for breakfast, and the like.

At this point, the antiutopian may play his trump card. Our problem, he may argue, is not one of logic but one of the dynamics of social structures. One cannot have planning without planners. What is to stop planning agencies from continually discovering new areas of life that require their attention or from seeking to extend their power until they totally dominate society? Planning organizations can become increasingly bureaucratic and authoritarian, even in social forms with the most egalitarian and democratic ideologies. This argument focuses on the crucial issue. The extent to which planning leads to regimentation depends on who plan and how they plan. We have already insisted that utopian planning must be collective and political; it is not the exclusive province of scientists or of bureaucrats. The concern over regimentation reinforces this position. Utopia must be defined through open participation, and such participation is a continuing obstacle to elitism in the construction of a new society. This strategy cannot guarantee that authoritarianism and regimentation will never arise, but it is the most promising method of assuring that these trends will be strongly resisted.

Political Impact

In the course of the above arguments, we have maintained that the design of a new society is a political project, beyond the purview of environmental science alone. In its application to political processes, environmental theory fundamentally serves as a critique. It demonstrates that particular activities cannot long be continued. In indicating that change is necessary, it raises the prospect of corrective action. However, a critique alone is politically insufficient, particularly when social restructuring is the long-term goal.

A critique can lead to political action, but the action is likely to be fragmented and inconsistent. It will often be individualist rather than collective. It may sacrifice major long-term objectives for minor short-term victories. Most important, a critique is seldom capable of mobilizing a political movement that can alter basic institutions. By their nature, critiques establish what one is against rather than what one is for. Thus, the simplest basis for unified action is a movement of resistance, which may produce immediate tangible results, such as a reduction in industrial pollution. However, moving beyond resistance requires a specific formulation of one's objectives. Organizations that rely solely on an environmental critique for their raison d'être lack a clear social alternative that can be offered as a program for positive action.

Movements founded on the environmental critique will probably find themselves unable to mobilize sufficient political power or to form sufficiently broad coalitions to achieve long-term goals. Within our present social structure, efforts to change environmental policy will impose significant costs on large numbers of people. They will interfere with the functioning of and perhaps require the elimination of major institutions. They will disrupt activities through which individuals satisfy basic needs. People who drive modern automobiles are acutely aware of the effects of smog-reduction equipment on the performance and the cost of maintenance of their vehicles. If a manufacturing plant cannot meet pollution-control standards and closes down, the people who worked there will be all too aware that environmental improvement requires high personal sacrifices.

The problem with environmental change, however, is not that it involves high costs. Large-scale social change is rarely accomplished easily, yet it is still possible to organize movements dedicated to such objectives. The problem for the environmentalist is to specify the benefits that make such costs worthwhile. And where costs are concrete and immediate, long-term benefits cannot be vague and indefinite. In addition to suggesting ways to preserve the environment, a political movement must be able to explain how the costs it demands are to be distributed. It must be able to explain how the institutions that are shut down will be replaced and what will happen to those whose lives were centered on those institutions. If old ways of meeting needs are to be terminated, new ways must be offered.

There is ample evidence to demonstrate the political consequences of seeking change without an accompanying positive social program. Automobile-emission standards are delayed because the industry cannot comply and maintain employment at adequate levels. The ecological impact of the development of energy sources is defined as of secondary status in relation to the need to provide fuel for continuing industrial production. Construction workers and loggers demonstrate because environmental-impact analyses threaten their source of income.

Thus, an analysis of present conditions, even when combined with a moral condemnation of their consequences, cannot provide direction for political and social action beyond that of a call to resistance. Those who would restructure a society must do more than resist. They must be capable of exercising political creativity and of transforming a critique into a statement of affirmation. They must devise a social model that can serve as a goal, as a focus for united action, and as a basis for judging between strategic alternatives. When political movements demand a model that lies beyond the limits of the prevailing order, they open the way to a call for utopia.

When a model of utopia develops in this fashion, through a political movement that combines environmental analysis with a concrete concern for human needs, it becomes a historical project rather than an idealist image. By directing attention to new forms of social organization, it suggests new directions for political action. Similarly, while utopian thought in itself cannot realize any historical possibility, it can influence the purposes of those who will change history. A utopia can proclaim the worth of objectives that lie beyond a movement's present strength. As a tantalizing vision of the unreal, it demands that men do what all those who would question a social order must do: test the sacred truths that define the present as immutable and portray the historical as eternal. The challenge is the first step toward the test. As the Polish philosopher Leszek Kolakowski reasoned:

> much historical experience, more or less buried in the social consciousness, tells us that goals unattainable now will never be reached unless they are articulated when they are still unattainable. It may well be that the impossible at a given moment can become possible only by being stated at a time when it is impossible. . . . *The existence of a utopia as a utopia is the necessary prerequisite for its eventually ceasing to be a utopia.* [7]

One cannot wait until a society crumbles under its own contradictions, be they economic or ecological, before beginning the task of devising an alternative. Chaos is the weakest of foundations for social reconstruction. The formation of a consensus capable of changing existing institutions must develop hand in hand with the creation of an outline of new structures. Only a group organized around a unified objective has any hope of maintaining its own stability while attempting to effect long-term social change. And whether or not political constraints restrict the immediate opportunity to experiment with new social forms, the ideas in question can still be circulated as a basis for discussion and planning. A utopia's political role, therefore, can and should begin early in the process of social reorganization, so early that its design may promptly be denounced as utopian.

If a utopia can have a significant political impact, what does the evidence from our case studies tell us concerning the way in which that impact can be made most effective? Many of the political lessons of the case studies coincide with other arguments we have already advanced.

Oneida's Perfectionists did bring a utopian model into history, albeit for only three decades. Noyes and his followers produced a mode of organization that combined two unorthodox but popular tendencies then prevalent in American culture: the interest in religious innovation and communitarian social life. The unique structure that resulted attracted adherents willing to accept economic hardship and public criticism to build and maintain their settlement. But Oneida's appeal was narrow. Only the firm disciple either desired or was permitted to join the Perfectionist ranks. Outside Oneida, other economic, political, and ideological forces developed; these movements dominated the community's social environment. Although Oneida attempted to adjust to external pressure, it could not do so and still maintain the internal balance necessary for its own stability.

Israeli kibbutzim continue to provide the most significant proof of the political viability of their vision: they endure. For a homeless people, perpetual foreigners in other lands, they raised the prospect of nationhood and, within that nation, the further objective of a new form of social organization and a new cultural standard. But, like Oneida, the kibbutzim were limited by the size of their potential membership. The kibbutzim arose as part of the nationalistic movement of a small ethnic group, and they appear to have proved uniquely attractive only to certain elements of that group. The kibbutzim, therefore, must also survive in an environment organized according to other social models. The kibbutzim can maintain their numbers by successfully winning the allegiance of new generations, but the external pressure always remains—economic, social, and ideological. And, therefore, the possibility that adjustment to these pressures will either disrupt the workings of the kibbutz system or require such extensive adjustment that the core of the original utopian ideal vanishes also remains.

Although *Walden II* is an enormously popular utopian novel, the social scheme it suggests has attracted few serious adherents. This is true despite the fact that the Walden model is extraordinarily broad in its membership policy: it is a society open to all but convicted criminals. Of course, Walden II is suggested as an alternative to a society on the verge of collapse. But even if the United States is not in its death throes, many citizens have considered the wisdom of exploring new forms of social organization. Why have these individuals not sought to adopt the Walden perspective? Perhaps the answer lies in the kinds of people who find fundamental social change to be a necessary political objective. As we have already suggested, groups willing to undertake such an awesome task arise from segments of the population that have found their aspirations blocked by existing structures. If we consider the concrete experiences of these individuals in modern society, we find that they have often been subjected to the dictates of scientific social planners. These planners, who regularly serve other more powerful interests, ignore their needs and manipulate their efforts at political organization. Thus, one can imagine the reaction of members of these groups to the idea of a society totally under the domination of scientific planners. In the last analysis, Walden II fails as a utopia because it appears antiutopian to the very forces that constitute a real base for a utopian movement. In fact, the techniques endorsed in Skinner's model have proved most attractive to elite institutions seeking to control the behavior of those who cannot or will not adjust to current social structures.

Columbia is a viable political project, probably capable of continuing stability over the short run. Indeed, Columbia has had to cope with only minimal political opposition, primarily because the New Town experiment challenges so few significant institutions and because the project's leaders have been willing to sacrifice their visions to the realities of profits and power.

Nevertheless, Columbia is unlikely to serve as a model for many other communities or as the goal of a broad utopian movement. Both in class composition and in outlook, the New Town's social base is ill-suited to either role. Columbia is a relevant social alternative to only a minority of upper-middle-class Americans. It does not appear to be an attainable prospect for the large majority, who know that they cannot afford to live there. In addition, Columbia's residents are generally successfully integrated into the higher echelons of modern social structures. Until the overall national socioeconomic system is shaken, these individuals are unlikely to believe the risk of participation in a utopian movement to be preferable to the status they already enjoy.

A utopist today can profit from these lessons from the past. If a utopian model is to have an impact that can contribute to its eventual realization, it must be oriented toward the aspirations of an appropriate social base. The members of this base must be so situated within the existing society that a utopian rather than a conservative or reformist perspective can best serve their interests. They must also be able to form a political coalition capable of social reorganization. Finally, they must be willing to support a macro-objective that attempts to satisfy their needs within the constraints imposed by environmental and economic conditions. When utopia is embraced by such a movement, it enters history as an idea whose time is coming.

REFERENCES AND NOTES

1. Polak, F. *The image of the future.* San Francisco: Jossey-Bass, 1973, p. 177.
2. Boulding, K. *The economics of the coming spaceship earth.* In G. Love and R. Love (Eds.), *Ecological crisis.* New York: Harcourt, Brace Jovanovich, 1970, p. 315.
3. Ibid., pp. 315–316.
4. Mead, M. Towards more vivid utopias. In G. Kateb (Ed.), *Utopia.* New York: Atherton Press, 1971, p. 45.
5. de Jouvenel, B. Utopia for practical purposes. In F. Manuel (Ed.), *Utopias and utopian thoughts.* Boston: Houghton Mifflin, 1966, pp. 219–220.
6. Commoner, B. *The closing circle.* New York: Bantam Books, 1971, p. 29.
7. Kolakowski, L. *Toward a Marxist humanism.* New York: Grove Press, 1968, pp. 70–71.

CHAPTER 9

Toward a Political
Ecological Utopia

We began with the premise that humanity can and must produce a deliberate design for its own future. In the preceding pages, we have sought to suggest that a synthesis of environmental and utopian thought might prove of value in developing that design. Here, in a final section, there remains the task of evaluating our findings.

A preliminary examination of environmental science and utopian speculation reveals formidable differences in their methods and viewpoints. Environmental thought holds rigorously to the scientific method; it concentrates mainly upon objective phenomena; it is empirical and descriptive in its conclusions. One consistent feature of environmental analyses is the recognition that environmental factors restrict and limit the options open to human endeavor.

Utopian thought, on the other hand, flows from the imagination. It is more concerned with social organization and values than with ecological forces; it is often stridently prescriptive in tone. Moreover, utopias always emphasize the openness, the unrealized potential, of the future. Their mission is to tempt mankind to test limits and to attempt new creative works.

Despite such formal differences, both perspectives have reached a stage in their historical development wherein the mutual exchange of ideas may be enlightening. Environmental science has recently come to reject determinist theses, with which utopianism is completely incompatible. The possibilist and ecological theories that have supplanted determinism still do not give man a free hand in planning his future; they set parameters our species dare not move beyond. However, within these parameters, a realm of speculation and inventiveness, utopian or otherwise, becomes legitimate. In addition, the development of social ecological analysis is beginning to provide new information about the functioning of human institutions and microenvironments, which are often the substantive foci of utopian design.

On the utopian side, early philosophical and theological models that depicted the ethics and the social relationships of utopian societies, while virtually ignoring ecological factors, have been supplanted, to some extent, by more secular frameworks. These modern projections consider such environmentally relevant issues as the side effects of technological innovation and the problem of balancing population and natural resources. Thus, on the basis of current trends, the prospect of a fruitful environmental–utopian dialogue appears promising.

However, the case for serious contact between these modes of thought can be made much stronger. Both perspectives have recently reached obstacles to their continued social usefulness that may be partially overcome by interaction with the other discipline. Environmental scientists have concluded that current patterns of economic activity in the developed world cannot continue within the limits set by basic ecological processes. If environmental stability is to be maintained, fundamental changes must take place in these economic institutions and processes and in the social and political formations that are based upon them. But the analytical tools of environmental science, or of any science, are ill-equipped to reshape a civilization. A deeper awareness and understanding of human values, social processes, hopes, and desires are needed, and these are, of course, the stock in trade of the utopian.

Utopians have been having difficulties of their own. Indeed, the impact of utopian scholarship has declined drastically in this century, except for a brief period in the late 1960s in the West. This lack of interest results largely from the perceived power, immutability, and ongoing "one-dimensionality" of current social systems. Utopian projections, which simply describe a brighter future but make no mention of how a new society is to be constructed, seem to be mere fantasies that may arouse transient intellectual interest but that cannot demand serious attention. Significantly, therefore, even groups genuinely committed to the need for large-scale social change tend to find utopian conjecture to be a futile pastime.

In order to reverse this attitude, utopia must sink its roots into reality. It must demonstrate its awareness that the structure of tomorrow develops out of present social and material dynamics, and it must clarify its connectedness with political and social forces emerging out of existing societal contradictions. Although environmental factors do not determine the totality of the relevant societal dynamics, they represent an essential subset thereof. A utopia figuratively "grounded" in environmental concerns has taken a major step toward attracting the consideration of those individuals and organizations capable of translating ideas into action.

If utopian creativity and environmental science could be brought together to focus on the possibilities for the human future, which shape might a design employing both perspective take? At the most abstract and general level, environmentalists and utopians seem to agree on the essential form (although not necessarily the specific content) of a model suitable for the contemporary era. First, a new social model should provide for a qualitative change in basic institutions. Throughout history, the mark of utopian thinking has been its willingness to "transcend reality," to move beyond "the bonds of the existing order." [1] Now, environmental theorists, fearful of the collapse of the ecological systems upon which human life depends, also support a major change in social organization. Instead of ameliorative reforms, totally new modes of social life—zero population growth, a steady-state economy—are being advanced as alternatives to an industrial juggernaut run amok.

Second, one cannot expect necessary new social structures simply to evolve out of current individual practices. Planning, and ongoing social feedback for subsequent planning, is needed to ensure sustained environmental and social stability. As noted above, the environmental case for planning and regulation is founded on the interrelatedness of ecosystem elements. Ecologically, no one is isolated from his community; individual actions reverberate, producing cumulative effects on others. If a society does not control important policies according to its own principles, personal autonomy cannot result. Rather, ecological dynamics will provide their own set of regulations without regard for human needs or desires. For their part, utopists have generally recognized the need for some degree of planning and for allocation and control of the power that may be used to make and enforce the necessary regulations to implement social plans. [2] In fact, the conviction that individual human actions are not fixed in nature but result from planned decisions made in concrete social contexts is intrinsic to the utopian notion of human betterment. The utopian reasons that a society that seeks to encourage new behavior patterns must plan an alternative social context in which the desired behavior becomes possible, satisfying, and meaningful. [3]

Third, a social model for the future can best avoid unintended consequences of well-meant designs by maintaining a holistic framework. Environmental science suggests that interconnectedness among ecosystems is as relevant as relations within ecosystems. Disturbances in one system can overflow into others. Similarly, at a microlevel, social ecological analysis suggests that communities can make more satisfactory use of man-made environments when they achieve intersystem congruence between physical structures and social patterns. It is therefore advisable to plan institutions, buildings, or neighborhoods in the context of a holistic perspective that examines the impact of such structures on related sectors. Here again, utopists find a technique to which they are accustomed. Utopists have traditionally attempted holistic designs, seeking to portray the essential elements of entire ongoing societies. To be sure, the completeness and the logic of the holistic patterns developed by utopists have often been inadequate. However, the utopian form is well suited to a holistic approach, and given the proper political and scientific input, it may substantially improve upon its prior record.

Finally, mankind must accept the responsibility of designing the criteria upon which a society is to be judged, as well as the responsibility of creating the specific structures that meet those criteria. Any plan of social transformation reflects a normative position; its proponents must be prepared to declare their values, to clarify why institutions should take on a precise form, and to explain the worth of the principles they seek to establish in social practice. On this issue, too, environmentalists and utopians can agree. Environmental theorists have increasingly noted that many of the fundamental norms of the West—the drive to dominate nature, the quest for ever-increasing levels of material growth—are incompatible with ecological stability. A new ethic, oriented toward balance with nature, is required. Utopists perceive such a normative challenge to the status quo as a call for their services. The true basis of a utopia is the set of ethical and philosophical premises of its founders. Basic patterns of cities and modes of social organizations are derived from these premises. Utopists would be the first to agree, for example, that it makes very little sense to attempt to reform a judicial system without having determined the concept of justice that that system is to serve.

In conclusion, modern environmental and utopian thought are both moving toward the design of a social model with four general attributes. This futurist framework would be qualitatively distinct from the existing social order, deliberately planned, holistic in perspective, and founded upon new values. One can certainly observe the outline of a utopia in these characteristics. But more than the traditional utopia is required. The merger of environmental science and utopian experiment must produce a model that is satisfactory to both disciplines in its mode of creation and in its specific content. If that merger is to lead to a social project relevant to contemporary needs, then it must bring forth a utopia that is unlike any developed heretofore: a political ecological utopia.

It is beyond the scope of this volume, or indeed of any single work, to fully define a utopia of this new type. However, evidence from our case studies and from our comparative analysis of the ecological and utopian viewpoints provides a basis for suggesting the kinds of processes that might bring this utopian model into existence and some of the principles of societal organization that it would have to satisfy.

A POLITICAL ECOLOGICAL UTOPIA

A political ecological utopia must differ from its historical forebears in the methods through which it is produced, as well as in the substantive form of its structures. To begin with, instead of developing as the brainchild of a single individual, the new utopia should arise out of collective creative processes. There are several compelling reasons for this recommendation. First, the basic nature of a political ecological utopia—the merger of environmental science and utopian thought—requires a planning process that enables men of science and men of the imagination to interact and strive to bridge the gaps between their "two cultures." Second, divergent opinions about the formation of a utopia are likely to encourage a holistic perspective, as specialists may focus attention on the possible effects of suggested innovations on sectors in which they have expertise. Failures of vision relating to the interaction among societal institutions, which may be related to the small number and the cultural homogeneity of social planners, might thus be avoided. Third, a collective procedure for utopian design is likely to yield a model of great diversity, capable of meeting the political demands of a broad spectrum of the population and also of satisfying the requirement of maintaining ecological variety. Thus, unlike Oneida or the kibbutz, the political ecological utopia would be able to attract adherents from diverse backgrounds with different political and social attitudes.

Importantly, the new utopia should be developed out of a particular type of collective process: a broad, participatory, political movement. Any collective decision-making procedure is likely to result in argument, disagreement, and conflict. When the fundamental norms upon which a society will rest are the subject of debate, the decision-making apparatus must be authoritative and eventually linked to societal power. If utopian planning is to be more than theoretical, if it is to be part of a genuine effort at social reconstruction, it will have to be political. In addition, an open, participatory process of utopian design is the best possible guarantee against bureaucratic rigidity in the planning mechanism and subsequent regimentation in the societal structure. The warnings of the antiutopians on this issue should not go unheeded. Nor should it be ignored that the kibbutz, the utopian experiment most democratic and political in its planning processes, has proved to be most capable of maintaining its nonbureaucratic and participatory character.

Finally, the utopian program must have an appropriate social base with concrete historical goals. As the objective of a movement for qualitative social change, a utopian project must appeal to a large segment of existing society. But it certainly cannot satisfy all interests or all social groups. Therefore, to maximize its prospects for eventual political realization, a utopia ought to be organized so as to motivate those groups that find their aspirations blocked in existing structures and that seek new opportunities through societal transformation. For example, the limited innovation and vision demonstrated at Columbia, Maryland is probably due to the fact that the community's primary market consisted of people tightly linked to the norms and the institutions of the status quo. Also, by being oriented to actual social groups with real needs, a utopia can establish the specific historical objectives it seeks to achieve. It can thereby avoid the trap encountered by earlier utopias that sought to meet all needs for all time—that is, the accomplishment of social perfection—and instead produced static and authoritarian models incapable of progress or change.

As our discussion of the process of utopian creation makes evident, we do not consider any single writer or collaborative team to be capable of designing a political ecological utopia. However, on the basis of the data and the arguments presented above, we can participate in the debate out of which such a utopia may arise by suggesting several principles of social organization that should be incorporated in a sound utopian project.

Diversity

High levels of social and ecological diversity may help a utopian society maintain stability and attract support from a multitude of human cultures. As has already been noted, environmental diversity probably helps ecosystems respond homeostatically to changes in their member elements. Catastrophic population shifts are certainly less likely in ecologically diverse systems. Social diversity is a requirement if a utopian model is to achieve mass cross-cultural appeal. Homogeneity remains the hallmark of small and short-lived sectarian utopian experiments. Thus, whatever its general characteristics, a utopia should be capable of functioning in a variety of different geographic environments and of satisfying the needs of widely varying sectors of humanity.

Flexibility

Utopia cannot be rigid and unchangeable. It must retain the capacity to innovate and to develop, without engendering social conflicts that tear it apart. From an environmental perspective, nature is neither so stable nor so predictable that man can possibly risk losing the ability to adapt to her mutations. From the standpoint of societal stability, any effort to totally block social changes virtually guarantees that such changes will be explosive when they finally do occur. Stasis is neither defensible nor adaptive. Each new generation has experiences and ideas distinct from those that have gone before and thus constitutes a potential for change that cannot be indefinitely contained. Among our case studies, the Oneida experiment provides an illustrative example of a social order that after 30 years of successful communal life, failed to survive because of the inflexibility of its institutions and ideology.

Social and Ecological Coherence

In the utopian design of urban and architectural forms, of organizational structure, and of social rules and practices, care must be taken to ensure that desired values and behavior patterns prove compatible with the physical and social structures that are established. Here, the findings of social ecological analysis may be used effectively. For example, if a high degree of communal interpersonal interaction becomes a utopian goal, then planners must understand what architectural frameworks are likely to facilitate such contact. Similarly, planners might decide to avoid modes of organization that foster a social climate conducive to competition and personal isolation. Our experimental utopias reveal the difficulty of maintaining such coherence within ongoing social systems. As a case in point, the experience of the kibbutz demonstrates the stresses that develop when a community seeks to combine forms of productive organization requiring specialization with an ideology demanding equality of occupational opportunity.

Balance

Utopia must exist in a state of environmental balance. This is not a static condition but rather a state in which certain basic limits to growth and innovation are observed. First and foremost, population growth cannot be permitted to exceed available resources, particularly food and space. Second, technology cannot be considered an end in itself, as in Walden II. On the contrary, technology would be a tool employed only to serve the values of a society. Third, the material resources of the earth must be considered whenever possible. Social institutions have to be designed to discourage waste, conspicuous consumption, or the stimulation of demand for material goods. According to this criterion, Columbia, Maryland fails badly as a utopian model. The kibbutz and Oneida, however, suggest that utopian practices may be quite efficient and frugal. Finally, the utopian ethos should reflect a concern for harmony among people and between people and nature.

World Scale

Utopia can no longer be envisioned as an isolated island in a remote sea. Today, both physical and social environments are recognized as worldwide and inescapable. In particular, utopian ventures cannot hope to maintain either ecological balance or social peace by isolating themselves from a nonutopian world. Sooner or later, they would fall victim to the environmental or political errors and excesses of neighboring social systems. Or perhaps, like the kibbutz and Walden II, they would have to reject ecological balance and adopt ideologies of growth as mechanisms of self-defense in order to preserve their own security. Therefore, as its final objective a political ecological utopia must seek the formation of a world political order.

These five principles represent only the barest of beginnings of an outline for a political ecological utopian form. What steps should be taken next?

For a utopian model to be created and realized, the quest for utopia must become a serious objective for scholars, for political activists, for artists, and indeed for men and women of all walks of life who are ready to take part in shaping their collective future. The prerequisite for such a quest is a radical change in attitude. Utopia demands a rejection of despair, a willingness to consider alternatives other than a continual extension of the status quo. Most of all, it requires a determination to move past negation to affirmation, to move beyond resistance (although resistance is often necessary) to construction. First, we must accept the obligation and the challenge to be builders. Then we can meet together to discuss the shape we will impress on things to come.

We join our colleagues in calling for increased emphasis on and support of futurism and future planning:

> Rather than ostracizing utopians, we should take advantage of their willingness to experiment, encouraging them with money and tolerance if not respect. . . . futurists should be attached to every political party, university, corporation, professional association, trade union, and student organization. We need to train thousands of young people in the perspectives and techniques of scientific futurism, inviting them to share in the exciting adventure of mapping probable futures.[4]

The computer simulation of alternative future scenarios has been popular, but a broadening of the cultural assumptions and parameters of the current computer models is needed.[5] It would also be useful to conduct alternative small-scale utopian experiments within existing societies. Of course, a diversity of "utopian" ventures does exist in our society, but we would favor outright economic and social support to ensure the development of a greater variety of social models. Speculation about the alternative physical and social forms of experimental "space cities" is a relevant development in this connection.[6]

Current environmental-assessment programs may soon provide the type of information that is necessary to plan a viable, environmentally based utopia. For example, the United Nations Earthwatch program was launched to focus on broad environmental problems such as climate change, the extent of man's influence on climate, water pollution, the effects of environmental pollution on human health, and the plight of human settlements. Solutions to these and other similar environmental problems require international participation, global monitoring systems, and facilities for communication and information exchange.[7] The fact that worldwide environmental-assessment centers may be developed for coordinating global environmental monitoring and information feedback is relevant to the construction of a viable utopia. The worldwide dissemination of information about environmental pollution will raise critical political issues beyond the competence of environmental scientists. It is at this point that the question of new values—and of participation by utopists—arises.

At another level, information on overall environmental quality is being compiled on an index basis analogous to currently available economic indices such as the Gross National Product. For example, the Canadian Environmental Quality Index (EQI) consists of four separate indices representing air quality, water quality, land quality, and the quality of miscellaneous aspects of the environment. Each has several subindices. For example, the land-quality index includes six subindices: overcrowding in cities, characteristics of forests, access to park land, erosion, strip mining, and sedimentation. The EQI is not simply a "pollution index." It attempts to take into account environmental benefits as well as problems and aesthetic considerations as well as those related to health.

A subindex of relative accessibility to regional and national parks incorporates people's perceptions of distances from environmental benefits or problems. Indices of human perception may give a much more accurate portrayal of the actual effect of environmental conditions on people's lives. Although the overall index value is purely relative, once a value has been established, a higher or lower value at a subsequent measurement would indicate that on the average environmental conditions were getting better or worse. Thus, an EQI might measure the "environmental health" of a country and could provide continuing relevant information to utopian planners.[8]

Although we have been duly warned about ecological disaster, most people are less concerned about what may happen in the distant future than they are with more immediate developments, partly because people do not fully appreciate their own ability to influence and control the future. Involvement in future planning could be enhanced by the dissemination of information about the extent to which we can control our own future development. People must be made aware that they can make a difference in the future course of human events. In this sense, it is important to develop methods for presenting information about alternative lines of environmental development in a way that will arouse people's interest and lead them to sustained effective action.

One step in the development of the social base necessary to a political ecological utopia is greater emphasis on environmental education. Environmental education should begin at the level of the individual and his immediate surroundings. Each individual must first feel competent to change and control at least some portion of his immediate environment. In fact, people usually can change their own home or apartment, their classroom or office, and even their street or neighborhood, at least to some degree.[9]

Enhancing environmental competence at the individual level may have beneficial consequences in developing an informed population base that can then tackle broader social problems. For example, there is no sharp distinction between solving broad ecological problems and improving one's immediate sociophysical milieu:

> One step toward solution . . . is to involve people in a problem-solving stance toward problems in their homes, schools, offices, and neighborhoods. This will inevitably mesh into larger environmental issues, but they are origi-

nally perceived at a scale where there is some likelihood of success. I would like to suggest that for most people the logical starting place is the person's immediate environment where the scale of problems is manageable and the effects of his efforts are apparent.[10]

A belief in the value and the creative potential of the human phenomenon is requisite to our survival. W. H. Murdy has argued that the greatest danger "is not that the human species will become extinct . . . but that the cultural values that make us human will become extinct." In this view, the ecological crisis is basically a social crisis. If the only alternative to extinction becomes a regimented ant-heap who is to doubt that a regimented ant-heap will in fact develop? This would be a "process of evolutionary retrogression in which higher emergent values are destroyed in behalf of the fundamental value of biological survival." [11] Murdy suggested that the value of the human enterprise transcends our individual lives and that we must form a collective bond of identity with future generations. He concluded that an anthropocentric belief in the meaningfulness and creative potential of the human phenomenon is a motivating factor necessary to participatory evolution, which, in turn, may be requisite to the future survival of the human species and its cultural values.

Once utopia becomes a goal, the long and difficult undertaking of defining the content for a new society can begin. At this stage, we cannot provide a program for further action in that direction. We can only emphasize the obvious. Through a variety of mechanisms—traditional and innovative—utopian frameworks must be presented, debated, and advocated. In the parlance of contemporary media, utopia must become an issue and, as an issue, receive a place on the political agenda of our society. At that point, utopia will face the fundamental test that confronts every proposal for social change. Are men and women, in sufficient number and with sufficient commitment, willing to take political action in support of a utopian design? The answer to that question determines whether utopia will exist as a dream or as a reality.

REFERENCES AND NOTES

1. Mannheim, K. *Ideology and utopia.* New York: Harcourt, Brace, 1936, p. 173.
2. Kinkade, K. Power and the utopian assumption. *Journal of Applied Behavioral Science, 10:*402–414, 1974.
3. Skinner, B. The steep and thorny way to a science of behavior. *American Psychologist, 30:*42–49, 1975.
4. Toffler, A. *Future shock.* New York: Random House, 1970, pp. 414–415.

5. See Mesarovic, M., and Pestel, E. *Mankind at the turning point.* New York: Dutton, 1974; Kahn, H., and Weiner, A. *The Year 2000.* New York: Macmillan, 1967.
6. Salgado, M. City in space no longer just fantasy. *Palo Alto Times,* Palo Alto, Calif., August 22, 1975.
7. Jensen, C., Brown, D., and Mirabito, J. Earthwatch, *Science, 190:*432–438, 1975.
8. Inhaber, H. Environmental quality: Outline for a national index for Canada. *Science, 186:*798–805, 1974.
9. Moos, R. *The human context.* New York: Wiley, Chs. 4 and 10.
10. Sommer, R. *Design awareness.* San Francisco: Rinehart, 1972, pp. 31–32.
11. Murdy, W. Anthropocentrism: A modern version. *Science, 187:*1168–1172, 1975.

Author Index

Subject Index